Lecture Notes of the Institute for Computer Sciences, Social Informatics and Telecommunications Engineering 556

The LNICST series publishes ICST's conferences, symposia and workshops.
LNICST reports state-of-the-art results in areas related to the scope of the Institute.
The type of material published includes

- Proceedings (published in time for the respective event)
- Other edited monographs (such as project reports or invited volumes)

LNICST topics span the following areas:

- General Computer Science
- E-Economy
- E-Medicine
- Knowledge Management
- Multimedia
- Operations, Management and Policy
- Social Informatics
- Systems

Paulo Jorge Coelho · Ivan Miguel Pires ·
Nuno Vieira Lopes
Editors

Smart Objects and Technologies for Social Good

9th EAI International Conference, GOODTECHS 2023
Leiria, Portugal, October 18–20, 2023
Proceedings

 Springer

Editors
Paulo Jorge Coelho ⓘ
Polytechnic University of Leiria
Leiria, Portugal

Nuno Vieira Lopes ⓘ
Polytechnic University of Leiria
Leiria, Portugal

Ivan Miguel Pires ⓘ
Instituto de Telecomunicações, Escola
Superior de Tecnologia e Gestão de Águeda,
Universidade de Aveiro
Águeda, Portugal

ISSN 1867-8211   ISSN 1867-822X (electronic)
Lecture Notes of the Institute for Computer Sciences, Social Informatics
and Telecommunications Engineering
ISBN 978-3-031-52523-0   ISBN 978-3-031-52524-7 (eBook)
https://doi.org/10.1007/978-3-031-52524-7

This Springer imprint is published by the registered company Springer Nature Switzerland AG
The registered company address is: Gewerbestrasse 11, 6330 Cham, Switzerland

Paper in this product is recyclable.

Preface

This volume comprises the proceedings of the ninth edition of the European Alliance for Innovation (EAI) International Conference on Smart Objects and Technologies for Social Good (EAI GOODTECHS 2023), held on October 18–20, 2023. Researchers, developers, and practitioners from all over the world attended this conference to share their experiences in designing, implementing, deploying, operating, and evaluating smart objects and technologies for social benefit. Social goods are commodities and services that may be offered by nonprofit organizations, the government, or private businesses. Many people with unique needs, including seniors, athletes, and children, will benefit from the results of the conference. Health care, safety, sports, the environment, democracy, computer science, and human rights are all examples of social goods. The primary institution of the General Chair that provided and actively assisted in the organizing of this conference was the Polytechnic University of Leiria, which organized the conference.

The EAI GOODTECHS 2023 technical program featured 13 full papers in oral presentation sessions across all tracks. As a result, there were two conference tracks: "Main Track" and "Late Track." In addition to the excellent technical papers' presentations, the technical program included four keynote speeches. Pétia Georgieva from Department of Electronics, Telecommunications and Informatics (DETI) at University of Aveiro, Portugal, Francisco Flórez-Revuelta from Department of Computer Technology, University of Alicante, Spain, Carina Dantas from SHINE 2Europe, and Radu-Ioan Ciobanu from National University of Science and Technology Politehnica Bucharest, Romania, delivered the four keynote sessions.

Coordination with the steering chair, Imrich Chlamtac, was essential for the success of the conference. We sincerely appreciate his constant support and guidance. It was also a great pleasure to work with such an excellent organizing committee team for their hard work in organizing and supporting the conference. In particular, the Technical Program Committee, led by our TPC Co-Chairs, Nuno M. Garcia, Norberto Jorge Gonçalves, Paulo Neves, and José Paulo Losado, completed the peer-review process of technical papers and made a high-quality technical program. We are also grateful to the Conference Manager, Kristina Havlickova, for her support and to all the authors who submitted their papers to the EAI GOODTECHS 2023 conference.

We are adamant that the GOODTECHS conference offers a suitable place for all researchers, developers, and practitioners to debate all science and technological issues pertinent to smart objects and technologies for social good. In addition, based on the papers included in this collection, we anticipate that subsequent GOODTECHS conferences will be as fruitful and interesting.

November 2023

Paulo Jorge Coelho
Ivan Miguel Pires
Nuno Vieira Lopes

Organization

Steering Committee

Imrich Chlamtac   University of Trento, Italy

Organizing Committee

General Chair

Paulo Jorge Coelho   Polytechnic University of Leiria, Portugal

General Co-chair

Ivan Miguel Pires   Universidade de Aveiro, Portugal

TPC Chair and Co-chairs

Nuno M. Garcia	Universidade de Lisboa, Portugal
Norberto Jorge Gonçalves	University of Trás-os-Montes and Alto Douro, Portugal
Paulo Neves	Polytechnic Institute of Castelo Branco, Portugal
José Paulo Lousado	Polytechnic Institute of Viseu, Portugal

Sponsorship and Exhibit Chair

Nuno M. Rodrigues   Polytechnic University of Leiria, Portugal

Local Chair

Nuno Vieira Lopes   Polytechnic University of Leiria, Portugal

Workshops Chair

Daniel Alexandre   University of Trás-os-Montes and Alto Douro, Portugal

Publicity and Social Media Chairs

Francisco Marinho	University of Trás-os-Montes and Alto Douro, Portugal
Maria Adelaide Andrade	University of Trás-os-Montes and Alto Douro, Portugal

Publications Chair

Joana Matos Dias	University of Coimbra, Portugal

Web Chair

António Jorge Gouveia	University of Trás-os-Montes and Alto Douro, Portugal

Posters and PhD Track Chair

Susanna Spinsante	Università Politecnica Delle Marche, Italy

Panels Chair

Valderi Leithardt	Polytechnic Institute of Lisbon, Portugal

Demos Chair

Eftim Zdravevski	Saints Cyril and Methodius University, Skopje, North Macedonia

Tutorials Chair

John Gialelis	University of Patras, Greece

Technical Program Committee

Abbas Aljuboori	University of Information Technology and Communications, Iraq
Abbas Jamalipour	University of Sydney, Australia
Abdul Hannan	University of Management and Technology, Pakistan
Alberto Taboada-Crispi	Universidad Central "Marta Abreu" de Las Villas, Cuba

Alessio Vecchio	University of Pisa, Italy
Alexandre Bernardino	Instituto Superior Técnico, Portugal
Amr Tolba	King Saud University, Saudi Arabia
Ana María Iglesias Maqueda	Carlos III University of Madrid, Spain
Ana Maria Mendonça	Universidade do Porto, Portugal
Ana Paula Silva	Instituto Politécnico de Castelo Branco, Portugal
Ana Sequeira	Institute for Systems and Computer Engineering, Technology and Science, Portugal
Ana Teresa Maia	University of the Algarve, Portugal
André Moraes	Universidade Federal de Santa Catarina, Brazil
Andrew M. Thomas	Birmingham City University, UK
Andrzej Janusz	University of Warsaw, Poland
Anna Sandak	University of Primorska, Slovenia
António Godinho	Instituto Superior de Engenharia de Coimbra, Portugal
António Pimenta	Monteiro da Universidade do Porto, Portugal
Argentina Leite	Universidade de Trás-os-Montes e Alto Douro, Portugal
Arlindo Silva	Instituto Politécnico de Castelo Branco, Portugal
Armando Pinho	Universidade de Aveiro, Portugal
Arnis Cirulis Vidzeme	University of Applied Sciences, Latvia
Aura Conci	Universidade Federal Fluminense, Brazil
Aurélio Campilho	Universidade do Porto, Portugal
Beata Godejord	Nord University, Norway
Beatriz Remeseiro	Universidad de Oviedo, Portugal
Beatriz Sousa Santos	University of Aveiro, Portugal
Bernardete Ribeiro	Universidade de Coimbra, Portugal
Birgitta Langhammer	Oslo Metropolitan University, Norway
Bruno Silva	Universidade da Beira Interior, Portugal
Catarina Reis	Instituto Politécnico de Leiria, Portugal
Catarina Silva	Universidade de Coimbra, Portugal
Catarina Silva	University of Coimbra, Portugal
Celia Ramos	University of the Algarve, Portugal
Ciprian Dobre	University Politechnica of Bucharest, Romania
Cláudio de Souza Baptista	Federal University of Campina Grande, Brazil
Cristina Portales Ricart	Universidad de Valencia, Spain
Cristina Santos	University of Minho, Portugal
Daniel Hernandez	Universidad Pontificia de Salamanca, Spain
David Lamas	Tallinn University, Estonia
Diego M. Jiménez-Bravo	University of Salamanca, Spain
Dimitrios Koutsouris	National Technical University of Athens, Greece
Diogo Marques	Universidade da Beira Interior, Portugal

Dominique Schreurs	KU Leuven, Belgium
Dustin van der Haar	University of Johannesburg, South Africa
Elizabeth Simão Carvalho	Open University, Portugal
Faisal Hussain	University of Engineering and Technology, Pakistan
Farhan Riaz	National University of Sciences and Technology, Islamabad, Pakistan
Federico Del Giorgio	Solfa National University of La Plata, Argentina
Fedor Lehocki	Slovak University of Technology, Slovakia
Fernando Monteiro	Instituto Politécnico de Bragança, Portugal
Fernando Ribeiro	Instituto Politécnico de Castelo Branco, Portugal
Filipe Caldeira	Instituto Politécnico de Viseu, Portugal
Francisco Garcia Encinas	University of Salamanca, Spain
Francisco Melero	CETEM, Spain
Frank Krüger	University of Rostock, Germany
Gabriel Pires	Instituto Politécnico de Tomar, Portugal
George Papadopoulos	University of Cyprus, Cyprus
Geraldo Braz Junior	Universidade Federal do Maranhão, Brazil
Graça Minas	University of Minho, Portugal
Gregory O'Hare	University College Dublin, Ireland
Hanna Denysyuk	Universidade da Beira Interior, Portugal
Hasan Ogul Østfold	University College, Norway
Hélder Oliveira	Universidade do Porto, Portugal
Henrique Neiva	Universidade da Beira Interior, Portugal
Hugo Silva	Instituto de Telecomunicações, Portugal
Inês Domingues	ISEC, Portugal
Isabel Sofia Brito	IP Beja, Portugal
Ivan Štajduhar	University of Rijeka, Croatia
Jaime Cardoso	Universidade do Porto, Portugal
Jake Kaner	Nottingham Trent University, UK
James C. Lin	University of Illinois at Chicago, USA
Jânio Monteiro	University of the Algarve, Portugal
João Dallyson Sousa de Almeida	Universidade Federal do Maranhão, Brazil
João Henriques	University of Coimbra, Portugal
João Paulo Costeira	IST, Portugal
João Paulo Cunha	Universidade do Porto, Portugal
João Paulo Papa	São Paolo State University, Brazil
João Pedrosa	Universidade do Porto, Portugal
João Tavares	Universidade do Porto, Portugal
Joel Guerreiro	University of the Algarve, Portugal
Johan Debayle	Ecole Nationale Supérieure des Mines, Saint-Etienne, France

Jonatan Lerga	University of Rijeka, Croatia
Jorge Calvo-Zaragoza	Universidad de Alicante, Spain
Jorge Oliveira	ISEP, Portugal
Jorge Semião	University of the Algarve, Portugal
Jorge Silva	Universidade do Porto, Portugal
José Alba Castro	University of Vigo, Spain
Jose Carlos Meireles Metrólho	Instituto Politécnico de Castelo Branco, Portugal
José Francisco Morgado	Instituto Politécnico de Viseu, Portugal
José Machado Silva	Universidade do Porto, Portugal
José Miguel Mota-Macías	Universidad de Cádiz, Spain
José Valente Oliveira	University of the Algarve, Portugal
Jose-Jesus Fernandez	CNB-CSIC, Spain
Juan José Rodríguez	Universidad de Burgos, Spain
Juan Manuel Dodero-Beardo	Universidad de Cádiz, Spain
Kalle Tammemäe Tallinn	University of Technology, Estonia
Kasim Terzic	University of St. Andrews, UK
Kerli Mooses	University of Tartu, Estonia
Koen Vermeer	Rotterdam Ophthalmic Institute, The Netherlands
Kuldar Taveter	Tallinn University, Estonia
Lei Guo Chongqing	University of Posts and Telecommunications, China
Leonel Morgado	Open University, Portugal
Lino Ferreira	Polytechnic of Leiria, Portugal
Lu Zhang	INSA, Rennes, France
Luís Alexandre	Universidade da Beira Interior, Portugal
Luis Augusto Silva	University of Salamanca, Spain
Luis Rosa	University of Coimbra, Portugal
Luís Teixeira	Universidade do Porto, Portugal
Marcelo Fiori	Universidad de la República, Uruguay
Marcin Szczuka	University of Warsaw, Poland
María García	University of Valladolid, Spain
Maria Graça Ruano	Universidade do Algarve, Portugal
Mário Marques	Universidade da Beira Interior, Portugal
Marta Chinnici	ENEA, Italy
Michael Burnard	University of Primorska, Slovenia
Miguel Coimbra	Universidade do Porto, Portugal
Miguel Velhote Correia	Universidade do Porto, Portugal
Mónica Costa	Instituto Politécnico de Castelo Branco, Portugal
Nicolai Petkov	University of Groningen, The Netherlands
Norbert Krugger	University of Southern Denmark, Denmark
Nuno Cruz Garcia	Universidade de Lisboa, Portugal
Nuno Miranda	Polytechnic of Leiria, Portugal

Octavian Postolache	ISCTE, Portugal
Oliver Montesdeoca	Universitat de Barcelona, Spain
Ouri Wolfson	University of Illinois at Chicago, USA
Panagiotis Kosmas	King's College London, UK
Paula Faria	Instituto Politécnico de Leiria, Portugal
Paulo Costa	Polytechnic of Leiria, Portugal
Paulo Mendes	University of Minho, Portugal
Paulo Novais	University of Minho, Portugal
Paulo Simoes	University of Coimbra, Portugal
Pedro Brandão	Universidade do Porto, Portugal
Pedro Cardoso	University of the Algarve, Portugal
Petre Lameski	Ss. Cyril and Methodius University, North Macedonia
Piotr Lasek	University of Rzeszów, Poland
Rafael Caldeirinha	Polytechnic of Leiria, Portugal
Rafael Maestre	Universidad Complutense de Madrid, Spain
Roberto Alejo	Instituto Tecnológico de Toluca, Mexico
Roberto Corizzo	American University, USA
Roberto Lam	University of the Algarve, Portugal
Rui Mesquita	CML, Portugal
Samuel Silva	Universidade de Aveiro, Portugal
Sandeep Pirbhulal	Norwegian Computing Center, Norway
Sébai Dorsaf	ENSI, Tunisia
Serge Autexier	Deutsches Forschungszentrum für Künstliche Intelligenz GmbH, Germany
Susana Catarino	Universidade do Minho, Portugal
Tânia Pereira	University of Porto, Portugal
Teresa Cardoso	Universidade Aberta, Portugal
Teresa Coimbra	Universidade Aberta, Portugal
Tiago Cruz	University of Coimbra, Portugal
Vaclav Skala	University of West Bohemia, Czechia
Vasco Ponciano	Instituto Politécnico de Castelo Branco, Portugal
Ventzeslav Valev	Institute of Mathematics and Informatics, BAS, Bulgaria
Víctor Muñoz Martínez	University of Malaga, Spain
Vitor Cardoso	Open University, Portugal
Xinbo Gao	Chongqing University of Posts and Telecommunications, China
Yueyue Dai	Nanyang Technological University, Singapore
Zhicheng Yang	PAII Inc., USA
Zuzana Berger Haladova	Comenius University, Bratislava, Slovakia

Contents

Computer Science and Information Technology

Zero Configuration Comfort and Accessibility in Smart Environments

Abdulkadir Karaagac$^{(\boxtimes)}$, Nicolas Coppik, and Rhaban Hark

ABB Corporate Research, Ladenburg, Germany
{abdulkadir.karaagac,nicolas.coppik,rhaban.hark}@de.abb.com

Abstract. By enabling more personalized hospitality services and adjustment of smart environments, the personalization of building and home automation systems can create better comfort, eased accessibility, improved user experience and greater energy efficiency for living and working environments. However, there is a lack of automation in nowadays systems, such that users must perform tedious manual interaction with the smart environments in order to personalize the environment according to their preferences and needs. In this regard, this paper presents the concept of *Zero Configuration Comfort and Accessibility*: portable and personalized smart space profiles which can be (i) configured, (ii) stored, (iii) accessed, (iv) transferred, and (v) applied to any smart environment in an automated manner. In addition to the concept, the main technical challenges and solution approaches for achieving portable personalization in smart spaces are presented. Moreover, the paper provides details about the design and implementation of a system prototype which demonstrates the feasibility and value of the proposed concept.

Keywords: Smart buildings · Personalization · Portable profiles · Building automation systems

1 Introduction

As smart environments and devices are becoming more capable and more common, people are expecting and demanding more personalization and increased comfort from smart environments. The personalization of smart environments includes the application of personal environmental preferences (such as temperature or lighting settings), automated routines, control, and/or accessibility requirements (voice commands, visual enhancements). The collection of these personal preference settings are referred as a *profile*.

Similarly, as many advanced technologies and systems, today's building and home automation systems are less accessible to people with disabilities, due to limitations of user interfaces and accessibility technology. Especially, considering the fact that smart environments are typically used by many different people, they are therefore usually not adapted to individual accessibility needs of users.

© ICST Institute for Computer Sciences, Social Informatics and Telecommunications Engineering 2024
Published by Springer Nature Switzerland AG 2024. All Rights Reserved
P. J. Coelho et al. (Eds.): GOODTECHS 2023, LNICST 556, pp. 3–16, 2024.
https://doi.org/10.1007/978-3-031-52524-7_1

This limits the benefits and usability of smart environments for people with disabilities.

Therefore, this work investigated the portable personalized profiles for smart environments and proposed the concept of *Zero Configuration Comfort and Accessibility* (*ZCCA*) which can enhance the accessibility, comfort and user experience in smart environments, especially for people with disabilities by enabling barrier-free and human-centered automation systems for smart spaces.

This paper is organized as follows. Section 2 describes some of the main use cases that the proposed concept can offer for social good. The key challenges that needs to be addressed to realize the proposed concept are presented in Sect. 3, which is followed by the potential solution approaches for those challenges in Sect. 4. After that, Sect. 5 provides a detailed description of the developed proof-of-concept. Finally, Sect. 6 concludes the paper with a short summary and outlook.

2   Use Cases for Social Good

The proposed concept of *Zero Configuration Comfort and Accessibility* (*ZCCA*) is the idea of portable and personalized smart space preferences which can be (i) configured, (ii) stored/accessed/transferred, and (iii) applied to any "smart" environment. By doing so, this concept enhances accessibility, comfort and user experience in smart environments, e.g., for people with disabilities, and deliver high-quality, barrier-free and human-centered home or building automation systems and applications.

Many technological advancements are less accessible to people with disabilities, including the usage of the Internet and smart devices [7], due to limitations of user interfaces and accessibility technology. Smart environments face another challenging development in this context, as they may be used by many different people and are therefore usually not adapted to individual accessibility needs. Apart from that, individuals may interact with a large number of smart environments on a regular basis and configuring each environment for their requirements is both practically challenging, given lack of accessibility, and would also present a large burden for environments that are only rarely interacted with. The proposed concept aims to address these concerns by making personal preferences and accessibility requirements easily portable and applicable across different smart environments. In the remaining of this section, three simple use cases are introduced to showcase the concept's application.

2.1   Personalized Spaces

The primary use case is the automated adaptation of environmental settings based on user preferences without requiring manual configuration of that environment, for instance in hotel rooms or office environments. By means of the proposed concept, the visitor's profile can be preloaded to the control system or automatically transfered upon their arrival, and the environment can be prepared based on their preferences and their type of trip. As this enables automatic application of personal preferences (profiles) to different smart environments and removes the need for manual configuration of control systems, thereby the *ZCCA* concept can enhance the comfort and accessibility of the smart environment and reduce the hurdles faced by people with disabilities in interacting with such environments. These personalized profiles may include environmental preferences (personalized control for temperature, humidity, light level etc.) and automated routines (alarm clock, lights, and heating cycles).

2.2 Personalized User Interfaces

In addition to environmental preferences, another aspect that can be personalized is how the user interacts with the smart environment: user interfaces for home/room/building automation systems. The user interfaces are one of the main components of smart environments which defines the usability and accessibility of the systems. A user may encounter several different smart environments, each with a different set of controllable devices and means to control those. At the same time each user has very individual capabilities (e.g. limitations due to disabilities, language) and personal demands when controlling smart environments. Therefore, temporary users of such systems typically first need to familiarize themselves with the interface, taking time and effort. If the controls are too complex, smart environment features may go unused.

The proposed concept can enable users to use their personalized interface to control any smart environment they encounter. This could include the customization of interfaces or presentation of unified user interfaces across different environments to improve the usability of the control/automation systems, especially for environments which are encountered only for short times. Also control capabilities can be adapted to the personal preferences and limitations of the present user by downloading a machine-readable description of those from a carried device or from a cloud share. Or, as illustrated in Fig. 1, control capabilities can be activated/deactivated and interface presentation can be adjusted based on the provided user preferences.

For instance, fonts sizes or altered colors in user interfaces for users with limited vision, changing language based on user preference or adjusted complexity level of the control functionalities. By offering personalized user interfaces, this concept can help to increase the acceptance of controllable smart environments, thus, also increased visibility and reputation of such systems.

2.3 Personalized Accessibility Method

Another aspect that can be personalized in a smart environment based on user profiles are the accessibility methods that user prefer or need. Based on the transferred accessiblity requirement information available in the user profile, different

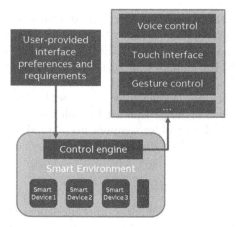

Fig. 1. User Interfaces adapting User Preferences and Accessibility Needs.

accessibility method can be activated or deactivated: e.g. voice recognition control for visually impaired users or visual enhancements for hearing impaired users.

3   Key Challenges

This section highlights some of the technical challenges that need to be addressed in order to realize the proposed concept of *Zero Configuration Comfort and Accessibility* (*ZCCA*) in smart environments. Potential approaches to the given challenges are discussed in the subsequent section.

Profile Portability. First of all, it is required to have appropriate means to make personal preference settings, so called profiles, portable. To this end, the profiles must be stored, transferred, and exposed in a secure and privacy-preserving manner. Within that a number of further sub-challenges arise. On the one hand, profiles should be always available with as little effort from the user as possible. Now, on the other hand, high availability options, such as cloud-based solutions, typically introduce considerable security efforts compared to manual transportation of profiles, e.g., in handheld devices.

Information Modeling. The modeling of the profile information is a twofold challenge: *(i)* First, it requires a suitable standardized, yet extensible meta-model for potential keys and values with accurately defined units. The model must be standardized (or be a candidate for such) in order to allow for interoperability of different systems and to prevent vendor lock-ins, a crucial acceptance criteria. On top of this, the meta-model must be extensible to allow for new and custom smart devices. The meta-model should additionally be organized in a hierarchical fashion to allow settings to be inherited from higher-level settings: As an example, the bedroom temperature can be refined, e.g., with a lower setting, while it also inherits the default room temperature in case it is not refined. *(ii)* Second, the stored per-user models must differentiate between different environments which a user may encounter. Within that, environments should also inherit settings from each other in a hierarchical fashion. A potential example here is the reuse of a home environment profile so it can be applied in a hotel room or office environment, without any special configuration if that is not desired.

Secure User Identification/Authentication and Access Management. In order to personalize the environment for user preferences, one of the main steps that needs to be taken is identifying the user and retrieving user-related data. For that reason, the presented concept and system requires appropriate methods to identify and authenticate users as well as provide access to selected data towards the smart environment. Again, this is a twofold challenge: *(i)* First, a user must be identified and authenticated through trustworthy means either by physical presence plus secret or using state-of-the-art online authentication mechanisms. *(ii)* Second, this includes the access to potentially privacy critical user profile for the environments encountered by the user. Thereby, the provided information may be limited to the extent required and configured for a certain environment.

Building Automation Systems Integration. Another key challenge is the integration of a *ZCCA* subsystem into existing building automation systems, where there is a plethora of different products. Besides a number of open-source solutions for building automation, several closed systems exist. Both need to be taken care of in order to ensure the user acceptance of the proposed concept and resulting system. Especially in the smart home sector, ensuring interoperability with the wide range of solutions available on the market poses a substantial challenge, which this work does not purport to fully address. Interoperability frameworks have been proposed as a solution to this issue [5], but have not seen widespread adoption. The adoption of the Matter standard may also indicate a move towards more standardized, interoperable solutions in the smart home space, which would alleviate this concern.

4   Solution Approaches

This section discusses potential approaches with their advantages and challenges. Those include the portability of profiles, user identification and how to model profiles internally.

4.1   Profile Portability and Storage

There are various options to store, transfer and expose preference data including cloud services, edge providers or directly on portable devices carried by users.

Firstly, a cloud-based service architecture can be an option. In this case, a central component serves as management unit and provides interaction between smart environment gateways and preference databases. The portability of the profiles comes from the availability of the data to all smart spaces via cloud access. An API (e.g., REST) as anchor point towards gateways and a web frontend allow access to the data. In case of any need for the modification of preferences, this API can be used by automation systems or by a web frontend.

In this approach, the created *ZCCA* system is available everywhere, highly reliable and not dependent on any particular device. However, as the preference data is stored in a cloud platform, care needs to be taken in order to address any privacy concern of users. Moreover, while the cloud service itself can be made highly reliable, overall reliability of the system also requires stable connectivity between a smart environment and the cloud service. A sample system architecture for such a *ZCCA* system with cloud-based services is provided in Fig. 2. As in Fig. 2, the cloud-based setup can include different backend vendors, allowing different environments to fetch preference settings from either of them after proper identification of a user. This design choice helps alleviate privacy concerns as users can choose between different backend services or even host their own.

Alternatively, an edge device, e.g., building automation system gateway, can also be used to store the user preferences locally (only and only with the consent of the user) and always close to the smart environment. This would eliminate the need of carrying a device and allow the system to work without cloud connectivity, but also limit the flexibility and availability of preference data cross different locations.

Thirdly, the profiles could be also stored and carried via mobile devices, such as smartphone, tablet or smartwatch. In this case, the data is carried together with the user as long as the mobile device is with them, which limits *ZCCA* functionality to scenarios where users have their device with them. However, the user data stays always with the user device, and the system can be designed to share as little data as necessary with the smart environment, making this a very privacy-friendly option.

After considering the advantages and limitations of these options for profile storage and portability, one can decide to use one of the cloud, edge or mobile-based profile portability solution or can also combine them to create more flexible solutions. In this case, the replication and synchronization of preference data needs to be handled carefully and properly.

4.2 User Identification and Access Management

Irrespective of where the preference data is stored and managed, users interact with the *ZCCA*-enabled smart environment locally, and user identification therefore also has to start with a local component. As the ultimate goal is minimizing user effort, this step should be as easy and convenient as possible.

A straightforward option for local identification of users is the use of hardware tokens, such as smart cards or phones, using Near-Field Communication (NFC) or Bluetooth Low Energy (BLE) beacons to detect a user's presence. As discussed above, some options, such as smartphones or more capable smart cards, can also be used to directly store preferences.

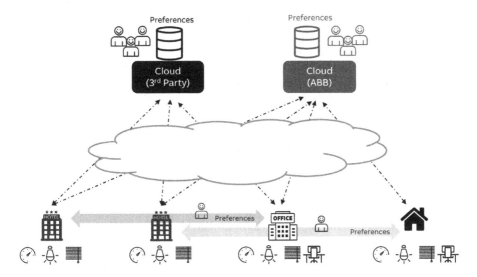

Fig. 2. Portable profiles using a Cloud-based Service Architecture. Two cloud backends are available from different providers. Multiple environments can access the backends.

Other options include biometric user identification, which may introduce privacy concerns, or, especially in enterprise environments, the integration of *ZCCA* concept with existing information technology (IT) infrastructure - for instance, in an office with desk sharing, users can be identified when they plug in their laptops, allowing their preferences (e.g., desk height or other ergonomic preferences) to be applied automatically.

In solutions using cloud or edge services to store and manage preferences, no matter what option for user identification is chosen, it must then be used to authenticate the user towards the backend service. The details of this process vary between options for user identification. A more detailed description of one example is provided in Sect. 5.3. Once the user is authenticated, their preferences can be retrieved from the backend service and applied to the smart environment.

Finally, all solutions must provide a way for users to manage their credentials, such as enrolling a new phone or revoking access for a lost smart card. Cloud-based solutions can easily provide this functionality as part of a web interface that users can also use to manage their preferences.

4.3 Information Modeling for Profiles

Looking at the information modeling for profiles, thus, for preference settings of users to control smart devices, a number of efforts already exist, which are targeting the modeling of Internet of Things (IoT) devices. To avoid the creation of yet another meta model, this paper refers to works such as HOMEML [6,8], the IEEE 1452.2 [1,10] and its adoption in IEEE 21450 [2], or IoT-LITE [3,4] as discussed in W3C. The interested reader may find more information summarized by da Silva and Hirmer [9].

As discussed in Sect. 3, the profile models must discern not only between users, but also environments and within that, allow to inherit settings. Environment settings can be inherited from other environments, e.g., *hotel* environment settings can inherit settings from *home* environment settings.

Furthermore, settings within an environment can inherit from one another. For example, room temperatures within one environment can get a default settings, but be refined based on their properties (cold bedrooms vs. warm living rooms).

In order to represent preference settings according to these requirements, this work set up a simple schema for settings depicted in Fig. 3. The schema exists per-user, while user settings are strictly isolated. For each user, all default settings can be set in the top level environment. Apart from this environment, sub-environments can be specified which inherit all settings from exactly one other environment. In each environment all settings can be individually configured or unset to cancel their inheritance.

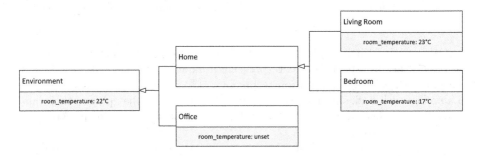

Fig. 3. Modelling of User Profiles based on Inheritance among Environments.

As example in the figure, the `room_temperature` is set initially with a default value of 22 °C. In the next layer, the environment splits up in a `home` environment and the `office`. Since the `home` environment does not refine the `room_temperature`, it will use the inherited 22 °C. The `office` environment unsets the `room_temperature` such that no value is given and the smart environment may apply any temperature, e.g., the company's default office temperature. Furthermore, the `home` splits up into different locations (sub-environments), namely the `living room` and the `bedroom`. In both cases the `room_temperature` value is refined with a low temperature of the bedroom and a more comfortable, warm temperature in the living room.

5 Proof of Concept

In order to demonstrate the feasibility of the *ZCCA* concept, a simple proto-type is developed, which presents the capability of automated adaptation and personalization of smart environments according to portable user profiles. This section provides details about the created system setup, architecture and result-ing demonstration flow.

5.1 Demo Setup

In the developed prototype system, a smart office environment with multiple control capabilities is mimicked. Within that, two separate working spaces with independent and different control systems and slightly different control function-alities are considered.

In the office environments, depicted in Fig. 4, the following control capa-bilities are integrated to enable accessibility and comfort: Both environments, *Workstation 1* (WS1) and *Workstation 2* (WS2), are equipped with a height adjustable desk such that users can sit with different heights, e.g., for office chairs but also wheelchairs as well as standing up. On top of this, one of the environments, namely WS2, has also smart control capabilities for the lighting, temperature and shutters. Both environments have an Radio Frequency Iden-tification (RFID) reader for the purpose of identifying the users and therewith fetching their profile.

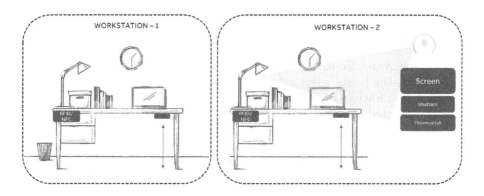

Fig. 4. Demo Setup to showcase a Proof of Concept for *ZCCA*.

5.2 System Architecture

Using the aforementioned setup, an automation system is created which can identify the user, obtain the user preferences, and apply those preferences on the desk height and other environmental settings.

In this *ZCCA*-aware automation system, a Cloud-based Service Architecture approach and deployment is used due to the omnipresent availability of profiles using this approach. The overview of the system architecture is provided in Fig. 5.

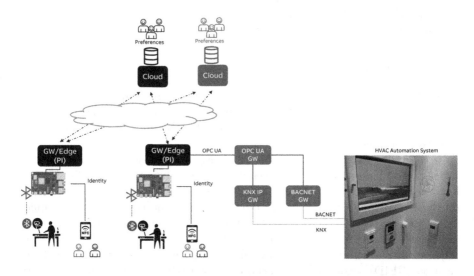

Fig. 5. The Architectural Overview of developed Proof of Concept.

As it is demonstrated in this figure, the setup includes two cloud instances (backend) which are being used by different users to store and access user profiles. On the other side, two local deployments with separate Gateways (e.g., edge devices) are created for each workstation: WS1 and WS2.

For WS1, the height-adjustable desk is integrated to the control system via *Bluetooth Low Energy* (BLE) and a smart card (i.e., NFC/RFID) reader that is directly connected to the gateway, which is used to identify the users. For WS2, in addition to height adjustable desk and smart card reader, a *Heating, Ventilation, and Air Conditioning* (HVAC) automation system is integrated by means of various industrial connectivity technologies (i.e. KNX IP and BACNET). This HVAC system allows the control of temperature, light and shutter system for the corresponding workstation.

5.3   User Identification and Access Management

The demo setup uses smart cards as user credentials, specifically Mifare Classic cards due to their broad availability and low cost. When a user presents their card to the system, the process shown in Fig. 6 starts.

First, the reader reads the card unique identifier (UID) and, since the system supports multiple, independent cloud instances, the URL of the backend service to use. This URL is stored on the card during credential enrollment, along

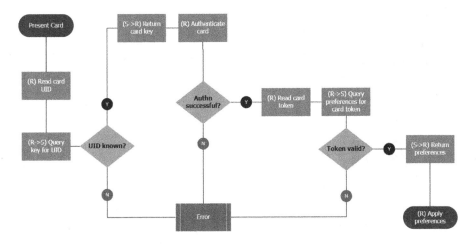

Fig. 6. Prototyped User Authentication Process.

with a unique token for that particular card generated by the backend service. The local system queries the backend service URL stored on the card for a key associated with that card's UID. If the service knows the card UID, it returns a corresponding key, which the reader can use to authenticate the card. From the authenticated card, it can then read the card-specific token. That token is sent to the backend service, as part of a request for the user's preferences. If the token is valid, the backend service returns the user's preferences, which can then be applied to the smart environment.

While the prototype implementation simply uses random bearer tokens, arbitrary other token formats could be supported. Similarly, although the prototype supports only a single kind of credential (classic smart cards), support for other kinds could easily be added. This would require implementing support in the backend service for the initial authentication steps, up to the point where the local system has access to the token. From this point, the token-based authentication and preference retrieval do not need to be adjusted.

5.4   Demo Scenario

The overview of the sample scenario and the demonstrated flow is illustrated in Fig. 7. As it can be seen in this figure, first, User 1 arrives to the working environment and checks-in to the workstation via the attached smart card reader and initiates the user identification process described in the previous subsection.

By using the acquired information (URL of the cloud instance, required credential data), the user profile is requested by the gateway from the corresponding cloud instance. Based on the user data and location information (specific location or its' type), the preference information is returned by the cloud server to the gateway.

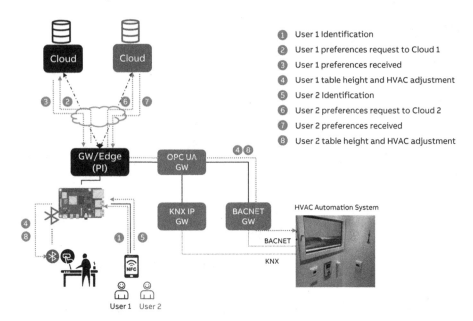

Fig. 7. Architectural Overview of the Demonstration Setup using two Instances of Cloud Services, a Gateway connected to the smart environment.

If the user information is not authenticated or if the access to the requested information is not granted by the user, the information request is declined. Upon the successful reception of the user profile, the environment settings and table height configuration is adjusted automatically. Some sample pictures from these steps and resulting changes on the proof of concept system is provided in Fig. 8.

Following User 1, another user identified as User 2, who utilizes an another cloud server, arrives and proceeds to check-in at the same workstation. By following the same automated procedures as for User 1, the same workstation is reconfigured according to the preferences of User 2. Similar to User 1, some sample pictures demonstrating each of these steps for User 2 are also available in Fig. 8.

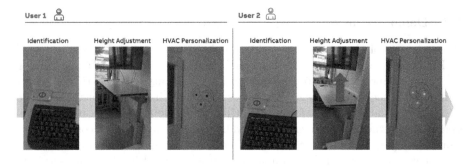

Fig. 8. Illustration of the Demo: The Environment adapts to the Profile that registered for an identified User.

6   Summary and Conclusion

Automated personalization and effortless adjustment of smart environments is an important step for improving the user experience and comfort for living and working. And it can enable to create more accessible, barrier-free and human-centered automation systems for smart spaces, especially for people with disabilities.

For that reason, this work investigated the feasibility and practicability of the proposed concept of *Zero Configuration Comfort and Accessibility (ZCCA)* which offers portable personalization in smart environments. A number of key challenges and research problems are identified. Consequently, the potential solution approaches for these challenges and problems are discussed. In summary, this includes *(i)* an architecture for storing and fetching user preferences, *(ii)* a concept for identifying users including access management for potentially privacy-critical profiles, *(iii)* a concept to model profiles with their relevant information. Last but not least, the conceptual architecture and description for one possible approach is detailed and a demo setup is created as a prototype to *(iv)* demonstrate the feasibility of the concept.

Even though this work takes an important step for more personalization, less configuration, improved comfort and accessibility, there are still a number of technical challenges that requires addressing. Especially standardized and widely adopted information models for user preferences, harmonized interfaces to enable interoperability and well-addressed privacy concerns will enable the true value of the proposed *ZCCA* concept.

References

1. IEEE Standard for a Smart Transducer Interface for Sensors and Actuators - Transducer to Microprocessor Communication Protocols and Transducer Electronic Data Sheet (TEDS) Formats. IEEE Std 1451.2-1997, pp. 1–120 (1998). https://doi.org/10.1109/IEEESTD.1998.88285
2. ISO/IEC/IEEE Information technology - Smart transducer interface for sensors and actuators - Common functions, communication protocols, and Transducer Electronic Data Sheet (TEDS) formats. ISO/IEC/IEEE 21450:2010(E), pp. 1–350 (2010). https://doi.org/10.1109/IEEESTD.2010.5668466
3. Bermudez-Edo, M., Elsaleh, T., Barnaghi, P., Taylor, K.: IoT-lite: a lightweight semantic model for the internet of things. In: 2016 INTL IEEE Conferences on Ubiquitous Intelligence & Computing, Advanced and Trusted Computing, Scalable Computing and Communications, Cloud and Big Data Computing, Internet of People, and Smart World Congress (UIC/ATC/SCALCOM/CBDCOM/IOP/Smartworld), pp. 90–97. IEEE (2016)
4. Bermudez-Edo, M., Elsaleh, T., Barnaghi, P., Taylor, K.: IoT-lite: a lightweight semantic model for the internet of things and its use with dynamic semantics. Pers. Ubiquit. Comput. **21**, 475–487 (2017)
5. Farooq, M.O., Wheelock, I., Pesch, D.: IoT-connect: an interoperability framework for smart home communication protocols. IEEE Consum. Electron. Mag. **9**(1), 22–29 (2020). https://doi.org/10.1109/MCE.2019.2941393

6. McDonald, H., Nugent, C., Hallberg, J., Finlay, D., Moore, G., Synnes, K.: The homeML suite: shareable datasets for smart home environments. Heal. Technol. **3**, 177–193 (2013)

7. Nam, S.J., Park, E.Y.: The effects of the smart environment on the information divide experienced by people with disabilities. Disabil. Health J. **10**(2), 257–263 (2017). https://doi.org/10.1016/j.dhjo.2016.11.001, https://www.sciencedirect.com/science/article/pii/S1936657416301741

8. Nugent, C.D., Finlay, D.D., Davies, R.J., Wang, H.Y., Zheng, H., Hallberg, J., Synnes, K., Mulvenna, M.D.: homeML – an open standard for the exchange of data within smart environments. In: Okadome, T., Yamazaki, T., Makhtari, M. (eds.) ICOST 2007. LNCS, vol. 4541, pp. 121–129. Springer, Heidelberg (2007). https://doi.org/10.1007/978-3-540-73035-4_13

9. Franco da Silva, A.C., Hirmer, P.: Models for internet of things environments - a survey. Information **11**(10), 487 (2020)

10. Song, E.Y., Burns, M., Pandey, A., Roth, T.: IEEE 1451 smart sensor digital twin federation for IoT/CPS research. In: 2019 IEEE Sensors Applications Symposium (SAS), pp. 1–6. IEEE (2019)

The Impact of the Evolution of Operating Systems on Older Web Applications

António Godinho[1]([✉])(iD), José Rosado[2,3](iD), Filipe Sá[2](iD),
and Filipe Cardoso[3,4](iD)

[1] Coimbra Business School, Polytechnic Institute of Coimbra, Quinta Agrícola - Bencanta, 3045-231 Coimbra, Portugal
agodinho@iscac.pt
[2] Coimbra Institute of Engineering, Polytechnic Institute of Coimbra, Rua Pedro Nunes - Quinta da Nora, 3030-199 Coimbra, Portugal
{jfr,filipe.sa}@isec.pt
[3] INESC Coimbra—Instituto de Engenharia de Sistemas e Computadores de Coimbra, Rua Sílvio Lima, Pólo II, 3030-790 Coimbra, Portugal
[4] Escola Superior de Gestão e Tecnologia, Politécnico de Santarém, Complexo Andaluz, Apartado 295, 2001-904 Santarém, Portugal
filipe.cardoso@esg.ipsantarem.pt

Abstract. At the beginning of 2020, the major browser-developing companies announced that newer software versions no more extended support for older TLS, 1.0 and 1.1. A warning message was displayed in older versions; the user could override it and enter the website. After implementing the deprecation of TLS 1.0 and TLS 1.1, the users can no longer enter those websites. It's becoming more unusual for websites to exist for over ten years and keep active, but there are legacy web platforms where the cost of updating an older platform may need to be revised.

The Microsoft .NET Framework has been used for almost twenty years and is supported by Microsoft Windows operating systems. In the last years, with the development of .NET Core and the release of .NET 5, Microsoft no longer develops ASP.NET Web Forms Framework. It's expected that existing web platforms will not run on newer operating systems from Microsoft and should be replaced and removed from active systems.

Keywords: ASP.NET Web Forms · Visual Basic .NET · Deprecation of TLS 1.0 and TLS 1.1 · Windows Server 2003 · IIS 6.0 · Operating System

1 Introduction

Over time, software applications and the underlying technologies or programming languages they depend on naturally undergo a process of aging, eventually becoming outdated [1]. This progression can result in a deterioration of the performance of these applications and, in certain instances, vulnerabilities [2,3].

P. J. Coelho et al. (Eds.): GOODTECHS 2023, LNICST 556, pp. 17–29, 2024.
https://doi.org/10.1007/978-3-031-52524-7_2

Additionally, these applications can be tethered to particular operating systems or technology versions, making upgrades infeasible [4].

Concurrently, as this technological aging occurs, development teams consistently confront difficulties associated with the acquisition and departure of team members [5,6]. The dynamics within these teams often revolve around the specialization of individuals in diverse technologies, a necessity driven by the rapid evolution of the technological landscape [7]. This aspect also needs to be revised to upgrade the existing systems.

Because of the economic consequences, numerous institutions and companies across various sectors offer outdated applications that operate on obsolete operating systems and technologies. It is essential to examine and assess this impact to determine whether the cost of replacing these legacy applications outweighs the benefits, especially when compared to creating new, supported applications through rewriting and redesigning [8]. All resources implicated in the process must be taken into account prior to undertaking such a venture. Nevertheless, this remains a crucial aspect within software development and system administration tasks, as the connection between outdated applications and the seriousness of vulnerabilities and glitches is significant [9,10].

Internet Information Services (IIS) 6.0 and Windows Server 2003 support ended in July 2015 [11]. Without updates, newer and modern encryption protocols used by Hyper Text Transfer Protocol Secure (HTTPS) cannot be used.

Browser developers like Google, Mozilla, Microsoft, and Apple made similar announcements that they were deprecating TLS 1.0 and TLS 1.1 around the spring of 2020 [12–15]. In April 2020, Google announced the release of Google Chrome 81, when the drop would happen, and almost by the same time, Mozilla released Firefox 74. Due to the COVID-19 pandemic, these changes were delayed for an undetermined time. Dropping the support during the pandemic could cause issues with critical government or healthcare sites that use somewhat outdated encryption protocols [16], and even Microsoft postponed the deprecation of TLS 1.0/1.1 for Microsoft 365/Office 365 for the same reasons.

In the middle of July, those changes were finally implemented, and website access was blocked automatically after the browsers updated to the latest stable version.

Almost in the same period, Microsoft announced the release of .NET Core 5 and, most importantly, the next release of their .NET family, .NET 5. With this new version, Microsoft will stop the development of the ASP.NET Web Forms Framework, making this technology obsolete [17]. Microsoft will continue to support .NET Framework (which ASP.Net WebForms is part of) for some time since much of its functionality is based on the core .Net Framework, even on modern Operating Systems like Windows 11 and Windows Server 2022 [18].

Nevertheless, the ASP .NET Web Forms Framework is a successful technology for developing web platforms. The framework has a set of built.in controls that provide visual components or functionalities to web applications.

After the time limit, a working platform was available, with all the main features working. The document is organized as follows: After this Introduction, the case study is presented in Sect. 2. The process for rebuilding the application is presented in Sect. 3. The results are shown in Sect. 4. For last, Sect. 5 gives the Conclusions.

2   Case Study - A Web-Based File Manager

The study was conducted on a higher education institution with a website that provided a file manager for all the institution's services. This application allowed all the regular file manager operations: upload, rename, delete, and, most importantly, provide the public URL to access the uploaded documents. This website was developed on ASP.NET Web Forms, using Visual Basic .NET 2.0 for the code behind it. The website serves as an internal tool for more than 3,500 users and is accessible to all visitors who download files from the site.

The website can be separated into three different components:

1. The login web page allows user authentication on Windows Active Directory.
2. The web page provides file management.
3. The file and directories repository, where the users upload the documents, and the folder organization.

2.1   Application End of Life

The institution workers have their systems configured to allow the browsers to be automatically upgraded. As refereed in Sect. 1, when browsers were updated in July, the users could no longer access the file manager, which posed a problem since all public documents, from forms for teachers and students to institution communications, weren't accessible. It was a problem that had to be fixed as soon as possible.

2.2   Upgrade Application or Develop a New Website

The original server was running Windows Server 2003 operating system, with IIS 6.0, and the website was over ten years old. The website could be moved to a new server with a recent version of IIS. Still, if the application was just copied to a newer server (running Windows Server 2019 or 2022), this would require setting up an Application Pool on .NET v2.0 Classic on IIS for the website to run. An Application Pool on .NET v2.0 Classic processes the requests in the app pool by using separate processing pipelines for IIS and ISAPI [19]. IIS7 and IIS8 were re-architected with the superior and faster Integrated Mode pipeline but retained the "Classic" mode for compatibility [19] (Fig. 1).

While the Application Pool on .NET v4.5 may run as an integrated pipeline, IIS and ASP.NET will take advantage of the improved features of IIS 7.0 using only one process. It will mean that the web platform will still be old and won't take advantage of all the potential of the newer Operating System and IIS. It wouldn't be more than a band-aid because some features were requested, and some minor bug fixes were required. Setting the application pool as v2.0 classic would still be the most straightforward task, as shown in Fig. 2.

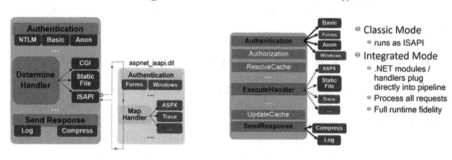

Fig. 1. Application Pools on IIS

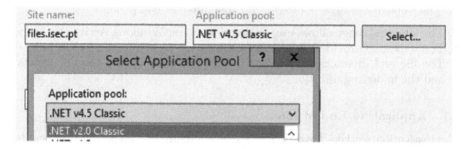

Fig. 2. Setting the Application Pool on IIS

2.3   VB vs C#

The update of the existing web platform had a significant problem. While Visual Basic .NET has not been deprecated, and there are still developers and applications that use it. Microsoft has continued to update and enhance Visual Basic .NET alongside C# in various versions of the .NET platform. However, C# has received more attention and new features in recent years, and it has become the primary language of choice for many developers working with the .NET framework. Microsoft has introduced many cutting-edge features and enhancements in C# to keep it competitive in the modern software development landscape. Microsoft has not abandoned Visual Basic .NET, but C# has become the dominant language in the .NET ecosystem, with more emphasis on its development and features.

Also, Visual Basic may not support future features of .NET Core that require language changes. Due to differences in the platform, there will be some differences between Visual Basic on .NET Framework and .NET Core [20]. Also, the webpage's code was complex due to limitations of the ASP.NET Web Forms platform version used to develop the website. One widespread mistake by web developers in the early 2000s was using inline styles. Inline styles don't separate content from design, with many locations to check when changing an element property. It also added complexity to the task of modernizing the platform to a new and more appealing design [21]. One crucial point to consider is that Microsoft no longer develops ASP.NET Web Forms and may be obsolete at any time soon. Other technology should be used if a new application is created from scratch.

2.4   IT Team Coding Expertise

The IT service staff at the institution had gradually lost their expertise in developing applications using Visual Basic (VB.NET). Over the past decade, as team members left and newcomers joined all development work shifted to C#. Consequently, Visual Basic .NET became an unfamiliar technology. Introducing a new coding language to the team was a challenging decision. It involved dealing with a learning curve, where team members required time to become proficient in the new language. Additionally, there were considerations regarding adopting specific development tools, libraries, and frameworks. This transition demanded resources and attention away from ongoing projects, and committing to a language fading into obsolescence seemed impractical.

Considering all these factors, the goal was to update the existing code from VB.NET to C# to a newer ASP.NET Web Forms running .NET Framework 4.8. The objective was to have a working website with only one developer involved within three days. A new platform should be planned and developed from scratch if this objective isn't achieved within the time limit.

3   Rebuild the Application

The existing web application is made of only two web pages. The first is the login page for user authentication on the Windows Active Directory, and the other web page is the file manager per se, with all the file and directory management features.

3.1   Tools

Developing reactive web pages or Responsive Web Design (RWD) from source is a complex process. Several frameworks provide generic functionality with already written modules and tailored components created traditionally. Web developers use front-end frameworks for implementing Cascading Style Sheets to facilitate the development of RWD [22]. Bootstrap is the most popular HTML, CSS, and JavaScript framework for developing a responsive and mobile-friendly website. It is free to download and use. It is a front-end framework for easier and faster web development [23]. Bootstrap [24] uses a grid system that allows a fluid grid system that appropriately scales up to 12 columns as the device or viewport size increases [23], allowing the implementation of the RWD. Bootstrap framework was chosen as the base for CSS formatting and visual elements to speed up the development process for this web platform. The JavaScript Framework JQuery and fontawsome icons were also added to provide visual details and user interaction.

3.2   Day One - Move from Visual Basic to C#

The first step was creating an Empty ASP.NET Web Forms solution, choosing C# for its code. The second step was the initial configuration of the application. This kind of application configuration is made by editing the web.config file, which defines the behavior of ASP.NET applications [25]. ASP.NET applications come with a default Web.config file that can be edited with the working IDE, in this case, and for this type of technology, it was Visual Studio.

Generally, Web.config files contain comments that make editing the file self-explanatory [25]. For this web application, and since the user authentication is made using Windows Active Directory, it was required to define a Connection String with the IP address and port of the LDAP server, with the credentials of a user with AD browsing access. This Connection String was then used by a platform's component, the Membership Provider, responsible for user management on the web application. Inside Authentication Mode Forms, this component allows the framework ASP .NET to authenticate users on the Windows Active Directory without needing extra coding.

3.3   Login Page

The first web page developed was the login page. It is a straightforward standard web page with an ASP .NET Web Forms Login Control. This framework component provides user interface elements for logging in to a website [26]. The control generates two input text boxes for the username and password, a "Remember me" option checkbox, and a submit button. This web page uses other controls from the framework, validating both text boxes to make both fields (username and password) required. Using the configuration defined on the web.config, this page is set as the default login web page. When an unauthenticated user tries to access a private area, it will be redirected to this web page.

3.4   File Manager Page

The second web page is the website's core, with all the directory and file management functionalities. With the slim timeline, rebuilding the whole application from scratch wasn't the objective, and the existing code would be used as a starting point. Again, to speed up the development process, the existing visual basic code was converted to C# with the help of an online tool from a company called Progress [27]. This company has a set of long-time successful tools for ASP.NET and provides this free service on its website. The output generated from the converter was incomplete and had many problems, but it served its purpose, Fig. 3. It was challenging because we started with a base code made by another developer. The next step was to analyze the generated code by the converter to understand all the features contained.

Fig. 3. Telerik code converter from visual basic to C#

Something stood out right from the beginning. The authorization options related to access levels were hard coded on the code behind the webpage. It used switch case statements with usernames or Services/Departments. It shouldn't be the way to restrict user access to specific areas, so the code blocks that provided this feature were removed entirely. To provide user authorization at a later stage of development, the framework's Authorization Manager Role Provider configuration using SQL Server was added to the web.config file.

The work developed on the first day allowed domain users to log in, access files, and do directory listing. Browsing through the directories tree failed to move up or down the hierarchy, as shown in Fig. 4.

3.5 Day Two - File/directory Operations and Design

With the login page already working, the focus was the file upload functionalities. The second page is the core of the application. The page is constituted of two sections side by side.

Left Section
Block with the information and file operation, composed of two different blocks. The one on the top has the following elements:

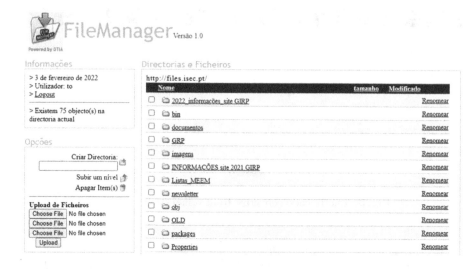

Fig. 4. Running website on a new server

– Information about the logged-in user.
– Logout button.
– A summary of the number of objects in the current directory.

The block below was the file and directory options, with multiple controls and components:

– A input textbox and button to create new directories.
– A button allows browsing up one level on the directories tree.
– Button to delete selected files and/or directories.
– Two file upload components and respective buttons permit the user to upload up to two files simultaneously to the current directory.

Right Section, the Directory Contents
This section is composed of a table with all directory files and sub-folders. They are marked with icons identifying folders and files using the font awesome icon pack. There are also columns with file size, creation/change date, and buttons to rename and obtain the public link. A checkbox on each line allows selecting a row to apply a single action to multiple rows. The page table and how the elements are disposed of can be seen in Fig. 5.

Developing the Second Page
File and directory are the main features of a file manager. At this point, only delete and file upload was working. The folder navigation needed to be addressed. When a user doubles and clicks a folder, the method that processed the click event fails, and the table with the current folder content will become empty. The

Fig. 5. Table with directory contents

original version used ASP.NET Web Forms Repeater Control to render the table with the folder contents. This control was changed to a GridView Control, and all the methods that list the files and directories were redone.

```
1  protected DataTable GetFiles ()
2  {
3      String dirMae = GetCurDir ();
4      DirectoryInfo dirInfo = new DirectoryInfo (dirMae);
5      FileInfo [] info = dirInfo.GetFiles ();
6      DirectoryInfo [] dirs = dirInfo.GetDirectories ();
7      DataTable dt = CreateDataSource ();
8      DataRow dr;
9      ...
10     curr = GetCurDir ();
11     foreach (var dir in dirs)
12     {
13         aux = curr + @"\" + dir.Name;
14         aux = aux.Replace (@"\\", @"\").ToUpper ();
15         location = InvisibleDirs.IndexOf (aux);
16         if (location < 0)
17         {
18             dr = dt.NewRow ();
19             dr ["filename"] = dir.Name;
20             ...
21             dr ["type"] = "0";
22             dt.Rows.Add (dr);
23         }
24     }
25     string auxExt;
26     foreach (var file in info)
27     {
28         dr = dt.NewRow ();
29         dr ["filename"] = file.Name;
30         ...
31         dr ["type"] = "1";
```

```
32    dt.Rows.Add(dr);
33  }
34  dt.AcceptChanges();
35  return dt;
36 }
```

Listing 1.1. Method to get dir contents, directories and files

The source data that feeds the GridView is now an instance of a DataTable object that is built in code behind, shown on Code 1.1.

There were several bugs across all the main features. The main task during the day was to correct all non-working features, with several exceptions sent to the web server while running the web platform.

4 Results

After the time limit, a working platform was available, with all the main features working. Some lingering problems will require significant code changes to fix. For example, the application used a session var that stores the current directory. This var was changed when a user entered a sub-folder by clicking on one of the folders on the table, as shown in Fig. 5. The session var could also be changed by pressing the "up one level" button, which allows changing to the parent directory. The problem with using a session var was that if the user used the back button from the browser instead of using the navigation buttons, the web page stopped working because the directory shown on the web page did not match the one on the session var. The multiple file upload failed when the total size exceeded the maximum defined on IIS. ASP.NET doesn't allow complete customization of its components. It led to some violations of the CSS framework Bootstrap, which resulted in some elements not being fully responsive. The results were satisfactory due to urgency, but several elements must be remade.

5 Conclusions

Upgrading older ASP.NET Web Forms applications from visual basic to C# for small websites/applications is possible, and it can be sustainable. But there are different aspects to be considered when trying to do this kind of update/upgrade. Other persons, over time, usually develop old applications with extended longevity; another issue may be existing documentation of these types of old web platforms. There are a couple of issues that will increase the understanding of code. Still, if the update/upgrade is decided, there are valuable tools that help convert the code from one language to the other to speed up the development. Still, this conversion results in extremely buggy code, requiring a deep analysis of the generated code, and on some occasions, it may take the same amount of time as developing a web page from scratch.

Over the years, web design has evolved, providing users with more friendly and appealing User Interfaces (UI). This approach can also make the UI modernization process more difficult because it is more connected to the old layout being used.

On more extensive applications, converting old code from a different language and using that generated code as a basis for an upgraded version of a web platform may be even more confusing than help full, and this approach should be disarted.

There is also the question of the longevity of the ASP.NET Web Forms platform. A newer technology should be used if the application has to be made from scratch. Choosing from the Microsoft ecosystem, more recent frameworks like .NET Core 3.1 and .NET 6/7 are considered LTS, but when this work was written, the last version was .NET 6 and should be chosen. There are also other options with different technologies. On the Microsoft ecosystem, there is Blazor, and on JavaScript full-stack Frameworks, there are several options like React, Angular, Vue, or Node.

The choice to upgrade or develop a new application has to be made case by case, considering the technologies where the IT team's skills are vital. Also, the time and effort required to upgrade an existing application following the path chosen in this work are to consider the complexity of the current web platform and probably the knowledge of the team of the application code and functionalities. The sum of all these factors has to be compared to the cost of developing a new web application.

Acknowledgements. This work is funded by FCT/MEC through national funds and co-funded by FEDER—PT2020 partnership agreement under the project **UIDB/50008/2020**. This work is partially funded by National Funds through the FCT - Foundation for Science and Technology, I.P., within the scope of the projects UIDB/00308/2020, UIDB/05583/2020 and MANaGER (POCI-01-0145-FEDER-028040). Furthermore, we would like to thank the Polytechnics of Coimbra and Santarém for their support.

References

1. Fürnweger, A., Auer, M., Biffl, S.: Software evolution of legacy systems. In: ICEIS 2016, p. 413 (2016)
2. Zerouali, A., Mens, T., Robles, G., Gonzalez-Barahona, J.M.: On the relation between outdated docker containers, severity vulnerabilities, and bugs. In: 2019 IEEE 26th International Conference on Software Analysis, Evolution and Reengineering (SANER), Hangzhou, China, pp. 491–501 (2019). https://doi.org/10.1109/SANER.2019.8668013
3. Narayana Samy, G., Ahmad, R., Ismail, Z.: Security threats categories in healthcare information systems. Health Inform. J. **16**(3), 201–209 (2010). https://doi.org/10.1177/1460458210377468
4. Zerouali, A., Cosentino, V., Mens, T., Robles, G., Gonzalez-Barahona, J.M.: On the impact of outdated and vulnerable Javascript packages in docker images. In: 2019 IEEE 26th International Conference on Software Analysis, Evolution and

Reengineering (SANER), Hangzhou, China, pp. 619–623 (2019). https://doi.org/10.1109/SANER.2019.8667984

5. Savor, T., et al.: Continuous deployment at Facebook and OANDA. In: Proceedings of the 38th International Conference on Software Engineering Companion (2016)
6. Goodman, E., Loh, L.: Organizational change: a critical challenge for team effectiveness. Bus. Inf. Rev. **28**(4), 242–250 (2011)
7. Acar, Y., Stransky, C., Wermke, D., Weir, C., Mazurek, M.L., Fahl, S.: Developers need support, too: a survey of security advice for software developers. In: 2017 IEEE Cybersecurity Development (SecDev), Cambridge, MA, USA, pp. 22–26 (2017). https://doi.org/10.1109/SecDev.2017.17
8. Christensen, C.M.: The innovator's Dilemma: When New Technologies Cause Great Firms to Fail. Harvard Business Review Press (2013)
9. Hossain, M.M., Fotouhi, M., Hasan, R.: Towards an analysis of security issues, challenges, and open problems in the internet of things. In: 2015 IEEE world Congress on Services. IEEE (2015)
10. Habibzadeh, H., et al.: A survey on cybersecurity, data privacy, and policy issues in cyber-physical system deployments in smart cities. Sustain. Cities Soc. **50**, 101660 (2019)
11. Microsoft. Internet information services (IIS) - microsoft lifecycle. Microsoft Lifecycle—Microsoft Docs. https://docs.microsoft.com/en-us/lifecycle/products/internet-information-services-iis. Accessed 15 Nov 2021
12. Benjamin, D.: Modernizing transport security. Google Online Security Blog (2018). https://security.googleblog.com/2018/10/modernizing-transport-security.html. Accessed 18 Nov 2021
13. Thomson, M.: Removing old versions of TLS. Mozilla Security Blog (2018). https://blog.mozilla.org/security/2018/10/15/removing-old-versions-of-tls/. Accessed 18 Nov 2021
14. Pflug, K.: Modernizing TLS connections in Microsoft edge and internet explorer 11. Microsoft Edge Blog (2020). https://blogs.windows.com/msedgedev/2018/10/15/modernizing-tls-edge-ie11/. Accessed 18 Nov 2021
15. Wood, C.: Deprecation of legacy TLS 1.0 and 1.1 versions. WebKit (2018). https://webkit.org/blog/8462/deprecation-of-legacy-tls-1-0-and-1-1-versions/. Accessed 18 Nov 2021
16. Laflamme, R.: Chrome 81 features and release date. Insightportal (2020). https://www.insightportal.io/news/all-news/chrome-81-beta-features-and-release-date. Accessed 18 Nov 2021
17. [MSFT], R., Rich Lander [MSFT] Program Manager, 6, A., Asthana, A., 6, S., [MSFT], S., Cheong00. Introducing.NET 5 (2021). https://devblogs.microsoft.com/dotnet/introducing-net-5/. Accessed 28 May 2022
18. Microsoft. Microsoft.NET Framework - Microsoft Lifecycle (n.d.). https://docs.microsoft.com/en-gb/lifecycle/products/microsoft-net-framework. Accessed 28 May 2022
19. Hanselman, S.: Moving old apps from IIS6 to IIS8 and why Classic Mode exists (2013). https://www.hanselman.com/blog/moving-old-apps-from-iis6-to-iis8-and-why-classic-mode-exists. Accessed 15 Nov 2022
20. .NET Team. Visual basic support planned for.NET 5.0 (2020). https://devblogs.microsoft.com/vbteam/visual-basic-support-planned-for-net-5-0/. Accessed 15 Nov 2022
21. Kyrnin, J.: Avoid inline styles for CSS design. ThoughtCo (2020). https://www.thoughtco.com/avoid-inline-styles-for-css-3466846. Accessed 24 Nov 2021

22. Shenoy, A., Prabhu, A.: CSS Framework Alternatives: Explore Five Lightweight Alternatives to Bootstrap and Foundation with Project Examples. Apress (2018)
23. Gaikwad, S.S., Adkar, P.: A review paper on bootstrap framework. IRE J. **2**(10), 349–351 (2019)
24. Mark Otto, J.: Bootstrap (2022). https://getbootstrap.com/. Accessed 17 Nov 2022
25. HaiyingYu. Edit configuration of an ASP.NET application - ASP.NET. Edit configuration of an ASP.NET application - ASP.NET—Microsoft Docs (n.d.). https://docs.microsoft.com/pt-PT/troubleshoot/developer/webapps/ aspnet/development/edit-web-config. Accessed 4 Mar 2022
26. Anderson, R.: Login class (system.web.ui.webcontrols). (System.Web.UI. WebControls)—Microsoft Docs (n.d.). https://docs.microsoft.com/en-us/dotnet/ api/system.web.ui.webcontrols.login?view=netframework-4.8. Accessed 7 Mar 2022
27. Code converter C# to VB and VB TO C#. Telerik. (n.d.). https://converter. telerik.com/. Accessed 29 Nov 2021

Method for Evaluating the Performance of Web-Based APIs

António Godinho[1]([✉]) [iD], José Rosado[2,3] [iD], Filipe Sá[2] [iD],
and Filipe Cardoso[3,4] [iD]

[1] Polytechnic Institute of Coimbra, Coimbra Business School Quinta Agrícola - Bencanta, 3045-231 Coimbra, Portugal
agodinho@iscac.pt
[2] Polytechnic Institute of Coimbra, Coimbra Institute of Engineering Rua Pedro Nunes - Quinta da Nora, 3030-199 Coimbra, Portugal
{jfr,filipe.sa}@isec.pt
[3] INESC Coimbra—Instituto de Engenharia de Sistemas e Computadores de Coimbra, Rua Sílvio Lima, Pólo II, 3030-790 Coimbra, Portugal
[4] Escola Superior de Gestão e Tecnologia, Politécnico de Santarém Complexo Andaluz, Apartado 295, 2001-904 Santarém, Portugal
filipe.cardoso@esg.ipsantarem.pt

Abstract. Application Programming Interfaces (APIs) are available in virtually every programming language. These interfaces make it easier to develop software by simplifying complex code into a more straightforward, manageable structure. APIs provide a standardized interface that allows different applications to communicate and connect easily, streamlining the software development process and making it more efficient and effective. Performance testing of a web API refers to evaluating the performance characteristics of an API accessible via the web. This process involves analyzing performance aspects such as response time, reliability, scalability, and resource utilization. This work defines a test battery using specific open-source tools to assess Web API performance. The tests used are load, stress, spike, and soak tests replicating various scenarios of the volume of users accessing the service or simulating a denial-of-service attack. These tests aim to determine how well an API can manage a substantial volume of traffic and transactions while upholding satisfactory performance standards. Applying Web API performance testing will also enable organizations to implement suitable measures for enhancing performance and guaranteeing smooth user interaction, pinpointing bottlenecks, constraints, or prospective problems in the API's architecture and execution. These tests can also demonstrate the technology's limitations and benchmarking, helping determine a more suitable production platform.

Keywords: web api · full-stack development · performance analysis · performance tools · linux operating systems

P. J. Coelho et al. (Eds.): GOODTECHS 2023, LNICST 556, pp. 30–48, 2024.
https://doi.org/10.1007/978-3-031-52524-7_3

1 Introduction

Full-stack development has seen tremendous growth recently due to the increasing demand for web development as the internet, and e-commerce continues to expand. Both mobile and web applications use RESTful Web APIs for authentication, data access, file management, and other resources. RESTful APIs are REST-based APIs that use resource identifiers to represent specific resources intended for interaction between components. The current state of a resource is referred to as a resource representation, which consists of data, metadata describing the data, and hypermedia links that allow for changing the state of the resource [1]. RESTful architectural design is a specific method for implementing APIs, introduced in 2000 by Roy Fielding. This design involves a set of constraints to improve an API's reliability, scalability, and performance [2]. APIs generally serve as interfaces with a set of functions, protocols, and tools to integrate software applications and services. Web APIs, in particular, can be accessed over the web through the HTTP/HTTPS protocols, allowing requesting systems to access and manipulate web resources using standard and predefined, uniform rules. REST-based systems interact through the Internet's Hypertext Transfer Protocol (HTTP) [3]. A Web API enables the front-end or multiple front-ends for different web application devices to communicate with the back-end by sending requests to specific endpoints and receiving data in response, as shown in Fig. 1. According to a survey from the developer nation in 2020, a staggering 90% of developers utilize APIs, demonstrating that the proliferation of APIs has played a crucial role in the growth of the developer ecosystem in recent years. The high adoption rate of APIs among developers serves as solid evidence that the rise of APIs has significantly impacted and contributed to the expansion of the developer ecosystem [4]. With an increasing number of programming languages, many with similar components and coding styles, performance should play a role in choosing a language/framework. The proper way to do this evaluation is to develop two different Web APIs using various technologies that use the same database and display the same output.

Analyzing the performance of web applications is a common practice, with most studies focusing solely on testing the application as a whole. However, it is essential to assess the entire solution, including isolating testing of the Web

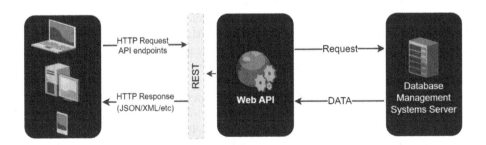

Fig. 1. Web API

API. This approach can effectively identify any potential issues specific to the Web API. This paper introduces a suggested suite of tests designed to evaluate how Web APIs behave across various CRUD (create, read, update, and delete) operations. These tests facilitate the examination of the application's performance under diverse circumstances, encompassing both typical and exceptionally high request rates, as well as prolonged and resource-intensive durations. Furthermore, we provide a collection of tools for assembling the test suite and for visualizing and interpreting the outcomes it generates.

The article is structured into six sections, starting with the Introduction. In this section, readers will gain an understanding of the article's objectives and the reasoning behind them. The second section describes RESTful Web API's technology's functionality, including its norms and practical applications, and an understanding of the key features that distinguish RESTful APIs from other APIs. In the third section, we introduce a set of tools utilized to construct and test the Web API and visualize the test results. The fourth section of API is performance testing, where the test battery is presented and why each test should be applied. The fourth section of the article focuses on performance testing, where the test battery is presented. It explains the reasoning behind each test's application, with the importance of performance testing and the specific tests. The fifth section provides insights into the possible outcomes of the performance testing and also how to visualize the test results. Finally, the sixth section is the Conclusions, which summarizes the importance of running the different tests on each CRUD operation.

2   Related Work

A previous study concentrated on assessing the latency and performance of Web APIs but encountered the challenge of defining a standardized set of tests that could be universally applicable across different technological contexts [5]. Similarly, various research efforts have attempted to compare performance across diverse technologies. Yet, they, too, have faced the limitation of needing a comprehensive test suite adaptable to various scenarios or technological environments [1,6,7].

In a separate line of investigation, some studies have compared performance between two prominent architectural styles for web service development: REST and SOAP/WSDL. However, these studies typically needed to include the utilization of multiple tests with varying loads, limiting the breadth of their performance evaluations. Conversely, numerous other research endeavors have honed in on assessing the performance of Web APIs in the context of microservices-based web applications [8–10].

Earlier studies have delved into Web API performance and benchmarking analysis, with certain ones outlining the methodologies employed to yield their results. However, these studies often grappled with the challenge of creating a standardized testing framework that could be universally applied across diverse technological contexts.

In contrast, the present research addresses these limitations by undertaking a comprehensive examination. This examination encompasses all CRUD (Create, Read, Update, Delete) operations within Web APIs and is intentionally designed to be platform and technology-agnostic.

3   RESTful Web API

A well-designed Web API can expose the functionality of the back-end to other applications and services, allowing for the reuse of existing code and easy integration of new services [11]. Web API has the advantage of allowing different teams and developers to work together more efficiently and build more powerful and flexible web applications [12]. For example, one team can focus on front-end development, another on back-end development, and a third on infrastructure or DevOps. This clear frontier allows each team to have a deeper understanding and expertise in their area of focus, which can result in better quality and more efficient development. Splitting the work across teams can make it easier to manage and scale larger projects [13]. The Web API can be developed using different technologies, from Java, .NET, or JavaScript, using web-development frameworks. A Web API is a set of rules and protocols that allows different software applications to communicate with each other. APIs provide a way for different programs to interact with one another without requiring direct access to the underlying code. APIs are often used to access web-based software, such as social media sites, weather services, and online databases. For example, when a client uses a mobile app to check the weather using a mobile phone, the app is likely using an API to retrieve the data from a weather service's servers [14]. Some web services provide APIs for clients to access their functionality and data. In such a scenario, the API is a set of functions, methods, and protocols that provide access to the functionality and data of a service, such as a database or a web application [15]. Then, Web API, when conforming to the REST architectural principles, are characterized by their relative simplicity and their natural suitability for the Web, relying almost entirely on the use of URIs for both resource identification and interaction and HTTP for message transmission [16].

3.1   Representational State Transfer (REST)

Following protocols, such as SOAP and RESTful web services, can implement Web APIs. The development of mobile applications was the initial driving force for RESTful, adopted over other protocols due to the simplicity of use [17]. There are clear advantages to the use of REST. Typically faster and uses less bandwidth because it uses a smaller message format. Another main reason is that it supports many different data formats, such as JSON, XML, CSV, and plain text, whereas SOAP supports only XML [18]. Representational State Transfer (REST) is a software architectural style that defines the rules for creating web services. RESTful Web APIs are based on the principles of REST architecture, which defines a set of architectural constraints that a web service must adhere to be considered RESTful, first described by Roy Fielding in his doctoral dissertation [2]. A RESTful Web API must follow these six architectural constraints [19]:

- Client-Server: Separate client and server concerns for independent evolution.
- Stateless: No client state retention, all needed data in requests.
- Cacheable: Clients can cache responses for improved performance.
- Layered System: Clients access API functionality consistently regardless of infrastructure.
- Code on Demand (Optional): Allows downloading executable code for client extension.
- Uniform Interface: Ensures an easy-to-learn and consistent client interaction.

Web APIs facilitate the seamless communication and collaboration of various software systems, which may have been developed using diverse technologies and programming languages. They foster interoperability across a broad spectrum of platforms and devices [20]. By leveraging APIs, developers can deconstruct intricate systems into more manageable, bite-sized components. This approach to modularity streamlines the processes of development, upkeep, and software updates. APIs empower applications to incorporate external services and data sources, broadening their capabilities and granting access to a broader array of services [21].

3.2 API HTTP Verbs

The API Interface should be simple, consistent, self-describing, and supports the most common standard HTTP methods (HTTP verbs): GET, POST, PUT, and DELETE. These verbs are used to indicate the intended action to be performed on the requested resource. Usually, they are translated into the CRUD operations - Create, Read, Update, and Delete [22].

4 Tools

A combination of Prometheus, Fluentd, and Grafana was utilized to facilitate monitoring this work. These tools were employed to collect statistics and create informative dashboards, providing insight into the performance and behavior of the system.

Prometheus is an open-source system monitoring and alerting toolkit. Provides real real-time monitoring and alerting on the performance of microservices-based applications in cloud-native environments. Prometheus uses a powerful query language and a flexible data model that makes it easy to collect and store metrics from various systems and applications. The tool also includes built-in alerting and visualization capabilities [23].

Fluentd is an open-source data collection and logging tool. It can collect data from a wide variety of sources using input plugins and store the data in various destinations using output plugins. For this work, it will be used to read Nginx logs, parsing them into specific fields to Prometheus. Prometheus can't process the NGINX logs to verify the accesses for each API. Fluentd can split the access logs into specific fields, such as IP, URL, and HTTP code. Then, Prometheus uses Fluentd as a data source. One of the fields relates to the path on the URL, which will be used on queries to Prometheus by Grafana to generate specific charts for each API.

Grafana is a popular open-source time-series data query, visualization, and alerting tool which was developed by Torkel Ödegaard in 2014. It has a highly pluggable data source model that supports multiple time-series-based data sources like Prometheus and Fluentd and SQL databases like MySQL and Postgres [24]. In this work, the data sources will be Prometheus, which provide the source for the virtual machine CPU and RAM, and Fluentd, for the NGINX reverse proxy.

For test and performance, the tools used were: cURL, Hey, and K6. cURL stands for "Client for URLs" and is a command-line tool for transferring data using various protocols. It is commonly used to send HTTP and HTTPS requests. Hey is an open-source load-testing tool for web servers developed by Jaana B. Dogan. It allows users to generate many HTTP requests to a specified endpoint to measure the endpoint's performance and the server it runs on. Hey can be used to simulate different types of traffic, such as concurrent users, and it provides metrics such as request rate, latency, and error rate [25]. K6 is an open-source load-testing tool that allows developers to test web applications and APIs' performance and scalability. It is written in Go, like Hey, and uses JavaScript as its scripting language for testing scenarios. It allows traffic simulation to a website or an API [26]. cURL and Hey was used for initial testing and to verify the testing environment, while K6 is the tool used in the examples in this work, with different setups for each test.

4.1 Test Scenario

The test scenario involved the setup of multiple virtual machines running Linux. Nginx was installed on the head node as a reverse proxy solution. The same VM hosted Prometheus, Grafana, and Fluentd to collect statistics and generate charts. Another VM housed a Java API connected to a third VM running a database engine, as depicted in Fig. 2.

5 WEB API Performance Testing

Performance testing is a task performed to determine how a system accomplishes responsiveness and stability under a particular workload. It can also investigate, measure, validate, or verify other system quality attributes, such as scalability, reliability, and resource usage [27]. It is also an important test to identify bottlenecks and ensure that the software can handle the expected usage and demand. Several tests used to measure website performance may also be applied to Web API. Each test uses the tools presented in Sect. 4, following the three phases of

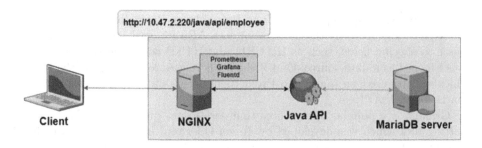

Fig. 2. Test scenario

traditional software testing: test design, test execution, and test analysis [28]. These steps should start by designing realistic loads for each type of test, simulating the workload that may occur in the field, or designing fault-inducing loads, which are likely to expose load-related problems. Once again, the tools from Sect. 4 will process logs, generating charts and tables with statistics [29].

5.1 The 99th, 95th and 90th Percentiles

The 99th percentile is often used as a benchmark for performance testing because it represents a high level of performance. It measures how well a system performs compared to others and helps identify any outliers or issues that need to be addressed. Additionally, using the 99th percentile instead of the average (mean) or median can provide a more accurate representation of system performance, as it eliminates the impact of a smaller number of extreme results. The 95th percentile is also a commonly used benchmark for performance testing because it represents a level of performance that is considered good but not necessarily the best. It can provide a more realistic measure of performance, as it believes there may be some variability in results. Similarly to the previous, using the 90th percentile instead of the average (mean) or median can provide a more accurate representation of system performance, as it eliminates the impact of a smaller number of extreme results. In this case, the 90th percentile can help identify if the system is not meeting the desired performance level and any issues or bottlenecks that must be addressed. The mean and percentiles will be utilized in Grafana to create charts from the tests defined in K6.

5.2 Number of Virtual Users

The initial step in creating testing scenarios is often determining the appropriate number of concurrent users to simulate, establishing the foundation for establishing performance objectives. Although estimating the maximum simultaneous users for a new website can be difficult, for an existing website, numerous data sources, such as Google Analytics, can be utilized to establish performance targets and provide valuable information about the number of concurrent users likely to be required. To ensure the correctness of the testing environment and to determine a consistent number of virtual users (VUs) for all future tests, multiple pilot tests using different numbers of virtual users should be conducted for new applications (Fig. 3). Analyzing hardware requirements across various VU numbers is crucial for achieving optimal performance, CPU utilization, memory usage, and latency response. Conducting tests with different VUs can reveal diverse CPU and memory requirements behaviors, as demonstrated in Figs. 3 and 4. Notably, in this example, the CPU requirements increase with the number of users. Still, the memory requirements remain similar or even decrease, which contradicts the initial impression, highlighting the importance of analyzing the various hardware components.

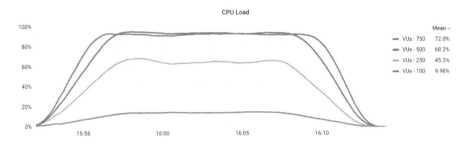

Fig. 3. Pilot tests - CPU requirements

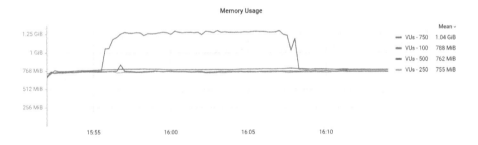

Fig. 4. Pilot tests - Memory requirements

A web API can be made available to clients through a web server or reverse proxy, which acts as a gateway to route incoming requests to the appropriate API endpoints and return responses to clients. These solutions can provide additional functionality like load balancing, caching, and security features that enhance API performance and security. Among the most popular web server and reverse proxy solutions are NGINX and Apache Web Server. The maximum number of concurrent connections for Apache2 is determined by the "MaxRequestWorkers" directive in its configuration file. The default value is 256 [30], but it can be adjusted according to specific requirements. On the other hand, the maximum number of concurrent connections for NGINX is set by the "worker_connections" directive in its configuration file. By default, NGINX can handle up to 512 connections per worker process, and this value can be increased to a maximum of 1024 connections per worker process [31]. Assuming that at least two workers are used, the number of allowed connections can be up to 2048.

5.3   Load Testing

Load testing primarily focuses on evaluating a system's current performance in terms of the number of concurrent users or requests per second. It is used to determine if a system is meeting its performance goals. By conducting a load test, you can evaluate the system's performance under normal load conditions, ensure that performance standards are being met as changes are made, and simulate a typical day in the business [32]. These tests are done using tools that use VUs to simulate the requests, as shown in Fig. 5. The configuration file in Fig. 6 specifies a maximum of 100 VUs for the test. As mentioned in Sect. 5.2, this value should be customized based on the expected traffic for a Web API or new applications. Figure 6 also shows that multiple endpoints can be tested simultaneously on the same instance using the same HTTP method.

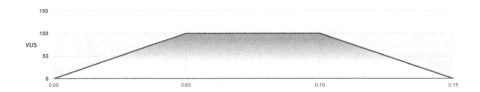

Fig. 5. Load testing - VUs progress over time

5.4   Stress Testing

Stress testing is a form of load testing used to identify a system's limits. This test aims to assess the system's stability and dependability under high-stress conditions. By conducting a stress test, it can determine how the system will perform under extreme conditions and the maximum capacity of the system in terms of users or throughput. Also, the point at which the system will break, how it will fail, and whether it will recover automatically after the stress test is complete without manual intervention, as shown in Fig. 7. The configuration file shown in Fig. 8 specifies the VUs for different time intervals during the stress test, as indicated by the chart in Fig. 7.

```
import  batch  from "k6/http";
import  sleep  from "k6";

export let options =
      insecureSkipTLSVerify: true,
      noConnectionReuse: false,
      stages: [
            { duration: "5m", target: 100 },
            { duration: "10m", target: 100 },
            { duration: "5m", target: 0 },
      ],
 ;

export default function () {
      batch([
            ["GET", "http://10.47.2.220/net/api/employee"],
            ["GET", "http://10.47.2.220/net/api/department"],
      ]);
      sleep(1);
}
```

Fig. 6. K6 Load testing

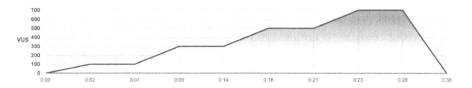

Fig. 7. Stress testing - VUs progress over time

```
import  batch  from "k6/http";
import  sleep  from "k6";

export let options =
      insecureSkipTLSVerify: true,
      noConnectionReuse: false,
      stages: [
            { duration: "2m", target: 100 },
            { duration: "5m", target: 100 },
            { duration: "2m", target: 250 },
            { duration: "5m", target: 250 },
            { duration: "2m", target: 500 },
            { duration: "5m", target: 500 },
            { duration: "2m", target: 750 },
            { duration: "5m", target: 750 },
            { duration: "10m", target: 0 },
      ],
 ;

export default function () {
      batch([
            ["GET", "http://10.47.2.220/net/api/department"],
      ]);
      sleep(1);
}
```

Fig. 8. K6 Stress testing

5.5   Spike Test

A spike test is a variation of a stress test that involves subjecting a system to extreme load levels in a very short period. The main objective of a spike test is to determine how the system will handle a sudden increase in traffic and identify any bottlenecks or performance issues that may arise. This type of test can help identify potential problems before they occur in a production environment and ensure that the system can handle expected levels of traffic [32–34]. By conducting a spike test, you can determine how the system will perform under a sudden surge of traffic, most frequently a Denial of Service (DOS) attack, and whether it can recover once the traffic has subsided. The success of a spike test can be evaluated based on expectations, and systems generally react in one of four ways: excellent, good, poor, or bad.

– "Excellent" performance is when the system's performance is not degraded during the surge of traffic, and the response time is similar during low and high traffic;
– "Good" performance is when response time is slower, but the system does not produce errors, and all requests are handled;
– "Poor" performance is when the system produces errors during the surge of traffic but recovers to normal after traffic subsides;
– "Bad" performance is when the system crashes and does not recover after the traffic has subsided, as depicted in Fig. 9.

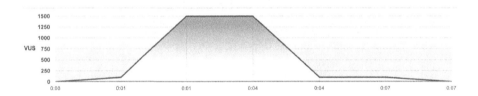

Fig. 9. Spike testing - VUs progress over time

Figure 10 shows the configuration file where it is defined that the VUs will peak at 1500 and sustain for 3 min.

5.6   Soak Testing

Soak testing is used to evaluate the reliability of a system over an extended period. By conducting a soak test, you can determine if the system is prone to bugs or memory leaks that may cause it to crash or restart, ensure that expected application restarts do not result in lost requests, identify bugs related to race

```
import | batch | from "k6/http";
import | sleep | from "k6";

export let options = |
    insecureSkipTLSVerify: true,
    noConnectionReuse: false,
    stages: [
                { duration: "10s", target: 100 },
                { duration: "1m", target: 100 },
                { duration: "10s", target: 1500 },
                { duration: "3m", target: 1500 },
                { duration: "10s", target: 100 },
                { duration: "3m", target: 100 },
                { duration: "10s", target: 0 },
            ],
};

export default function () {
    batch([
            ["GET", "http://10.47.2.220/net/api/department"],
    ]);
    sleep(1);
}
```

Fig. 10. K6 Spike testing

conditions that occur sporadically, confirm that the database does not exhaust allocated storage space or stop working, verify that logs do not deplete the allotted disk storage, and ensure that external services that the system depends on do not stop working after a certain number of requests [34]. To run a soak test, you should determine the maximum capacity that the system can handle, set the number of VUs to 75–80% of that value, and run the test in three stages: ramping up the VUs, maintaining that level for 4–12 h, and ramping down to 0, as shown on Fig. 11. A capacity limit of 75% to 80% for the soak test may place too much strain on the database, potentially causing the test to fail. To prevent this, the test should be conducted with a lower number, for example, using the default capacity limit for the Apache web server, which amounts to 400 connections when set to 80% capacity. The file configuration in Fig. 12 displays the VUs reaching 400 and staying at that level for approximately 4 h.

Fig. 11. Soak testing - VUs progress over time

5.7 Tests to All CRUD Operations

The tests outlined in Sect. 5 are exclusively related to the GET method. When evaluating an API's performance, testing the other HTTP verbs used for the

```
import | batch | from "k6/http";
import | sleep | from "k6";

export let options = |
    insecureSkipTLSVerify: true,
    noConnectionReuse: false,
    stages: [
            { duration: "2m", target: 400 },
            { duration: "3h56m", target: 400 },
            { duration: "2m", target: 0 },
    ],
|:

export default function () {
    batch([
            ["GET", "http://10.47.2.220/net/api/department"],
    ]);
    sleep(1);
|
```

Fig. 12. K6 Soak testing

CRUD operations, such as the POST method for creating new records or the PUT method for updating existing ones, is essential. In these cases, a valid JSON payload must be added and sent to the server, as demonstrated in the example in Fig. 13. This example also showcases using environment variables and virtual users for iteration. The PUT method needs a present identifier to update a record successfully. Testing for deletions is challenging, as most web APIs include the identifier of the record to be deleted in the URL. It necessitates a distinct strategy for deleting a valid existing record, and various methods exist. For testing purposes, you can define the inserted identifier and use only identifiers that combine the iteration and virtual user. Alternatively, you can eliminate the identifier parameter and erase the identifier with the highest value on the database.

6   Results

The tests run on a linux console, using K6 provide initial results via command shell, as shown in Figs. 14 and 15. The results provide valuable performance information, particularly for HTTP request duration - median, percentile 99, and 90, as well as the number of test iterations and iterations per second and the number and percentage of failed HTTP requests. This information reveals the latency of requests at each percentile and the performance and potential bottlenecks of the Web API, as demonstrated by the results. The GET method in Fig. 14 ran without any issues, while with the PUT method (Fig. 15), over 10% of the requests failed due to 40x HTTP errors. Running the test only on the GET method could be deceiving, and it shows the importance of testing all methods, helping to identify potential technology or code problems. Using Grafana helps to gain a deeper understanding of the performance data. Grafana provides charts and visualizations and can be used to cross information such as VU numbers with the number of failed requests. It can also be used to visualize key metrics such as the latency of HTTP requests at the 99th and 90th percentiles, as demonstrated in Fig. 16. In addition to that, it also provides insight

```
import http from 'k6/http';
import  sleep  from 'k6';
import exec from 'k6/execution';

export let options = {
      insecureSkipTLSVerify: true,
      noConnectionReuse: false,
      stages: [
            { duration: "5m", target: 100 },
            { duration: "10m", target: 100 },
            { duration: "5m", target: 0 },
      ],
};

export default function () {
      const url = 'http://10.47.2.220/net/api/employee';
      const payload = JSON.stringify({
            fullName: "Teste - " + __ITER + " - " + __VU,
            idDepartment: 4,
            salary: '250000',
            hireDate: '17/02/2018'
      });

      const params = {
            headers: {
                  'Content-Type': 'application/json',
            },
      };

      http.post(url, payload, params);
      sleep(1);
}
```

Fig. 13. K6 POST load test

```
root@openvpn:~/K6# k6 run java-get-spike-test.js --summary-trend-stats="med,p(90),p(99)"

execution: local
   script: java-get-spike-test.js
   output: -

scenarios: (100.00%) 1 scenario, 1500 max VUs, 8m10s max duration (incl. graceful stop):
         * default: Up to 1500 looping VUs for 7m40s over 7 stages (gracefulRampDown: 30s, gracefulStop: 30s)


   data_received..................: 198 MB 429 kB/s
   data_sent......................: 21 MB  47 kB/s
   http_req_blocked...............: med=5.67µs  p(90)=8.05µs  p(99)=378.28µs
   http_req_connecting............: med=0s      p(90)=0s      p(99)=252.04µs
   http_req_duration..............: med=2.25s   p(90)=2.48s   p(99)=2.72s
     { expected_response:true }...: med=2.25s   p(90)=2.48s   p(99)=2.72s
   http_req_failed................: 0.00%  ✓ 0         ✗ 225344
   http_req_receiving.............: med=79.89µs p(90)=101.01µs p(99)=180.84µs
   http_req_sending...............: med=25.76µs p(90)=37.18µs p(99)=94.19µs
   http_req_tls_handshaking.......: med=0s      p(90)=0s      p(99)=0s
   http_req_waiting...............: med=2.25s   p(90)=2.48s   p(99)=2.72s
   http_reqs......................: 225344 489.287271/s
   iteration_duration.............: med=3.29s   p(90)=3.54s   p(99)=3.81s
   iterations.....................: 112672 244.643636/s
   vus............................: 10     min=6      max=1500
   vus_max........................: 1500   min=1500   max=1500
```

Fig. 14. K6 GET Spike test

```
root@openvpn:~/K6# k6 run java-put-spike-test.js --summary-trend-stats="med,p(90),p(99)"


        /\      |‾‾|  /‾/  /‾/
   /\  /  \     |  |/ / / /
  /  \/    \    |   (  ‾ )
 /          \   |  |\  \ ‾‾\
/_____\  |__| \_\___/  .io


  execution: local
     script: java-put-spike-test.js
     output: -

  scenarios: (100.00%) 1 scenario, 1500 max VUs, 8m10s max duration (incl. graceful stop):
           * default: Up to 1500 looping VUs for 7m40s over 7 stages (gracefulRampDown: 30s, gracefulStop: 30s)


  running (7m40.6s), 0000/1500 VUs, 133520 complete and 0 interrupted iterations
  default ✓ [======================================] 0000/1500 VUs  7m40s

         data_received..................: 43 MB  94 kB/s
         data_sent......................: 36 MB  79 kB/s
         http_req_blocked...............: med=5.58µs  p(90)=7.12µs  p(99)=347.24µs
         http_req_connecting............: med=0s      p(90)=0s      p(99)=233.8µs
         http_req_duration..............: med=1.65s   p(90)=1.9s    p(99)=2.29s
           { expected_response:true }...: med=1.65s   p(90)=1.89s   p(99)=2.28s
         http_req_failed................: 10.84% ✓ 14474       ✗ 119046
         http_req_receiving.............: med=77.85µs p(90)=96.49µs p(99)=180.94µs
         http_req_sending...............: med=32µs    p(90)=44.31µs p(99)=98.93µs
         http_req_tls_handshaking.......: med=0s      p(90)=0s      p(99)=0s
         http_req_waiting...............: med=1.65s   p(90)=1.9s    p(99)=2.29s
         http_reqs......................: 133520 289.874794/s
         iteration_duration.............: med=2.65s   p(90)=2.9s    p(99)=3.29s
         iterations.....................: 133520 289.874794/s
         vus............................: 1      min=1     max=1500
         vus_max........................: 1500   min=1500  max=1500
```

Fig. 15. K6 PUT Spike test

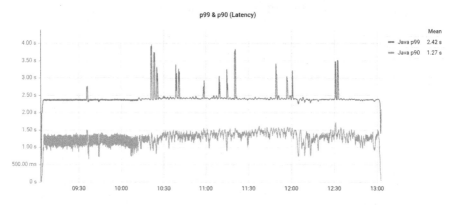

Fig. 16. Grafana - Latency p99 and p90

into the CPU and memory utilization, as shown in Fig. 17. This complete picture of the Web API's performance allows for quick and easy identification of any potential bottlenecks or areas for improvement. Using multiple sources on Grafana, it is possible to compare different APIs on the same chart, allowing direct comparison, shown in Fig. 18.

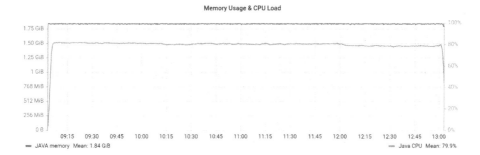

Fig. 17. Grafana - CPU and memory

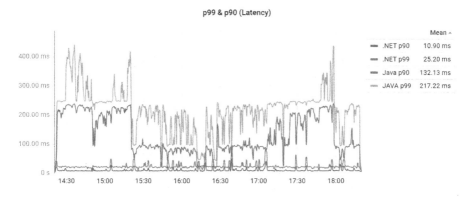

Fig. 18. Soak test .NET vs Java Spring

7   Conclusions

Web API performance is essential because it directly affects the user experience and the application's overall success. Poor API performance can result in slow response times, error messages, and frustrated users. It can decrease user engagement, and e-commerce websites may reduce revenue. On the other hand, fast and reliable API performance can provide a better user experience, increase customer satisfaction, and drive business growth. In addition, efficient Web API performance is crucial for scalability and sustainability. As the number of users and API requests increase, the API must be able to handle the increased load without slowing down or crashing. A well-optimized API can handle significant traffic and requests, allowing smooth and seamless growth. Therefore, monitoring and improving Web API performance should be a priority for any organization that relies on APIs to power their applications and services.

One of the critical aspects of performance testing is defining the number of virtual users that will be used to simulate real user traffic. The number of virtual users required for performance testing will depend on several factors, including the system's nature, the expected user load, and the testing goals.

There are several factors or steps, but conducting a pilot test with a few virtual users ensures that the testing environment is set up correctly and establishes a baseline for the system's performance. From that point, gradually increase the number of virtual users, monitoring the system's performance at each stage. Gradually increase the number of users until the system reaches its maximum capacity or until the testing goals have been achieved.

The tests outlined in this work aim to evaluate a Web API under varying workloads thoroughly. The tests should cover the primary HTTP verbs, including GET, POST, PUT, and DELETE. The GET test should address the most demanding scenario: retrieving all entities from a single endpoint. The POST test focuses on creating new records in the database, the PUT test focuses on updating existing resources, and the DELETE test focuses on removing resources. The comprehensive test suite must be run on the four CRUD (Create, Read, Update, and Delete) operations to identify and eliminate potential performance problems. By thoroughly testing each of the CRUD operations, you can gain confidence in the reliability and scalability of the system and prevent any unexpected issues from arising during production use. Testing all HTTP methods may also help to determine the appropriate number of virtual users for the tests.

The tools presented in this work are a valid method for obtaining real-world results and testing the response limits of the application. The results may be visualized through charts generated by these tools, clearly representing any issues detected during the testing process. Running multiple queries on a single chart allows running the same test on numerous Web APIs, visualizing the results on a single graph, and providing a tool for direct comparison.

Acknowledgements. This work is funded by FCT/MEC through national funds and co-funded by FEDER—PT2020 partnership agreement under the project **UIDB/50008/2020**. This work is partially funded by National Funds through the FCT - Foundation for Science and Technology, I.P., within the scope of the projects UIDB/00308/2020, UIDB/05583/2020 and MANaGER (POCI-01-0145-FEDER-028040). Furthermore, we would like to thank the Polytechnics of Coimbra and Santarém for their support.

References

1. Hong, X.J., Yang, H.S., Kim, Y.H.: Performance analysis of restful API and RabbitMQ for microservice web application. In: 2018 International Conference on Information and Communication Technology Convergence (ICTC), Jeju, Korea (South), pp. 257–259 (2018). https://doi.org/10.1109/ICTC.2018.8539409
2. Fielding, R.T.: Architectural Styles and the Design of Network-Based Software Architectures. University of California (2000)
3. Karlsson, O.: A Performance comparison Between ASP. NET Core and Express. js for creating Web APIs. [Dissertation] (2021). http://urn.kb.se/resolve?urn=urn:nbn:se:hj:diva-54286
4. Voskoglou, C.: APIs Have Taken over Software Development: Nordic Apis —. Nordic APIs, 20 October 2020. https://nordicapis.com/apis-have-taken-over-software-development/

5. Bermbach, D., Wittern, E.: Benchmarking web API quality. In: Bozzon, A., Cudre-Maroux, P., Pautasso, C. (eds.) ICWE 2016. LNCS, vol. 9671, pp. 188–206. Springer, Cham (2016). https://doi.org/10.1007/978-3-319-38791-8_11

6. Kronis, K., Uhanova, M.: Performance comparison of Java EE and ASP. NET core technologies for web API development. Appl. Comput. Syst. **23**(1), 37–44 (2018)

7. Karlsson, O.: A Performance comparison between ASP. NET Core and Express. js for creating Web APIs (2021)

8. Rathod, D.: Performance evaluation of restful web services and soap/wsdl web services. Int. J. Adv. Res. Comput. Sci. **8**(7), 415–420 (2017)

9. Akbulut, A., Perros, H.G.: Performance analysis of microservice design patterns. IEEE Internet Comput. **23**(6), 19–27 (2019)

10. El Malki, A., Zdun, U.: Combining API Patterns in Microservice Architectures: Performance and Reliability Analysis (2023)

11. Geewax, J.J.: API design patterns. Simon and Schuster (2021)

12. Maleshkova, M., Pedrinaci, C., Domingue, J.: Investigating web APIs on the world wide web. In: 2010 Eighth IEEE European Conference on Web Services, Ayia Napa, Cyprus, pp. 107–114 (2010). https://doi.org/10.1109/ECOWS.2010.9

13. Vainikka, J.: Full-stack web development using Django REST framework and React (2018)

14. Richardson, L., Amundsen, M., Ruby, S.: RESTful Web APIs: Services for a Changing World. O'Reilly Media, Inc., Sebastopol (2013)

15. Ong, S.P., et al.: The materials application programming interface (API): a simple, flexible and efficient API for materials data based on representational state transfer (REST) principles. Comput. Mater. Sci. **97**, 209–215 (2015)

16. Neumann, A., Laranjeiro, N., Bernardino, J.: An analysis of public REST web service APIs. IEEE Trans. Serv. Comput. **14**(4), 957–970 (2018)

17. Halili, F., Ramadani, E.: Web services: a comparison of soap and rest services. Mod. Appl. Sci. **12**(3), 175 (2018)

18. Sohan, S.M., Anslow, C., Maurer, F.: A case study of web API evolution. In: 2015 IEEE World Congress on Services. IEEE (2015)

19. Archip, A., Amarandei, C.M., Herghelegiu, P.C., Mironeanu, C.: RESTful web services-a question of standards. In: 2018 22nd International Conference on System Theory, Control and Computing (ICSTCC), pp. 677–682. IEEE, October 2018

20. Noura, M., Atiquzzaman, M., Gaedke, M.: Interoperability in internet of things: taxonomies and open challenges. Mob. Netw. Appl. **24**, 796–809 (2019)

21. Michel, F., Faron-Zucker, C., Corby, O., Gandon, F.: Enabling automatic discovery and querying of web APIs at web scale using linked data standards. In: Companion Proceedings of the 2019 World Wide Web Conference, pp. 883–892, May 2019

22. Ozdemir, E.: A general overview of RESTful web services. Applications and approaches to object-oriented software design: emerging research and opportunities, pp. 133–165 (2020)

23. Coarfa, C., Druschel, P., Wallach, D.S.: Performance analysis of TLS web servers. ACM Trans. Comput. Syst. (TOCS) **24**(1), 39–69 (2006)

24. Chakraborty, M., Kundan, A.P.: Grafana. Monitoring Cloud-Native Applications, pp. 187–240. Apress, Berkeley, CA (2021)

25. Dogan, J.: RAKYLL/Hey: HTTP Load Generator, ApacheBench (AB) Replacement. GitHub, Rakyll. https://github.com/rakyll/hey/

26. Deliver Fast and Reliable Digital Experiences with K6. k6, K6 Grafana Labs. https://k6.io/deliver-fast-and-reliable-digital-experiences-with-k6/

27. Khan, R., Amjad, M.: Web application's performance testing using HP LoadRunner and CA Wily introscope tools. In: 2016 International Conference on Computing, Communication and Automation (ICCCA), Greater Noida, India, pp. 802–806 (2016). https://doi.org/10.1109/CCAA.2016.7813849

28. Harrold, M.J.: Testing: a roadmap. In: Proceedings of the Conference on the Future of Software Engineering (2000)

29. Jiang, Z.M., Hassan, A.E.: A survey on load testing of large-scale software systems. IEEE Trans. Softw. Eng. **41**(11), 1091–1118 (2015). https://doi.org/10.1109/TSE.2015.2445340

30. Apache MPM Common Directives. mpm_common - Apache HTTP Server Version 2.4, The Apache Software Foundation. https://httpd.apache.org/docs/2.4/mod/mpm_common.html#maxrequestworkers

31. NGINX - Core Functionality. NGINX. http://nginx.org/en/docs/ngx_core_module.html#worker_connections

32. Malik, H., Jiang, Z.M., Adams, B., Hassan, A.E., Flora, P., Hamann, G.: Automatic comparison of load tests to support the performance analysis of large enterprise systems. In: 2010 14th European Conference on Software Maintenance and Reengineering, Madrid, Spain, pp. 222–231 (2010). https://doi.org/10.1109/CSMR.2010.39

33. Malik, H., Hemmati, H., Hassan, A.E.: Automatic detection of performance deviations in the load testing of large scale systems. In: 2013 35th International Conference on Software Engineering (ICSE). IEEE (2013)

34. Hasanpuri, V., Diwaker, C.: Comparative analysis of techniques for big-data performance testing. In: 2022 Seventh International Conference on Parallel, Distributed and Grid Computing (PDGC). IEEE (2022)

Application of Traditional and Deep Learning Algorithms in Sentiment Analysis of Global Warming Tweets

Dragana Nikolova$^{(\boxtimes)}$, Georgina Mircheva, and Eftim Zdravevski◉

Faculty of Computer Science and Engineering, Ss Cyril and Methodius University, Skopje, Macedonia
dragana.nikolova.1@students.finki.ukim.mk,
{georgina.mircheva,eftim.zdravevski}@finki.ukim.mk

Abstract. The Earth's surface is continuously warming, changing our planet's average balance of nature. While we live and experience the impacts of global warming, people debate whether global warming is a threat to our planet or a hoax. This paper uses relevant global warming tweets to analyze sentiment and show how people's opinions change over time concerning global warming. This analysis can contribute to understanding public perception, identify misinformation, and support climate advocacy. This paper proposes a data processing pipeline encompassing traditional and deep learning based methods, including VADER, TextBlob, Doc2Vec, Word2Vec, LSTMs, to name a few. The extensive testing shows that the combination of document embeddings and neural networks yields the best results of up to 97% AUC ROC and 93% accuracy. The findings enable the comprehension of human attitudes and actions related to this worldwide issue in production environments.

Keywords: natural language processing · sentiment analysis · global warming · machine learning · deep learning

1 Introduction

Increased temperatures, severe storms, drought, rising oceans, loss of species, and health risks are threats imposed by global warming. Our planet is at risk, and we must fight for the health of our planet. But to fight, people must understand why and how global warming is happening and what we can do to slow down the process of it. The emission of greenhouse gases is one of the biggest drivers of global warming, of which more than 90% is the emission of carbon dioxide [17]. In the emission of CO_2, we humans influence with burning fossil fuels for energy consumption, transportation, deforestation, manufacturing [3]. Knowing the causes of global warming helps us understand climate change and how we can all contribute to avoiding worse harm.

Classifying tweets based on sentiment analysis in the context of global warming is an interesting and beneficial activity with potential impacts on climate

P. J. Coelho et al. (Eds.): GOODTECHS 2023, LNICST 556, pp. 49–61, 2024.
https://doi.org/10.1007/978-3-031-52524-7_4

communication, policy development, and public awareness. The results obtained from such an analysis can provide valuable insights for addressing one of the most pressing challenges of our time.

In this paper, we conduct sentiment analysis on tweets related to global warming. Twitter serves as a platform where individuals express their opinions in raw and informal texts. Analyzing tweets has been a prevalent practice over the years. Notably, a relevant study [14] addresses a similar challenge using tweets, focusing on abusive language detection. Another study [15] employs distant supervision techniques and word embeddings on tweets with additional unlabeled data to enhance stance classification. Sentiment analysis on tweets is used even in health care, as explained in a paper [6] that investigates public sentiments surrounding COVID-19 vaccination using Twitter data. By employing natural language processing, the authors identify different sentiment categories and analyze the sentiment trends over time and in response to vaccination-related events.

Our approach starts with preprocessing the tweets and extracting features from the same. Starting with traditional supervised models, we compare the results of Naïve Bayes, Decision Trees, and Random Forest models. Then we train a neural network, comparing the results of using word embeddings and document embeddings. Additionally, we perform an unsupervised clustering model.

The paper's organization is as follows. We begin by reviewing the relevant literature on sentiment analysis for global warming in Sect. 2. Next, in Sect. 3, we describe the dataset used for our analysis. Section 4 provides a detailed overview of the preprocessing steps undertaken. The models trained and the methodology employed are presented in Sect. 5. In Sect. 6, we present the outcomes of our sentiment analysis for global warming-related tweets, followed by a discussion of the findings in Sect. 7. Finally, in Sect. 8, we present our conclusions and summarize the key takeaways from this study.

2   Related Work

Sentiment analysis allows us to gain insights into specific topics and therefore it is broadly used, especially in social media monitoring. With sentiment analysis on global warming tweets, we gain an understanding of the public's perception of global warming and in which hands is our planet.

In [19], seven lexicon-based approaches were used for sentiment analysis on climate change. Namely, SentiWordNet, TextBlob, VADER, SentiStrength, Hu and Liu, MPWA, and WKWSCI were used in combination with classifiers such as Support Vector Machine, Naïve Bayes, and Logistic Regression. They have reached the best accuracy using hybrid TextBlob and Logistic Regression. Additionally, they discovered that using lemmatization improved the accuracy by 1.6%.

In 2017, a paper for sentiment analysis on global warming was published, where participants proved that positive tweets are increasing after 2014 [16]. They have used global warming tweets worth ten years and applied Naïve Bayes,

Support Vector Machines, and Linear Support Vector classification (SVC). They reached the best accuracy using Linear SVC with unigram and bigram combinations.

The same year a paper was published for real-time Twitter sentiment analysis using an unsupervised method [5]. They have used a variety of dictionaries to calculate the polarity and intensity of opinion in a tweet. With great focus on the preprocessing part, they established slang correction, acronyms replacement, POS tagging, phonetic inconsistencies correction, and noun standardization. With the unsupervised approach, they developed a system for visualizing opinions on tweets in real-time. In our paper, we also focus on the preprocessing part which is known to have a huge effect on the results, as explained in a paper [10] where they go in-depth about how the selection of appropriate preprocessing methods can enhance the accuracy of sentiment classification.

In [18] the authors explore topic modeling and sentiment analysis of global warming tweets using big data analysis. This paper analyses the discussion of global warming on Twitter over a span of 18 months and concludes that there are seven main topics. The sentiment analysis shows that most people express positive emotions about global warming, though the most evoked emotion found across the data is fear, followed by trust. Another recent study [8] deals with the topic of sentiment analysis on global warming tweets using naïve Bayes and RNN.

3   Dataset

Our analysis will involve two types of data. First, we will preprocess the text data, which will be used to train an unsupervised model through clustering. Next, we will perform supervised learning using neural networks. Once we have identified the highest accuracy model, we will use it to analyze how people's understanding of global warming is changing over time.

The first dataset contains labeled global warming tweets. This dataset was downloaded from Kaggle [1]. These tweets are between April 27, 2015 and February 21, 2018. In total, 43,943 tweets are available. For each tweet, the identifier, text, and sentiment are available.

The second dataset contains 308,371 unlabeled tweets published between September 21, 2017 and May 17, 2019 from the Twitter API, which is publicly available [11]. Since only tweet identifiers are available from this dataset, we used tweepy python library to retrieve text and publication date for each tweet.

The main goal is to perform classification, where we have negative sentiment or class 0, and positive sentiment or class 1. We will use the processed texts as input to the machine learning models and the dates will serve to analyze the results and see if people's opinion about global warming is gradually changing to positive or if people see it as a hoax. To present a more comprehensive picture of public sentiment, future studies could incorporate neutral sentiment analysis alongside positive and negative sentiment.

4   Data Preprocessing

The initial stage in our analysis involves preprocessing textual data. The aim here is to prepare the text in a manner that can be utilized as input for a machine learning model. We have outlined the steps involved in the process in Fig. 1. By following this ordered sequence of preprocessing steps we ensure that the text data is optimally prepared for analysis.

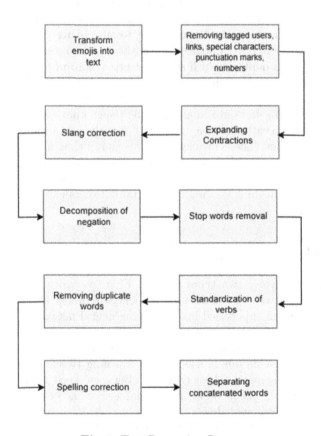

Fig. 1. Text Processing Steps.

4.1   Transforming Emojis in Text

The first step in preprocessing is the detection of emojis and their transformation into appropriate text. Emojis can have a significant impact on sentiment analysis for several reasons as adding context, or introducing subjectivity as explained in a study [20]. We iterate through each sentence and each word and see if the characters match any of the existing emojis in the python library emoji, which are then transformed into words.

4.2   Text Cleaning

The next step in our analysis is cleaning the text data. This involves removing tagged users, links, special characters, punctuation marks, and numbers. Furthermore, we ensure that each word in the dataset is represented in lowercase letters to avoid any discrepancies caused by variations in capitalization. By performing this cleaning process, we can improve the quality and consistency of our data, thereby enhancing the accuracy of our subsequent analyses.

4.3   Expanding Contractions

Shortened form of a group of words forms a contraction. When a contraction is written in English, letters are replaced by an apostrophe. Expansion of these words is achieved by using the python library contractions. By using the fix function from this library, the words are simplified and an example of that is given in Table 1, where on the left side we have contractions and on the right side we have the extended words. The examples are from our dataset.

4.4   Slang Correction

In the dataset we have spotted slang abbreviations which consist of a couple of letters. For figuring out which words are contained in the abbreviations, we needed to translate each slang in its long form. For translating the slangs, we have first extracted all existing English slangs from a web page [4]. Using the Python library BeautifulSoup we iterate through the web page HTML and store each slang and the translations in a dictionary. Then we compare each word in our dataset with the stored slang and replace each with their correct meaning.

4.5   Decomposition of Negation

To deal with negation, antonym replacement using WordNet was used to replace the word that comes after the words "not" and "never". An example of such a transformation is given in Table 2 where the sentences have the same meaning before and after the transformation, but words on the right side have negation words obtained as antonyms of those on the right side. The purpose of this step is to give more meaning to negative words. This step positively influenced our results by enhancing the accuracy of sentiment classification and reducing ambiguity.

4.6   Stop Words Removal

English stop words are removed using the python library nltk. By ignoring these words, we ignore giving meaning to words that are used often in English sentences, for example conjunctions and pronouns, such as "I", "me", "myself", "we", "you", "because", etc.

4.7   Verb Standardization

We perform verb standardization to represent all verbs in the future or past tense in their lemma. In morphology and lexicography, a lemma is a canonical form or a form used in dictionaries. The en_core_web_sm [2] module from spacy python library is used for this purpose.

4.8   Spelling Corrections

The dataset is downloaded from twitter in the form of tweets where people express their opinion, in our case it is the opinion on global warming. Because people have the absolute freedom to write their opinions, there may be spelling mistakes. Such mistakes in the words contribute to the fact that the words themselves do not exist in the dictionary of the English language, and thus do not have a role and meaning in the sentiment analysis. To deal with this, we introduce automatic word spelling correction using the spell function from the python autocorrect library. An example of corrected words from the data set is given in Table 3.

4.9   Separating Concatenated Words

During the text preprocessing, we encountered instances where multiple words had been concatenated into a single word, which does not exist in the English language and thus lack a clear meaning. To address this issue, we developed a method in which we iterated through each concatenated word letter by letter and checked if the words exist using the check function from the enchant python library. An example of how we separated concatenated words in our dataset can be found in Table 4. By implementing this step, we enhanced the tokenization process, ensuring that each word in a concatenated sequence is treated as a separate entity. This, in turn, led to more accurate and meaningful text analysis.

Table 1. Expanding Contractions

Contractions	Extended words
Here's my harsh reality	Here is my harsh reality
Today I'm much more worried	Today I am much more worried
It's a lesson	It is a lesson
We wouldn't have forest fires	We would not have forest fires

5   Machine Learning Models

We will elaborate on three different strategies for solving sentiment analysis using the labeled data. In each strategy we are using set of lexicon-based features

Table 2. Decomposition of Negation

Before decomposition	After decomposition
Has not earned any votes	Unearned any votes
He not accept the evidence	He refuse the evidence
Not prepared for global warming	Unprepared for global warming

Table 3. Spelling Correction

Wrong spelling	Correct Spelling
possition	position
individuen	individual
beweging	begging
earthi	earth
kmart	smart
healthcaren	healthcare
societys	society
crite	write

Table 4. Separating Concatenated Words

Concatenated words	Separated words
urbanplanning	urban plan
resillienceforall	resilience for all
greatbarrierreed	great barriers reef
climatechangeisreal	climate change is real
didyouknow	did you know
savethereef	save the reef
natureseedle	nature seed
recordbreak	record break
scientistgobhi	scientist gob hi

and we are performing word and sentence embeddings. Using the best accuracy model, we will predict the unlabeled data and give insights in the results. Additionally, we will perform clustering on the unlabeled data as an unsupervised learning. For evaluation we used accuracy, macro average F1-score calculated using precision and recall, and AUC ROC (Area Under the ROC curve).

5.1   Classification

VADER + TextBlob + Traditional Models. First, for each of the tweets, we find VADER (Valence Aware Dictionary and Sentiment Reasoner) features. VADER is a lexicon and rule-based sentiment analysis tool specifically attuned for sentiment expressed in social media [7]. It uses a combination of list of lexical features that are labeled according to their semantic orientation as positive or negative. For each tweet we get how positive it is, how negative it is, and compound metric that calculates the sum of all ratings that are normalized between −1 (extremely negative) and +1 (extremely positive). Then for each tweet we extract the polarity and subjectivity using TextBlob. Polarity is the output from TextBlob that lies between −1 and 1, where −1 refers to a negative feeling and +1 refers to a positive feeling. Subjectivity is the output that lies between 0 and 1 and refers to personal opinions and judgements [13]. With VADER and TextBlob we have 5 features in total.

Only 9.08% tweets of the whole dataset are labeled as negative tweets, which makes our dataset unbalanced. To solve that, the data set was balanced using oversampling with the SMOTE python library. With oversampling we duplicate the data from the minority class, which in our case is the class with tweets labeled as negative.

Using VADER and TextBlob metrics we trained classifiers whose accuracy metrics are given in Table 5. We trained the classifiers on the labeled data, of which 20 used for testing. The highest accuracy was obtained with Random Forest classifies.

VADER + TextBlob + Doc2Vec + Neural Network. To represent each tweet numerically, we employed the use of Doc2Vec. By doing so, we were able to map each tweet to a vector of size 100. We then supplemented these vectors with additional features from VADER and TextBlob, which increased the vector size to 105 for each tweet. These enhanced vectors were then used as inputs for a sequential neural network. This approach demonstrates the importance of combining diverse techniques in order to achieve best possible results. 60% of the dataset was used for training, 20% for validation and 20% for testing. With this model we have reached maximum accuracy of 92.9%, as indicated in Table 6.

VADER + TextBlob + Word2Vec + Neural Network. We constructed a neural network that included an LSTM layer and Word2Vec vectors as the embedding layer. Each word was represented by a vector of size 200. In addition to the embedding vectors, we also utilized VADER and TextBlob features as additional input to the neural network. To train and evaluate the model, 60% of the data was reserved for training, 20% for validation, and 20% for testing. After testing, we found out that with this model we achieved the minimum accuracy for all evaluation metrics.

5.2   Clustering with K-Means

We conducted clustering on the 308,371 unlabeled tweets in our dataset. For each tweet, we extracted VADER and TextBlob features, and added a TF-IDF vector to each tweet. TF-IDF estimates how relevant a word is to a document in a collection of documents. If a word appears frequently in one document but not in others, it is likely to be highly relevant to that document. To further enhance our analysis, we also represented each tweet as a vector of size 100 using Doc2Vec. By combining these features (VADER, TextBlob, TF-IDF, Doc2Vec), we trained a clustering model (kmeans) with k = 2, which resulted in two categories: positive and negative tweets. Through this approach, we were able to classify 28,919 negative tweets out of 308,371.

Table 5. Accuracy Scores For Traditional Models

Model	Accuracy	Macro Average F1-score	AUCROC
Bernoulli Naive Bayes	54.58%	54%	54%
Complement Naive Bayes	53.59%	53%	53.57%
Multinomial Naive Bayes	53.63%	53%	53%
Kneighbors	71.51%	71%	71%
Decision Tree	77.37%	77%	77.3%
Random Forest	78.61%	79%	78.6%
Logistic Regression	54.11%	54%	54%
Multi-layer Perceptron	59%	59%	58.98%
Ada Boost	62.20%	62%	62.18%

6   Results

Figure 2 presents the percentage of negative tweets from the total number of tweets, grouped by year. To generate Fig. 2, we used labeled data and supplemented it with our own classification of unlabeled data. Our analysis reveals that the number of negative tweets in 2017, 2018, and 2019 is considerably lower than in 2015 and 2016, as shown in the graph. Therefore, it can be inferred that people's attitudes towards global warming have become more positive in recent years, potentially indicating a shift towards more proactive measures to address the issue.

Table 6. Final Accuracy Scores

Model	Accuracy	Macro Average F1-score	AUC ROC
VADER + TextBlob + Doc2Vec + Neural Network	92.9%	93%	97.2%
VADER + TextBlob + Random Forest	78.61%	79%	78.6%
VADER + TextBlob + Word2Vec + Neural Network	59.04%	59%	58.69%

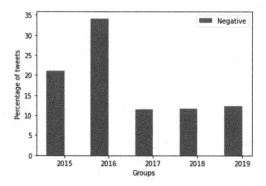

Fig. 2. Percentage of negative tweets.

It's important to note that a reduction in negative tweets may not solely signify a positive shift in public perception of global warming. Several factors could contribute to this trend, which requires further investigation. These factors may include overexposure and decreased attention.

7   Discussion

One of the limitations of the paper is that only two classes are considered, namely positive and negative tweets, while neutral could also be equally important. In future research, it is essential to explore the incorporation of a much broader semantic representation of language. This can be achieved by leveraging advanced approaches like deep learning architectures and state-of-the-art language models.

Recent advancements in natural language processing, such as the XLNet [9] model, have shown promising results in training high-performing sentiment classifiers. XLNet, a transformer-based model, addresses the limitation of BERT's unidirectional context by employing permutation-based training. By considering all possible permutations of input tokens, each token can effectively attend to any other token in the sequence, capturing a more comprehensive context for sentiment analysis [21].

Another model that holds potential for sentiment analysis is RoBERTa, a variant of BERT. RoBERTa fine-tunes the pretraining process to enhance performance. This involves utilizing more data, employing larger batch sizes, and eliminating the next-sentence prediction task present in BERT. These improvements contribute to RoBERTa's ability to achieve better results on various NLP tasks, including sentiment analysis [12].

However, it's important to acknowledge that models like XLNet and RoBERTa often require large datasets for effective training, which can be a challenge in certain domains, such as our case of analyzing social media data related to global warming. As the discussions surrounding global warming have gained momentum in recent years, it has become a pertinent topic on social media. However, due to the relatively recent surge in these discussions, the availability of labeled data remains limited, hindering the development of sentiment analysis models for this specific context.

To address this scarcity of labeled data, our study focused on carefully preprocessing the available data. Additionally, we adopted a combination of multiple approaches and incorporated techniques tailored for analyzing social media content, such as VADER.

In conclusion, while the paper highlights some crucial limitations, such as the exclusion of neutral sentiment and the challenges of limited data availability, it provides a foundation for future research to explore more advanced language models and innovative strategies to improve sentiment analysis on social media data related to global warming. By leveraging the power of transformer-based models like XLNet and RoBERTa, and by adapting to the unique characteristics of social media language through techniques like VADER, we can enhance sentiment analysis and gain valuable insights into public perceptions and attitudes towards global warming.

8   Conclusion

The world is currently experiencing the effects of global warming, which is partially caused by human activities that emit greenhouse gases, such as carbon dioxide. As a result, the number of tweets about global warming has been on the rise, and there is a sharp divide between those who believe in its existence and those who deny it. To better understand this phenomenon, we developed machine learning models that classify global warming related tweets using both labeled and unlabeled data. After testing various methods, we found that the best results were achieved using document embeddings and neural networks. By harnessing the power of machine learning, we can better understand the patterns of human behavior and opinions surrounding this global concern.

Acknowledgements. This article is based upon work from COST Action CA19121 (Good Brother: Network on Privacy-Aware Audio- and Video-Based Applications for Active and Assisted Living), supported by COST (European Cooperation in Science and Technology). COST is a funding agency for research and innovation networks. COST Actions help connect research initiatives across Europe and enable scientists to grow their ideas by sharing them with their peers. This boosts their research, career, and innovation. More information at https://www.cost.eu.

References

1. Climate change. https://www.kaggle.com/datasets/edqian/twitter-climate-change sentiment-dataset
2. English pipeline. https://spacy.io/models/en
3. Global emissions. https://www.c2es.org/content/international-emissions
4. Internet slang. https://www.internetslang.com/
5. Azzouza, N., Akli-Astouati, K., Oussalah, A., Bachir, S.A.: A real-time twitter sentiment analysis using an unsupervised method. In: Proceedings of the 7th International Conference on Web Intelligence, Mining and Semantics, pp. 1–10 (2017)
6. Dandekar, A., Narawade, V.: Twitter sentiment analysis of public opinion on COVID-19 vaccines. In: Bansal, J.C., Engelbrecht, A., Shukla, P.K. (eds.) Computer Vision and Robotics. Algorithms for Intelligent Systems, pp. 131–139. Springer, Singapore (2022). https://doi.org/10.1007/978-981-16-8225-4_10
7. Hutto, C., Gilbert, E.: Vader: a parsimonious rule-based model for sentiment analysis of social media text. In: Proceedings of the International AAAI Conference on Web and Social Media, vol. 8, pp. 216–225 (2014)
8. Joy, D.T., Thada, V., Srivastava, U.: Sentiment analysis on global warming tweets using Naïve Bayes and RNN. In: Nanda, P., Verma, V.K., Srivastava, S., Gupta, R.K., Mazumdar, A.P. (eds.) Data Engineering for Smart Systems. LNNS, vol. 238, pp. 225–234. Springer, Singapore (2022). https://doi.org/10.1007/978-981-16-2641-8_21
9. Khurana, D., Koli, A., Khatter, K., Singh, S.: Natural language processing: state of the art, current trends and challenges. Multimed. Tools Appl. **82**(3), 3713–3744 (2023)
10. Krouska, A., Troussas, C., Virvou, M.: The effect of preprocessing techniques on twitter sentiment analysis. In: 2016 7th International Conference on Information, Intelligence, Systems & Applications (IISA), pp. 1–5 (2016). https://doi.org/10.1109/IISA.2016.7785373
11. Littman, J., Wrubel, L.: Climate change tweets ids. In: GWU Libraries Dataverse. Harvard Dataverse (2019). https://doi.org/10.7910/DVN/5QCCUU
12. Liu, Y., et al.: Roberta: a robustly optimized bert pretraining approach. arXiv preprint arXiv:1907.11692 (2019)
13. Loria, S., et al.: Textblob documentation. Release 0.15 **2**(8), 269 (2018)
14. Markoski, F., Zdravevski, E., Ljubešić, N., Gievska, S.: Evaluation of recurrent neural network architectures for abusive language detection in cyberbullying contexts. In: Proceedings of the 17th International Conference on Informatics and Information Technologies. Ss. Cyril and Methodius University in Skopje, Faculty of Computer Science (2020)
15. Mohammad, S.M., Sobhani, P., Kiritchenko, S.: Stance and sentiment in tweets. ACM Trans. Internet Technol. (TOIT) **17**(3), 1–23 (2017)

16. Mucha, N.: Sentiment analysis of global warming using twitter data. In: Computer Science Masters Papers. North Dakota State University (2018)
17. Olivier, J.G., Schure, K., Peters, J., et al.: Trends in global co2 and total greenhouse gas emissions. PBL Net. Environ. Assess. Agency **5**, 1–11 (2017)
18. Qiao, F., Williams, J.: Topic modelling and sentiment analysis of global warming tweets: evidence from big data analysis. J. Organ. End User Comput. (JOEUC) **34**(3), 1–18 (2022)
19. Sham, N.M., Mohamed, A.: Climate change sentiment analysis using lexicon, machine learning and hybrid approaches. Sustainability **14**(8), 4723 (2022)
20. Shiha, M., Ayvaz, S.: The effects of emoji in sentiment analysis. Int. J. Comput. Electr. Eng. (IJCEE) **9**(1), 360–369 (2017)
21. Yang, Z., Dai, Z., Yang, Y., Carbonell, J., Salakhutdinov, R.R., Le, Q.V.: XLNet: generalized autoregressive pretraining for language understanding. Adv. Neural Inf. Process. Syst. **32** (2019)

3D Simulation and Comparative Analysis of Immune System Cell Micro-Level Responses in Virtual Reality and Mixed Reality Environments

Hanifi Tugsad Kaya[1]([✉]) [iD], Elif Surer[2] [iD], and Aybar C. Acar[1] [iD]

[1] Department of Health Informatics, Graduate School of Informatics, Middle East Technical University, 06800 Ankara, Turkey
tugsad.kaya@metu.edu.tr

[2] Department of Modeling and Simulation, Graduate School of Informatics, Middle East Technical University, 06800 Ankara, Turkey

Abstract. When working on any informatics topic, it is critical to understand the primary mechanism of the domain. This is no different in bioinformatics, which necessitates a fundamental grasp of the biological phenomena under consideration. Understanding biological phenomena, on the other hand, is not always easy since the intricacy of the events and the difficulty in picturing the events can often lead to difficulties in gaining insight, which is especially important in education. For teaching purposes, many biological processes are shown in written and visual form. New technologies such as virtual reality (VR) and mixed reality (MR) are occasionally used to increase the efficacy and ease of use of the training. In this study, a 3D interactive simulation of white blood cells, one of the body's defense system components, battling bacteria in a blood artery, was used. Twenty-two participants tested the interactive demonstration of how these cells function in Personal Computer (PC), VR, and MR settings, and an answer to which platform was favored for this sort of visualization was sought. The findings highlight the potential of such interactive experiences, in which participants effectively evaluate usability, immersion, and presence.

Keywords: Virtual Reality · Mixed Reality · Multimedia Applications · Biological Applications · System Usability Scale

1 Introduction

The basic building blocks are essential for learning in almost any field, and this is even more prominent in the field of informatics. Because the data at hand must be analyzed and interpreted, while doing this, it is necessary to have knowledge about the process under consideration and to evaluate the proposed solution, procedure, or outcome from this perspective. Otherwise, it is possible to evaluate the values incorrectly and reach a wrong conclusion. This also applies to the field of bioinformatics and it is

P. J. Coelho et al. (Eds.): GOODTECHS 2023, LNICST 556, pp. 62–78, 2024.
https://doi.org/10.1007/978-3-031-52524-7_5

necessary to understand the biological process under consideration and to make sense of the acquired values. However, sometimes it takes effort to understand biological processes as some biological processes contain very complex structures and are almost impossible to examine visually. In this case, delays in understanding and misconceptions regarding these biological phenomena may arise.

With a focus on education, biological processes can sometimes be explained by narrowing down the focus, or subject comprehension can be made more efficient by visualization [1–3]. These techniques allow the learners to better understand the complex interactions of biological phenomena and explore how these interactions affect system functions [4]. This is particularly important in education, where visualizations can facilitate better comprehension of complex phenomena. Different technologies are used in this direction, and educators attempt to use the most effective methods for the users [5–7]. Different studies have been performed on the visualization of biological processes for this purpose[1], and there is evidence showing that these studies have positive effects on users [8]. Technologies like Virtual Reality (VR) and Mixed Reality (MR), which enable direct interaction with the users where the users can observe the results of their actions in the environment, provide a new experience to the users in this regard. With these technologies, studies have been carried out to show and simulate various biological phenomena [9–11].

There are currently many different biological simulations that can be used for different purposes. Andrews et al. [18] developed detailed simulations of cell biology. They developed algorithms to simulate the diffusion, membrane interactions, and reactions of individual molecules and implemented these in the Smoldyn[2] program. Ghaffarizadeh et al. [19] developed an open-source agent-based simulator called PhysiCell and they stated that it provides the stage to the players for studying many interacting cells in dynamic tissue microenvironments. In most of these simulations, users can set simulation parameters and get simulation outputs. Some simulations show the images of real experiments for this purpose. However, many existing simulations remain at a high level and have a structure that can be used by people with knowledge in the field and can include steep learning processes too. Therefore, it is not very suitable for the beginner level, it is difficult for people to understand at first sight. In addition, most of the existing simulations are static and do not contain real-time interaction and movement. This makes it very difficult for users to examine the cause-and-effect relationship in real-time. Also, the existing biological simulations are mostly in 2D but simulations in 3D virtual environments are still a very new field and do not have a widespread prevalence. New studies and simulations are being developed in this regard and there is lots of research on these topics.

This study aims to interactively simulate the defense mechanism of phagocytes, which are one of the important aspects of the body's defense against bacteria and other pathogens. The activity of these cells in a 3D environment is simulated so that users can effectively understand the dynamics of these white blood cells. Users can see the basics of the defense of white blood cells in the vessel, interact with this system, and directly

---

[1] White Blood Cell Differential Simulator, https://www.medialab.com/case-simulator-wbc, Last accessed: 2023–04-30.

[2] Smoldyn. (n.d.). Home - Smoldyn. Retrieved from https://www.smoldyn.org/.

observe the effects of different factors. This interactive experience provides a simple explanation of the activity of these white blood cells in a blood vessel (a capillary). The interactive simulation was presented for three different platforms, and one of the research questions was to determine which platform would be more effective and usable for users. The three platforms, PC (Flat Display), VR, and MR, have been used so that a comparison regarding the clarity of the proposed simulation is possible. For this purpose, a 3D capillary environment was created in the Unity 3D engine[3], and a one-way laminar blood flow was simulated in this vein. A customized version of Unity's experimental Spline package was used to enable unidirectional laminar flow. Although the movements of the bacteria and white blood cells in the vein follow the flow, it is also possible for the white blood cells to target and migrate toward the bacteria and to try to destroy them in the simulation. A density factor is used to model this movement. When a white blood cell enters a bacterial area, it calculates this value. If the calculated value is above a certain limit, it begins migrating toward the source and tries to destroy that bacterium. In addition, users can create different situations and observe the effects of these trials. With these interactions, users can create a permanent bacterial field and perform a basic disease simulation, observing that white blood cells are vulnerable to new threats in a situation where they are on active defense. In addition to that, users can follow the changes and interactions in the environment by creating more bacteria in the environment. They can interact with the world and see the results of these interactions in real-time. We surveyed 22 participants who interacted with the simulation and filled out standard questionnaires such as Technology Acceptance Model, System Usability Scale, Immersion Tendency Questionnaire, and Presence. The results show that users found the application useful and that their priority platform preference was VR. Overall, this study demonstrates the potential of VR and MR technologies in bioinformatics education and highlights the potential use of these technologies in the bioinformatics domain.

2 Materials and Methods

2.1 Development Process

During the development of the simulation, the Unity3D game engine has been used since the Unity3D game engine can easily be adapted to different platforms in a fast and efficient way. Initially, prototypes of the interactions between bacteria and white blood cells have been visualized. White spheres are used to represent white blood cells in the simulation, red spheres to represent bacteria, and green areas around the bacteria to represent their chemical trail intensity (i.e., the "odor" that the white blood cells use for chemotaxis). Initial implementation starts with an empty development environment and spheres representing bacteria and cells.

2.2 Movement Algorithm

At the beginning of the study, white blood cells were instantiated in random positions in an environment with defined borders and moved using random walks. Then, bacterial

---

[3] Unity Real-Time Development Platform, https://unity.com, Last accessed: 2023-04-30.

cells were created at random points in the environment. The OnTrigger function in the Unity3D library was used to target bacteria. First, the bacterial cells were directly targeted, and the white blood cells were allowed to follow them until they reached the center of the bacterial cells. However, it has been observed that this movement is unnatural, and the method is insufficient to perform this movement in case of a flow in the environment. Therefore, an alternative movement algorithm has been developed to give a sense of movement in a natural flow structure and support flow vectors in different directions. In this way, both the flow in the vessel is represented, as well as the movements of the targeted cells are shown more naturally. Spline structures are used to represent the flow within the vessel so that the main paths to be followed by the cells over the predetermined main routes and to generate different random deviations over these routes are determined. Different ready-made Spline packages and a manual Spline algorithm have been developed and tested for the creation of paths. Manual additions were made to satisfy the project requirements by using the experimental version of Unity3D's official Spline package (v2.1.0.)[4]. The working logic of the movement system of the cells is as follows: The main waypoints that the white blood cells will travel through the vessel were determined manually, and different paths were produced for each cell centered around these main waypoints. Each cell thus moves on one of these pathways. If the cell encounters any chemical signal during the movement and decides to follow it, it leaves this path and starts to follow its target. If the target cell is destroyed, it returns to its original spline path and continues that path (Fig. 1).

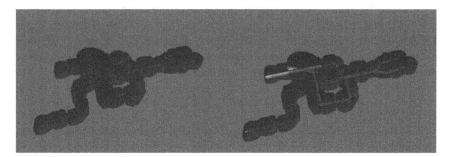

Fig. 1. Main spline paths (left panel), each cell creating its path in the veins (right panel)

2.3 Environment Models

Since the simulation takes place inside the vessel, modular models that can represent the vessel's interior and simultaneously allow the creation of different environments quickly are used. To speed up the development, ready-made and free-to-use packages (i.e., Unity3D's official Creator - FPS Kit[5]) were selected. FPS Kit has a vein-like shaped

---

[4] About Splines, https://docs.unity3d.com/Packages/com.unity.splines@2.0/manual/index.html, Last accessed: 2023–04-30.

[5] Creator Kit: FPS, https://assetstore.unity.com/packages/templates/tutorials/creator-kit-fps-149310, Last accessed: 2023-04-30.

game level model for prototyping while containing various tools and models to teach how to make a game in the first-person camera mode in an environment set in Unity3D. The vessel models included in the package were examined and it was decided that they could be used with minor changes in the simulation environment both in terms of model and appearance. After the environment models were extracted from the package, changes were made to the custom shader to suit the desired environmental background texture (i.e., the interior of a blood capillary).

2.4 Targeting Algorithm

After the cell's movement systems were developed, the targeting and migration algorithm that the white blood cells will use to follow the bacteria was developed. The default trigger structures in Unity3D were used up to this point, and each cell was set to be activated directly during an interaction with a target cell. However, in this study, realism has been an important design parameter while creating the simulation environment. For this purpose, the responses and movements of white blood cells were studied, and it was seen that white blood cells detect the chemical trails of bacteria (e.g., through endotoxins secreted by these bacteria) in the environment through their receptors. When an offending cell is detected, it migrates toward the pathogen and tries to destroy it by engulfing and digesting it—i.e., by phagocytosis [12, 13]. To show this structure in the virtual environment, the following structure has been developed: As soon as white blood cells enter the chemical trail of any bacteria (in other words, when its receptors detect a bacterium in the area), a density factor is calculated depending on the distance from the center of that area. Depending on the value of this density factor, a decision is made as to whether it will follow the bacterium. For the calculation of the density factor, the exponential fog formula (Eq. 1) from the Microsoft DirectX library was taken as a basis, and the values were updated according to the number scale in the environment.

$$f = 1/e^{d*density} \tag{1}$$

The higher the calculated value, the higher the probability of following and destroying the bacterium involved. The value is directly related to the distance from the point where it enters the center of the bacterial area. While moving toward the center of the area, if it encounters another bacterial area and the targeting score calculated at that point in this area is higher than the one it is currently following, the probability of following the newly encountered bacteria will also increase. In this way, a dynamic cell tracking system within the field is developed. White blood cells target the bacteria they touch during their movement and destroy them in turn. When a target cell is destroyed, all white blood cells migrating to the cell return to the path, they continue their movement in the flow.

2.5 Environment and Units

White Blood Cell. White blood cells represent the main defense cells in the vein, and they are modeled as white spheres in the environment (Fig. 2). They move in the direction of flow in the vein, and if they encounter the chemical trail of a bacterium, they may migrate toward the target and kill it, with probability based on the calculated density value. When the target is destroyed, a white blood cell continues its movement in the flow from where it leaves off. The velocity of each white blood cell in the flow is calculated randomly and thus differs from one another. When the cell is created, a new path of its own is created in the flow over the main turning points, and the cell follows this path.

Fig. 2. White Blood Cell Visualization

Bacteria. Bacteria represent the harmful elements in the vein (e.g., bacteria or dead cells). The red sphere in the middle represents the bacterium, and the green sphere around it represents the chemical field of the bacterium (Fig. 3). The chemical field volume grows over time. The duration and limit of this growth vary from cell to cell, so the probability of targeting each bacterium is different. The speed of each bacterium is different in the flow, thus increasing the randomness in the environment. When the cell is created in the environment, a new path specific to each cell is created by using the main turning points, and the cells follow this path. In addition to this movement in bacteria, there is also the possibility of turning to different points on the path at random time intervals.

Fig. 3. Bacteria Visualization

Vessel Walls. Vessel walls serve as the limiting elements of the space in the environment. Cells, both white blood cells, and bacteria, are limited to moving in the volume enclosed by the vessel walls—migrating into tissue is not simulated. The material of the vessel wall model has been made so that the interior of the model can be seen from the outside (Fig. 4). In addition, the shader on the model offers a lively look and contributes to the feeling of the environment. Vessel walls are used when the movement path-related variables like spline shape, creation points, and flow direction parameters are set within the limits of the environment.

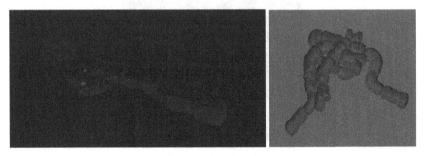

Fig. 4. Vessel Walls Representations

2.6 User Interactions

The 3D simulation is developed for three different platforms (Personal Computer (PC), Virtual Reality (VR), and Mixed Reality (MR)) so that a thorough comparison based on the differences between these modalities could be made by the users. Given that each platform has a different control scheme and there are different user inputs, the impact of these features on the user experience is investigated. User inputs for PC are taken directly from the keyboard and mouse, and the OVRInput package[6] is used to get user inputs for VR and MR platforms. Initially, 50 WBCs and 20 bacteria are created in the environment. As soon as the user enters the scene, these cells are present in the environment and they interact with each other. After a while, all the bacteria die, and WBCs continue their actions. The user can create changes in this process with various inputs. However, the WBC number is constant, and the total bacteria count cannot exceed 45 in the run-time because of visual understandability and optimization perspectives.

User entries. User entries on the platforms are as follows:

1. **Bacteria Creation**: The user can create bacteria for observation while in various positions and monitor their interactions with white blood cells. There is an upper limit on the number of bacteria that can be created in the environment to maintain a minimum viable frame rate.
2. **Creating a Permanent Bacterial Field:** The user can experience a small-scale infection simulation by creating a permanent bacterial field. The white blood cells that start

---

[6] Map Controllers | Oculus Developers, https://developer.oculus.com/documentation/unity/unity-ovrinput/, Last accessed: 2023–04–30.

to follow this area remain closed to the area created and are not able to interact with other bacteria, which shows the effect of weakening the defense system at the time of illness. Users can destroy this area at any time.

3. **Interacting as Bacteria:** In the first-person camera mode, users can interact as bacteria and observe the white blood cells targeting them. While in this mode, white blood cells are not able to destroy the bacterium assigned to the user.

4. **Camera Mode Switching:** Users can switch between first-person and third-person camera modes on supported platforms and experience the environment from different perspectives.

5. **Third-Party Camera Mode Position Changing:** Users can try the simulation environment from different positions and observe the results of interacting with the environment by changing their positions in the third-person mode (Fig. 5).

The environment, the number of cells, and the behavior of the cells are common to all platforms, and the platforms are differentiated in terms of user inputs and the hardware they work with. The user inputs for each of the platforms are listed below:

PC: This is the default environment for the simulation, and it includes both a primary and a third-person camera viewpoint. The PC version has the features of creating new cells with keyboard inputs, creating a permanent bacteria area, interacting as bacteria, and switching between camera modes and positions. There is no frame rate limit.

Virtual Reality (VR): VR has all the user inputs as in the PC environment, but the speed of the simulation can be controlled and is directly proportional to the time of holding the trigger. The frame rate is limited to 60 frames per second.

Mixed Reality (MR): Unlike the other two versions, the MR version only has a third-person perspective. In this way, simulations can be made and observed on the real-world images taken from the cameras. Other user inputs were used in the same way as the VR. The frame rate is limited to 60 frames per second.

Optimizations. Sphere Shapes. The default sphere in the Unity3D game engine was used for the trials and initial studies in the development process, but the performance was found to be very low in the trials with the VR system (on Oculus Quest 2). After it was determined that the performance was not satisfactory, optimizations were made in the models used. Namely, to represent cells, an IcoSphere with 32 segments was created on the open-source program Blender[7], and this optimization was used in place of a sphere. Following this substitution, the performance increased significantly and reached a satisfactory level.

Environment Modeling. Environment models were used from Unity3D's official FPS kit asset, and changes were made to them. The custom environment shader included in the package was customized for two-sided rendering and lighting. However, no changes were made to the motion and animation parts in the shader.

Lighting. Ambient lighting is used as bake lighting considering performance. There is no dynamic lighting in the environment. While developing the ambient lighting, care was taken to ensure that the cells and vessel walls were clear and not obstructing the

---

[7] Blender.org | Home of the Blender project, https://www.blender.org/, Last accessed: 2023-04-30.

users' line of sight. After adjusting the colors and powers of the lights in the scene, they were baked, and the light data were applied to the scene.

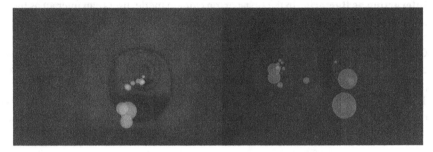

Fig. 5. User View in The Scene

2.7 Evaluation

After the development of the simulation, working versions for three different platforms were implemented: PC, VR, and MR using the Oculus Quest 2 device. An open space was arranged like a workshop where users could experience the application on each platform in turn (Fig. 6). To gather data on user experiences with each platform, the participants were asked to fill out several standard questionnaires after each trial. The questionnaires used are the Technology Acceptance Model (TAM) [14], System Usability Scale (SUS) [15], Presence Questionnaire [16], and Immersive Tendency Questionnaire [17]. The TAM questionnaire was used to measure the participants' acceptance of the technology and it includes questions about the perceived usefulness and ease of use of the system. The SUS questionnaire was used to measure the overall usability of the system. The Presence questionnaire was used to measure the users' sense of being present in the simulation environment. Finally, the Immersive Tendency Questionnaire was used to

Fig. 6. User Experience Tests with Oculus Quest 2 for VR and MR Simulations

measure the degree to which users were immersed in the simulation. After completing the experiments and filling out the questionnaires, the collected data were analyzed.

3 Results and Discussion

In this study, a 3D simulation environment of immune system cell micro-level responses has been developed and tested by 22 participants. The age range of the participants is between 20–32 and all the participants have at least a Bachelor's degree. In addition, the male-female ratio among the participants was approximately 50%. Most of the participants are graduates of different engineering disciplines, but there are also graduates of architecture, sound design, animation design, and bioinformatics departments. The results, based on 22 participants' responses to the Technology Acceptance Model, System Usability Scale, Presence Questionnaire, and Immersive Tendency Questionnaire, are shown in Table 1. The table contains the means and standard deviations of the user feedback. The participants stated that the educational study was effective and that they would be interested in experiencing different biological processes in this way. It was also among the comments that an interactive learning method could be easier to retain.

The infection simulation, done by creating a permanent bacterial density area, was stated to be the most effective interaction method by the volunteers. A frequent request received was that there should be more interaction in this kind of direct environment, where the effect can be seen. The participants also stated that being able to interact with more features in the environment and seeing their results would be more effective. In addition, users also stated that their first choice was the VR platform, and they would try it if there were a more interactive and advanced MR version. This is also seen in our results. Users who experienced problems such as motion sickness with virtual glasses stated that they preferred the PC version more.

When we applied the t-test on the System Usability scale, results revealed that the usability of the system was high among the users. For the System Usability Scale results for the VR platform, the median value was 2.84, the standard deviation was 0.25, and the IQR was 0.35. In addition, system usability scores for the platforms were found to be 76.0 for PC, 78.0 for VR, and 75.25 for MR, respectively, showing that the application was found usable by the users based on the System Usability Scale. Considering the scores, it is seen that in general, users find the VR platform more usable than the other two platforms with a slight difference. This strengthens the opinion that users find the VR platform more effective, considering the results of other tests and the verbal feedback given by the participants. Another point seen in the system usability score results is that the PC platform score is slightly ahead of the MR platform. This value is consistent with the verbal feedback given by the users, especially about the MR platform. Users frequently stated that it was interesting to use the MR platform, but they preferred the PC platform because the interaction in the environment was insufficient as it is. The distributions of the feedback given by the users to the system usability questionnaire are given in Fig. 7. Considering these distributions, it is seen that the answers given to the VR platform had less variance stability. More interactive platforms such as VR and MR can offer more options in terms of user experience. However, the differences and preferences between the platforms based on Technology Acceptance Model scores are analyzed, and no significant difference was detected. The VR platform is slightly ahead of the other two platforms, as shown in Fig. 8.

A two-tailed t-test was conducted on the TAM questionnaire results. The test results are shown in Table 2. According to these results, there were significant differences between the PC-VR and VR-MR values, but no such difference could be observed between the PC-MR values. These values also match with the verbal feedback of the users and strengthen the result that the users primarily find the VR platform effective. The calculated TAM scores were 6.86 for PC, 7.02 for VR, and 6.84 for MR; thus, it can be concluded that the participants found all platforms usable. Table 2, Table 3, Table 4, and Table 5 show the t-test results of the participants given to the Technology Acceptance Model, System Usability Scale, Immersive Tendency, and Presence questionnaires, respectively. Figure 7, Fig. 8, Fig. 9, and Fig. 10 show the answers given to the System Usability Scale, Technology Acceptance Model, Immersive Tendency, and Presence questionnaires as boxplots, respectively. When the overall survey results are evaluated in general, it is seen that the VR platform is found most effective by the participants, followed by PC and MR.

Table 1. Mean and Standard Deviation Values of Presence, Technology Acceptance, Immersive Tendency, and System Usability Questionnaires

	Presence (Out of 7)	Technology Acceptance Model (Out of 10)	Immersive Tendency (Out of 7)
Personal Computer (PC)	4.74 ± 1.21	7.19 ± 1.55	4.78 ± 0.77
Virtual Reality (VR)	5.20 ± 0.96	7.02 ± 1.86	4.55 ± 1.03
Mixed Reality (MR)	4.89 ± 1.46	6.83 ± 1.91	5.14 ± 1.11

Table 2. Two-tailed t-test results for the Technology Acceptance Model Questionnaire

	PC-VR	PC-MR	VR-MR
n	22	22	22
t	2.210	0.881	2.708
p	0.038	0.389	0.013
df	21	21	21
Std. Error	0.15	0.16	0.07

Participants (denoted by *P*, followed by participant number) gave verbal and written feedback in addition to the survey questions.

P1: "MR version is very different and exciting to see compared to the other platforms, but currently it does not have enough interactions for the simulation."

Table 3. Two-tailed t-test results for the System Usability Scale Questionnaire

	PC-VR	PC-MR	VR-MR
n	22	22	22
t	1.636	0.324	1.873
p	0.130	0.752	0.088
df	11	11	11
Std. Error	5.99	0.75	1.87

Table 4. Two-tailed t-test results for the Immersive Tendency Questionnaire

	PC-VR	PC-MR	VR-MR
n	22	22	22
t	1.521	3.768	2.761
p	0.143	0.001	0.012
df	21	21	21
Std. Error	0.15	0.17	0.15

Table 5. Two-tailed t-test results for the Presence Q uestionnaire

	PC-VR	PC-MR	VR-MR
n	22	22	22
t	0.016	0.546	1.479
p	0.016	0.546	0.154
df	21	21	21
Std. Error	0.02	0.55	1.48

Based on verbal feedback from participants, there is also the possibility that the enhanced MR version may have an impact on the results, as it is possible that an MR simulation allowing users to interact using real-world objects, without the need for any controller, has been a positive experience.

P2: "I wish I could control the number of bacteria and the white blood cells because it is very fun to see bacteria creation."

P3: "We want more cell types."

Participants stated that they could not especially choose the number of cells in the simulation among the negative feedback they gave verbally. Therefore, they stated that they could not see the large-scale movements as they wanted to do, and in some cases, they would want to see the bacteria winning and the situations where the white blood cells were insufficient, so they thought it would be a more comprehensive simulation.

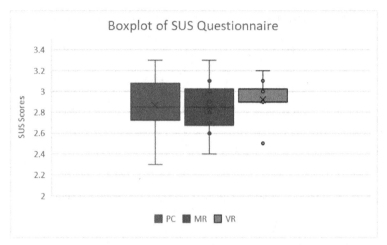

Fig. 7. Boxplot Visualization of System Usability Scale Questionnaire responses given by participants to each platform that shows the distribution of the calculated SUS Scores

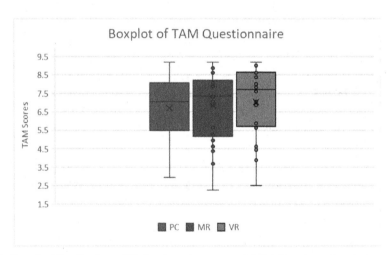

Fig. 8. Boxplot Visualization of Technology Acceptance Model Questionnaire responses given by participants to each platform that shows the distribution of the calculated TAM Scores

P4: "I think the existing camera angles are not enough, I would like to see more camera angles."

P5: "It was really fun watching white blood cells attacking me and watching bacteria getting spawned. But I wish I could move myself to dodge bacteria."

Some participants also stated that it would be more effective to have more camera angles in different positions. In addition, some users stated that they wanted to be able to move, especially in the first-person camera mode. They wanted to avoid white blood cells when the bacteria mode was enabled, so they thought this modality would be more effective.

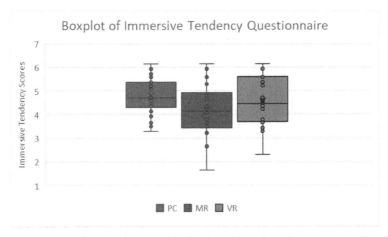

Fig. 9. Boxplot Visualization of Immersive Tendency Questionnaire responses given by participants to each platform that shows the distribution of the calculated Immersive Technology Scores

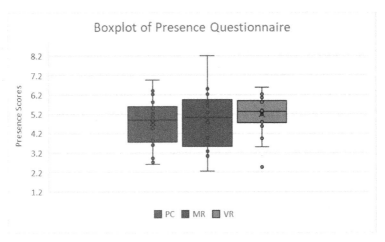

Fig. 10. Boxplot Visualization of Presence Questionnaire responses given by participants to each platform that shows the distribution of the calculated Presence Scores

P6: "In-game inputs need to be shown. A button can toggle that interface."

P7: "I would like to toggle for the user interface (UI) system because I want to see information about the current status of the simulation."

Some participants stated that there should be an informative UI system, that they want to change the variables in the simulation environment, and that they want to follow the results through this interface.

P8: "Maybe a laser pointer can be used to select where to create new bacteria or select existing bacteria for control."

P9: "It was fun, but I would like to have more control over the cells."

Another frequently spoken improvement suggestion was that users want to control the bacteria they want specifically; they want to move the bacteria with the controllers and see the results of their movements. With this, the white blood cells can follow the path created by the users in the vessel (while chasing the bacteria), and they will be able to experience the results.

P10: "More visual effects and feedback are needed."

P11: "Sound would make things easier and more immersive."

P12: "Sound effects for actions would make it much better."

P13: "The lack of sound impacted my feedback."

In addition to these, it was also among the feedback that it would be nice to have sound and visual effects to increase impressiveness. The positive and negative verbal feedback given by the participants for the application is included in Fig. 11 as a word cloud so that it can be understood more easily. Topics on which users gave feedback regularly are shown in a larger format. Since these keywords are from the feedback regarding the simulation, they can be of utter importance to guide and indicate areas for development in future studies.

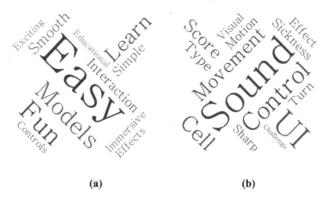

(a)   (b)

Fig. 11. (a) Word cloud of participants' positive verbal feedback, and (b) Word cloud of participants' negative verbal feedback

4 Conclusion

This study shows a 3D interactive environment created for the PC, VR, and MR settings that demonstrates the defense mechanism of white blood cells against pathogen cells. The use of such an interactive simulation shows the potential to enhance the understanding of biological phenomena. A 3D vessel structure was developed for interactive experiments, allowing cells to move in laminar flow and interact with each other within that vessel. As a result of the study conducted with 22 participants, it has been seen that such an interactive simulation can become a promising visualization framework. Following the user experiments, it was seen that participants expected more interaction with the environment, and they found the VR platform to be the most effective of the evaluated platforms, whilst the MR platform provided insufficient interaction. However, there is still an opportunity for advancement in terms of enhancing the interactions of the simulation and establishing additional real-world interactions, particularly for MR. Our findings add to the corpus of knowledge about the effectiveness of employing 3D interactive environments to visualize biological activities. Overall, this study represents a promising step toward the utilization of 3D interactive settings for biological visualization and research. With sustained work and further development, interactive simulations will most certainly become crucial tools in improving knowledge of complex biological phenomena.

References

1. Chi, S., Wang, Z., Liu, X., Zhu, L.: Associations among attitudes, perceived difficulty of learning science, gender, parents' occupation and students' scientific competencies. Int. J. Sci. Educ. **39**(16), 2171–2188 (2017)
2. Pigozzo, A.B., Macedo, G.C., Dos Santos, R.W., Lobosco, M.: On the computational modeling of the innate immune system. BMC Bioinform. **14**, 1–20 (2013)
3. Harb, A., Fakhreddine, M., Zaraket, H., Saleh, F.A.: Three-dimensional cell culture models to study respiratory virus infections including COVID-19. Biomimetics **7**(1), 3 (2022)
4. Marino, S., Hogue, I.B., Ray, C.J., Kirschner, D.E.: A methodology for performing global uncertainty and sensitivity analysis in systems biology. J. Theor. Biol. **254**(1), 178–196 (2008)
5. Zhang, J.F., Paciorkowski, A.R., Craig, P.A., Cui, F.: BioVR: a platform for virtual reality assisted biological data integration and visualization. BMC Bioinform. **20**, 1–10 (2019)
6. Wu, H.K., Lee, S.W.Y., Chang, H.Y., Liang, J.C.: Current status, opportunities and challenges of augmented reality in education. Comput. Educ. **62**, 41–49 (2013)
7. Bower, M., Howe, C., McCredie, N., Robinson, A., Grover, D.: Augmented reality in education–cases, places and potentials. Educ. Media Int. **51**(1), 1–15 (2014)
8. Cassidy, K.C., Šefčík, J., Raghav, Y., Chang, A., Durrant, J.D.: ProteinVR: web-based molecular visualization in virtual reality. PLoS Comput. Biol. **16**(3), e1007747 (2020)
9. Mazurek, J., et al.: Virtual reality in medicine: a brief overview and future research directions. Human Movement **20**(3), 16–22 (2019)
10. Yeung, A.W.K., et al.: Virtual and augmented reality applications in medicine: analysis of the scientific literature. J. Med. Internet Res. **23**(2), e25499 (2021)
11. Amini, H., et al.: Feasibility and usability study of a pilot immersive virtual reality-based empathy training for dental providers. J. Dent. Educ. **85**(6), 856–865 (2021)
12. Segal, A.W.: Europe PMC funders group how neutrophils kill microbes. Ann. Rev. Immunol. 2 (2007)
13. Janeway, C.A., Travers, P., Walport, M., Shlomchik, M.J.: Immunobiology: The Immune System in Health and Disease, 5th edn. Garland Science, New York, NY (2001)
14. Venkatesh, V., Davis, F.D.: A theoretical extension of the technology acceptance model: four longitudinal field studies. Manage. Sci. **46**(2), 186–204 (2000)
15. Brooke, J.: SUS-A quick and dirty usability scale. Usability Eval. Ind. **189**(194), 4–7 (1996)
16. Witmer, B.G., Singer, M.J.: Measuring presence in virtual environments: a presence questionnaire. Presence **7**(3), 225–240 (1998)
17. Jerome, C.J., Witmer, B.: Immersive tendency, feeling of presence, and simulator sickness: formulation of a causal model. In: Proceedings of the Human Factors and Ergonomics Society Annual Meeting, vol. 46. no. 26, pp. 2197–2201. SAGE Publications Los Angeles (2002)

18. Andrews, S.S., Addy, N.J., Brent, R., Arkin, A.P.: Detailed simulations of cell biology with smoldyn 2.1. PLoS Comput. Biol. **6**(3), e1000705 (2010)
19. Ghaffarizadeh, A., Heiland, R., Friedman, S.H., Mumenthaler, S.M., Macklin, P.: PhysiCell: an open source physics-based cell simulator for 3-D multicellular systems. PLoS Comput. Biol. **14**(2), e1005991 (2018)

Developing a 3D Laparoscopy Training Application to Assess the Efficacy in Virtual Reality Environments

Ege Yosunkaya[1]([✉]) [iD], Sebahat Selin Şahin[2], Elif Surer[1] [iD], and Hasan Onur Keleş[2] [iD]

[1] Department of Modeling and Simulation, Graduate School of Informatics, Middle East Technical University, 06800 Ankara, Turkey
ege.yosunkaya@metu.edu.tr

[2] Department of Biomedical Engineering, Ankara University, 06830 Ankara, Turkey

Abstract. This study aims to develop a multimodal understanding of transferring an established method of laparoscopy training to the virtual reality domain. The virtual reality version of the laparoscopic box trainer is developed and tested with 15 participants. Post-experiment questionnaires showed the version of the simulation with tutorial and haptic feedback is acceptable in terms of usability and received better feedback in the technology acceptance model questionnaire. Furthermore, the kinematic behavior of participants' hands showed a significant distinction between above-average and below-average completion time groups similar to the physical and computer-based non-immersive simulation counterparts. The physiological response of the participants is investigated between rest state and during the task with an Electrocardiogram (ECG) and indicators of increased mental workload are observed with increased heart rate and decreased heart rate variability. The interest in assessing the physiological and kinematic features of trainees in a virtual reality (VR) environment is on the rise and the proposed study is very promising in terms of enhancing the development of improved training and assessment methodologies.

Keywords: Virtual Reality · Assessment · Laparoscopy · Training · System Usability Scale

1 Introduction

Virtual reality (VR) technology has rapidly advanced, offering immersive and realistic simulated environments. These virtual platforms have been extensively utilized in various fields, including aviation, military, and gaming, for training and skill development purposes. The application of VR in surgical training has shown promising results, particularly in laparoscopy by creating a safe and controlled environment for trainees to practice surgical techniques, refine their psychomotor skills, and gain experience before operating on patients. During the last several decades, laparoscopy, the most common form of minimally invasive surgery, has spread widely in high-income countries, although some of the training still takes place in a master-apprentice format. The

P. J. Coelho et al. (Eds.): GOODTECHS 2023, LNICST 556, pp. 79–90, 2024.
https://doi.org/10.1007/978-3-031-52524-7_6

advantages of laparoscopy include lower cost, short hospital stay, and rapid return to work. Many surgeons have acquired laparoscopic abilities in an informal fashion ("see one, do one"), ultimately compromising patient safety. Proper training for laparoscopy is not cheap, especially for lower-middle-income countries, and creates an accessibility barrier [1]. Moreover, laparoscopy training has been identified as one of the obstacles to the adoption of laparoscopy where resident surgeons in the USA reported a lack of case volume, unexpected scenarios, and technical familiarity with using devices such as depth perception and video-eye-hand coordination as limiting factors [2]. Laparoscopy training is different from situational awareness training because the trainee not only gains situational awareness but improves their skill by developing hand-eye coordination and getting familiar with the shift from a three-dimensional operating environment to a two-dimensional camera as well. There are specialized simulations for laparoscopy training in various levels of virtualization, and box trainers [3] provide a fully physical experience. VR-based training in laparoscopy allows trainees to interact in a real-time learning environment, which would be nearly impossible to do in the physical world. VR-based training methods have shown to be an effective means of enhancing laparoscopic skills both in the operating room and in the laboratory compared to non-VR training methods [4–7]. Commercially available VR training systems are currently accessible in a variety of forms. Two known VR systems employed in laparoscopy training are MIST-VR® and LapSim®[1]. MIST-VR® incorporates a screen and physical graspers [8], while LapSim® employs physical laparoscopic graspers in conjunction with a head-mounted display. Moreover, Diesen et al. concluded there is no significant difference between box trainers and VR in terms of time to learn and after training skill level after a long period of training [9]. However, the computer-based VR systems in the aforementioned studies use a semi-virtual environment with physical graspers, mainly because it is not possible to provide force feedback in a generic VR controller and create a virtual environment that closely simulates the real world while eliminating the necessity for physical materials to operate on.

Advances in wearable technologies allow easy physiological data collection from the surgeon during the training in the physical box and the VR-based methods. Although several studies focused on the effect of the physical box on human physiology [10, 11] the assessment of VR-based training is still new and has many unknown questions regarding human physiology. In addition, there is a lack of deep understanding of how Virtual Reality can influence complex learning in medical education. Our preliminary results will help to assess how skills acquired through Virtual-Reality enabled training transfer to the field.

In surgical education, objective assessment of surgical skills is essential because performance in training and performance is difficult to correct without objective feedback. Traditional approaches to studying skills use bulky equipment, behavioral metrics to measure performance, and surveys of subjective experience. These inhibit the ability to collect data in realistic settings or provide only intermittent data, or intrusive methodologies. In the literature, heart rate (HR), and heart rate variability (HRV), have been correlated with mental workload scores as well as task complexity in similar simulation-based

---

[1] Surgical Science Ltd., Gothenburg, Sweden, https://surgicalscience.com/simulators/lapsim/, Last accessed: 2023–07-01.

tasks [12, 13]. Few studies focused on combining VR environments and physiological sensors during general virtual reality learning context and surgical training [14–16].

In this study, we developed VR-based training environments using standardized tasks including Peg Transfer and String Pass. We evaluated the VR-based training on human subjects using kinematic, psychological, and subjective measures. Our aim is to develop the VR-based training platform as a multimodal assessment tool rather than just a laparoscopic trainer.

This study proposes methods for transferring established methods of psychomotor training into a virtual reality environment and investigates how skill evaluation methods translate for fully immersive environments. The simulation is implemented using the Unity3D game engine[2] and Oculus Quest 2 as VR hardware. To evaluate the usability and technology acceptance aspects of the simulation, 15 higher education students performed the tasks and answered System Usability Scale (SUS) [17] and Technology Acceptance Model (TAM) [18] questionnaires. Motion tracking is implemented into the game to track the position and rotation of both hands and the head-mounted display to find relations between task performance and kinematics. Moreover, a three-channel ECG is recorded during the tasks for each participant.

Our work integrates kinematics, psychological responses, and subjective feedback to provide multi-dimensional understanding for fully immersive simulations in psychomotor training. Furthermore, this study has been expanded upon in a Master's thesis [19], incorporating a larger number of participants. Additionally, the simulation's design phase has been thoroughly examined, and the topics addressed in this study have been discussed.

2 Methods

2.1 Task Design

Two laparoscopy standardized training tasks, peg transfer and string pass are selected to be implemented in a virtual reality environment. The peg transfer requires the user to pick a small object using the graspers, change hands without dropping the object, and insert the object into the target location. In string pass, the user grasps a thin rope and moves it between circles in a pre-determined order. Both tasks are designed by medical professionals to help entry-level trainees develop the required motor skills, depth perception, and hand-eye coordination to conduct minimally invasive surgeries. Moreover, both tasks require the user to develop depth perception with the two-dimensional camera and hand-eye coordination for both hands. The users are evaluated by completion time, and the task is ended after six minutes if not finished.

2.2 Game Design

The game was developed with the Unity3D game engine and tested with Oculus Quest 2. We used official integration libraries to establish communication between the Quest and the game engine. The grasper models are open-source and used from Unity Asset

---

[2] Unity Real-Time Development Platform, https://unity.com, Last accessed: 2023–06-28.

Store. The operation room, task materials, and all other UI elements are designed from scratch. The objective of the simulation is to replicate the authentic experience provided by the box trainer. Consequently, initial trials are conducted on the physical box trainer prior to the commencement of simulation development.

The controls are mapped to reflect the box trainer, where the user holds the grasper with the "PrimaryHandTrigger" button on the controller and controls the tip of the grasper with the "PrimaryIndexTrigger" button. Moreover, the thumbstick of the controller controls the rotation of the tip of the grasper.

We implemented two versions; the first version has no tutorial, and the physics of the graspers is more realistic. The second version has the tutorial, and the grasper physics is eased with snapping. Moreover, the second version has haptic feedback to help the user understand if the tip of the grasper touches a solid object to mimic force feedback. Given that the VR training version does not have force feedback to restrict the movement of trainees' hands during collisions, it becomes crucial to replicate this tactile sensation in an alternative manner. The implementation of haptic feedback from the controllers presents a viable method to address this issue. We designed a minimal user interface to not intervene with the immersion, the tutorials have a button for skipping the tutorial and on-screen guidance text, whereas the real task only shows the elapsed time, the number of targets remaining, and the number of errors made.

The tutorial part of both tasks is divided into subtasks that show the required movement, for the peg transfer, the user needs to grab one peg, switch hands, and drop into the target location. The tutorial for string pass uses one solid object that subrogates the tip of the string. The user is required to grab the object, pass it through the ring, grab it with the other grasper, and drop it into the target zone. User is guided with texts in each step of the tutorial and can reset their state to initial if needed. The task starts after the user clicks the "Finish Tutorial" or "Skip Tutorial" buttons, and an automatic timer is started when the user grabs both graspers and records the finish time when all required tasks are completed. Moreover, with the grabbing of two graspers, the simulation starts to record the positions of both hands in 3D space and the rotation as a quaternion. It is saved to the device file system with unique identifiers when the task finishes or if the user quits the application. Sample scenes from the game for tasks and their respective tutorials can be seen in Fig. 1.

2.3 Experiment Setup

All subjects voluntarily participated and were briefed about the ECG and motion data collection as well as post-experiment questionnaires and properly instructed before the experiment began. Ethical approval of this research was initially granted by the Middle East Technical University Human Subjects Ethics Committee in December 2021 (454-ODTU-2021) and revised to include physiological data collection in April 2023 (0171-ODTUİAEK-2023).

The experiment is carried out with the participant assuming a standing position and wearing the Oculus Quest 2 head-mounted display together with the controllers. The second version is performed subsequent to the completion of the first one. In the second version, the user proceeded to engage in each task by initially completing the related tutorial section. Following this, a resting ECG was collected for a duration of one minute,

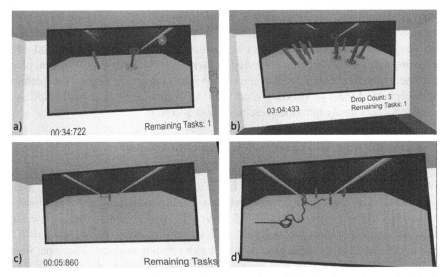

Fig. 1. Sample in-game point-of-view screen captures from the (a) Peg Transfer tutorial, (b) Peg Transfer task, (c) String Pass tutorial, and (d) String Pass task.

after which the user resumed the real task. An observer watched the user's perspective while the user was playing. The playing of the first version took about 15 min. The second version, with the preparation of ECG, resting records, and tutorials took about an hour. Thus, the total process was approximately 90 min per participant. The questionnaires are filled out by the participants after the procedures are done. The flow of the experiment can be seen in Fig. 2.

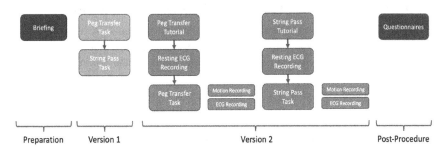

Fig. 2. Flow of the experiment procedure.

2.4 User Experience Evaluation

The implemented simulation is an immersive experience, and it is important to receive feedback on how users felt during the tasks. Moreover, usability and acceptance of the system are important for the simulation to be effective and used as a valid replacement for physical methods. The experience is evaluated on two aspects; the usability of the system, which is evaluated by the System Usability Scale (SUS), a 5-point Likert scale questionnaire of 10 questions. SUS has both negative and positive questions and it has the scoring method that is commonly used in literature. The other aspect is technology acceptance, which focuses on self-perceived usefulness and ease of use. The Technology Acceptance Model (TAM) questionnaire is a 7-point Likert scale and helps us to understand if this newly introduced technology is accepted.

2.5   Kinematic Analysis of Participants' Hand Movements

The motion of both hands is captured during the tasks to analyze the relationships between motion and participant success in a VR environment. It has been previously shown that there are significant relations between velocity and jerk and psychomotor skill level in a box trainer environment [20]. Moreover, the motion capture data is processed the extract significant kinematic features, such as velocity, acceleration, and jerk. The mean velocity of a participant's hand is calculated by finding position change per frame and differentiating by the time between each frame and calculating the sample mean of the observed velocities by difference of position between frames (Eq. 1), where n is the number of frames. Likewise, the mean jerk is calculated as the second derivative of the velocity (Eq. 2).

$$\frac{1}{n}\sum\sqrt{\left(\frac{dx_i}{dt}\right)^2 + \left(\frac{dy_i}{dt}\right)^2 + \left(\frac{dz_i}{dt}\right)^2} \tag{1}$$

$$\frac{1}{n}\sum\sqrt{\left(\frac{d^3x_i}{dt}\right)^2 + \left(\frac{d^3y_i}{dt}\right)^2 + \left(\frac{d^3z_i}{dt}\right)^2} \tag{2}$$

2.6   Analysis of Participants' Heart Rate and Heart Rate Variability

The ECG recording starts after the tutorial finishes. Participants are verbally briefed before the procedure starts and warned again about staying still until the observer presses the button located on the wireless recorder to mark the end of the 1-min resting period. The raw ECG signals collected from the participants are cleaned with the NeuroKit2 python package [21]. The peaks of QRS complexes are identified and heart rate (HR) and heart rate variability (HRV) are calculated. In some studies, a decrease in HRV is found as an indicator of mental workload [22]. Moreover, frequency domain features of HRV are also shown to be indicators of mental and physical load [23], thus low frequency (LF) and high frequency (HF) components of the HRV signal are calculated and included in the study.

3   Results

3.1   User Experience

The post-experiment questionnaire for system usability for version 1 and version 2 shows average scores of 57.5 and 69.17 respectively with the positive-negative scoring of the SUS questionnaire. Moreover, the scores per participant of the first and second versions are statistically different from each other according to the two-tailed t-test (p = 0.016). The TAM questionnaire also shows statistical significance with p-value < 0.001 increase in the second version with mean scores 4.561 and 5.789 respectively, indicating more acceptance for the second version. Moreover, for the second version, the mean value of ~ 5.8 with a standard deviation of 0.85 shows a good acceptance outcome on a 7-point scale. The participants are asked "What is your general opinion about the application?" after the questionnaires and free text responses are collected. Sample answers in Table 1 suggest that haptic feedback, tutorials, and assistance in grabbing mechanics improve the overall user experience.

Table 1. Sample Responses Version 1 and Version 2 to Question "What is your general opinion about the application?"

Topic	Version 1	Version 2
Controls	Overhaul of the controls would definitely benefit the game	It is way better than version 1 in terms of controls. The only issue I faced was it assisted a bit too much while grabbing the objects
Haptic Feedback	Adding vibrations, flashing lights, and setting controllers to be more sensitive can make it easier to use	Adding vibrations greatly improved the user experience
Tutorial	It would be good to add a description of the tasks before starting, explaining how to do them	This version felt generally similar to Version 1. The tutorials made it easier to get the point and what the subject had to do in the steps

3.2 Kinematic Analysis

The mean completion time of Peg Transfer was ~ 2 min 9 s and ~ 1 min 35 s for String Pass among participants who were able to finish the task. Whereas three participants for each task did not finish the task in time. Moreover, one user has not been recorded in the Peg Transfer task, and one has not been recorded in both tasks due to an issue in the test device, thus those users are excluded from the kinematic analysis. Users are split into two groups according to their finish times, where we consider the top half successful. In Fig. 3, we can see the mean velocity distributions of the participants for both hands and each task. The difference in mean velocity of the two groups is statistically significant in the left hand and right hand for Peg Transfer with p-values 0.003 and 0.025. In the String Pass task, the two groups are different in terms of the mean velocity of the left hand (p = 0.026), however, the right-hand mean velocity did not show any significant difference (p = 0.06).

The jerk, a frequently used kinematic parameter, shows significance in assessing the smoothness of movement across several tasks and for both hands (see Fig. 4). This significance is supported by statistical analysis, with p-values less than 0.03 for both

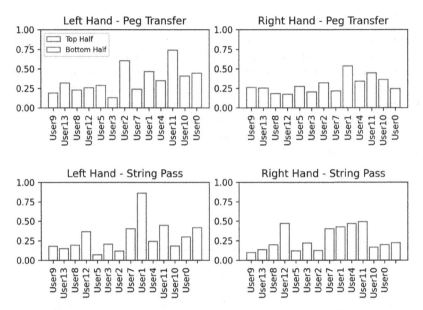

Fig. 3. Mean velocities (m/s) of each hand of the users for both tasks.

hands in the Peg Transfer task and p-values less than 0.04 in the String Pass task, measured using a two-sided t-test.

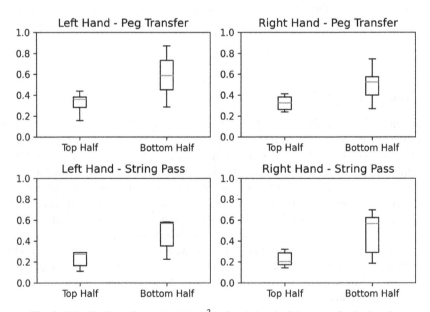

Fig. 4. Distribution of mean jerk (m/s^3) of each hand of the users for both tasks.

3.3 ECG Analysis

The heart rate of the participants is investigated to understand the physical response to doing the procedure in a VR environment. The mean heart rates of the participants are significantly less in resting than during the play according to the one-sided t-test. However, there is no significant difference is found between successful and unsuccessful groups in terms of heart rate for both tasks while playing. Furthermore, the mean distance between normal RR peaks (MeanNN) is also significantly decreased between resting and playing states as shown in Table 2. However, the frequency domain features of HRV; low-frequency component of the signal 0.04 Hz and 0.15 Hz (LF), the high-frequency component of the signal 0.15 Hz to 0.4 Hz (HF), and the ratio of LF and HF (LF/HF), did not show any significant difference between rest and playing.

Table 2. Descriptive statistics of mean HR and mean distance between normal RR peaks (MeanNN) of the participants for each task between resting and playing states.

		Mean	SD	t	p	df
Heart Rate (bpm)						
Peg Transfer	Resting	84.78	10.4	−3.87	< 0.001	13
	Playing	89.11	9.94			
String Pass	Resting	86.88	11.55	−2.18	< 0.025	13
	Playing	89.22	10.70			
MeanNN (ms)						
Peg Transfer	Resting	717.64	84.42	4.50	< 0.006	13
	Playing	681.58	79.71			
String Pass	Resting	702.08	91.88	2.44	< 0.030	13
	Playing	682.61	87.91			

4   Discussion

In the developed VR application, post-procedure questionnaires showed that the second version with haptic feedback and tutorials made the application more usable. The first version was "not good" in terms of usability whereas the second version is acceptable according to SUS. Moreover, significant improvements in acceptance scores are observed in the second version compared to the first. Haptic feedback is an important tool for VR environments in laparoscopy training because of the lack of real graspers and their interaction with solid objects. It is used in the study to mimic the force feedback and is seen to improve user experience along with the other changes done in the second version. Moreover, even though the participants were briefed about the task and the required motion to accomplish the tasks verbally, tutorials still improved the usability according to the questionnaires and free text responses. It can be said that using the advantages of virtual reality by integrating the methods that are commonly used in games can improve the experience of the users in VR-based laparoscopy training.

The motion analysis is thoroughly used for predicting or evaluating the skill level of the trainees in literature both in box trainers and computer-based simulations with physical graspers. The analysis shows that the same pattern of motion exists even without the need for a physical device. Mean velocity and jerk are distinguishing factors between the top half and the bottom half of the participants according to their finish times in both tasks, where the mean jerk inversely related to the smoothness of the motion is significantly less in the more successful group. Showing the parallel between the kinematics of training with physical devices and training in VR paves the way for automatic skill evaluation, personalized training, and other benefits of immersive environments.

HR and HRV comparison between resting state and during training can provide insight into the mental workload (MWL) of the trainee. Estimating MWL is important for proper training because studies showed that mental MWL is inversely correlated with task performance in laparoscopy training and experienced surgeons can perform the tasks with less MWL [24, 25]. Thus, MWL is both a differential factor and a parameter to reckon with to design a training procedure. We found out that HR increased and HRV decreased significantly during the training. The mean HR increase between rest and training was about 4% and is not sufficient to suggest physical load. However, an increase in HR and a decrease in HRV combined suggest increased MWL in participants during the training. However, the LF, HF, and LF/HF indices of HRV did not show significant differences, therefore our results did not indicate MWL difference between the top and bottom half groups. This might be due to a lack of practice and familiarity between both groups since we cannot distinguish them as experts and novices as in previous studies. The HR and HRV can be measured with wearable devices and estimations on MWL can be integrated into training in real time.

5   Conclusions and Future Work

Ours is a preliminary work for immersive psychomotor training in various fields. Laparoscopy is an important way of minimally invasive surgery and making its training more accessible with customer-grade products, more scenarios and personalized training is important for achieving broader adaptation. Our work shows the parallels between currently used methods and VR-based training and suggests ways to understand physiological responses during training and analysis of kinematic behavior in an automatic fashion.

We intend to increase the sample size of the participants and study the differences between groups with different levels of virtual reality experience and familiarity with games. Also, we are planning to conduct experiments with surgeons with various levels of expertise to understand if the real-life skills are translating into immersive VR performance. The kinematic analysis can be done in real-time during the training and the effects of personalized learning performance tasks can be investigated.

References

1. Choy, I., Kitto, S., Adu-Aryee, N., Okrainec, A.: Barriers to the uptake of laparoscopic surgery in a lower-middle-income country. Surg. Endosc. **27**(11), 4009–4015 (2013). https://doi.org/10.1007/S00464-013-3019-Z
2. Lim, S., Ghosh, S., Niklewski, P., Roy, S.: Laparoscopic suturing as a barrier to broader adoption of laparoscopic surgery. JSLS : J. Soci. Laparoendosc. Surg. **21**(3) (2017). https://doi.org/10.4293/JSLS.2017.00021
3. Dhariwal, A., Prabhu, R., Dalvi, A., Supe, A.: Effectiveness of box trainers in laparoscopic training. J. Minim. Access Surg. **3**(2), 57 (2007). https://doi.org/10.4103/0972-9941.33274
4. Logishetty, K., Rudran, B., Cobb, J.P.: Virtual reality training improves trainee performance in total hip arthroplasty: a randomized controlled trial. Bone Joint J. 101-B(12), 1585–1592 (2019). https://doi.org/10.1302/0301-620X.101B12.BJJ-2019-0643.R1
5. Gurusamy, K.S., Aggarwal, R., Palanivelu, L., Davidson, B.R.: Virtual reality training for surgical trainees in laparoscopic surgery. Cochrane Database Syst. Rev. 1 (2009).https://doi.org/10.1002/14651858.CD006575.PUB2
6. Gallagher, A.G., et al.: Virtual reality simulation for the operating room: proficiency-based training as a paradigm shift in surgical skills training. Ann. Surg. **241**(2), 364 (2005). https://doi.org/10.1097/01.SLA.0000151982.85062.80
7. Seymour, N.E., et al.: Virtual reality training improves operating room performance: results of a randomized. Double-Blinded Study. Ann. Surg. **236**(4), 458 (2002). https://doi.org/10.1097/00000658-200210000-00008
8. Wilson, M.S., Middlebrook, A., Sutton, C., Stone, R., McCloy, R.F.: MIST VR: a virtual reality trainer for laparoscopic surgery assesses performance. Ann. R. Coll. Surg. Engl. **79**(6), 403 (1997)
9. Diesen, D.L., et al.: Effectiveness of laparoscopic computer simulator versus usage of box trainer for endoscopic surgery training of novices. J. Surg. Educ. **68**(4), 282–289 (2011). https://doi.org/10.1016/J.JSURG.2011.02.007
10. Zakeri, Z., Mansfield, N., Sunderland, C., Omurtag, A.: Physiological correlates of cognitive load in laparoscopic surgery. Sci. Rep. **10**(1), 1–13 (2020). https://doi.org/10.1038/s41598-020-69553-3
11. Keles, H.O., Cengiz, C., Demiral, I., Ozmen, M.M., Omurtag, A.: High density optical neuroimaging predicts surgeons's subjective experience and skill levels. PLoS ONE **16**(2), e0247117 (2021). https://doi.org/10.1371/JOURNAL.PONE.0247117
12. Hirachan, N., Mathews, A., Romero, J., Rojas, R.F.: Measuring cognitive workload using multimodal sensors. In: Proceedings of the Annual International Conference of the IEEE Engineering in Medicine and Biology Society, EMBS,pp. 4921–4924. (2022). https://doi.org/10.1109/EMBC48229.2022.9871308
13. Zhou, T., Cha, J.S., Gonzalez, G., Wachs, J.P., Sundaram, C.P., Yu, D.: Multimodal physiological signals for workload prediction in robot-assisted surgery. ACM Trans. Hum.-Robot Interact. (THRI) **9**(2), 1–26 (2020). https://doi.org/10.1145/3368589
14. Dey, A., Chatourn, A., Billinghurst, M.: Exploration of an EEG-based cognitively adaptive training system in virtual reality. In: 26th IEEE Conference on Virtual Reality and 3D User Interfaces, pp. 220–226 (2019). https://doi.org/10.1109/VR.2019.8797840
15. Yu, P., et al.: Cognitive load/flow and performance in virtual reality simulation training of laparoscopic surgery. In: Proceedings - 2021 IEEE Conference on Virtual Reality and 3D User Interfaces Abstracts and Workshops, VRW, pp. 466–467 (2021). https://doi.org/10.1109/VRW52623.2021.00115
16. Antoniou, P.E., et al.: Biosensor real-time affective analytics in virtual and mixed reality medical education serious games: cohort study. JMIR Serious Games **8**(3), e17823 (2020). https://doi.org/10.2196/17823

17. Brooke, J.: SUS-A quick and dirty usability scale. In: Patrick, W., Jordan, B., Thomas, Ian Lyall McClelland., Weerdmeester, B (eds.), Usability Evaluation In Industry, pp. 189–196. CRC Press (1996)

18. Venkatesh, V., Davis, F.D.: A model of the antecedents of perceived ease of use: development and test. Decis. Sci. **27**(3), 451–481 (1996). https://doi.org/10.1111/J.1540-5915.1996.TB0 0860.X

19. Yosunkaya, E.: Developing a virtual reality adaptation of the laparoscopic surgical training: A multimodal study (Master's Thesis). Middle East Technical University, Ankara, Türkiye (2023)

20. Ebina, K., et al.: Motion analysis for better understanding of psychomotor skills in laparoscopy: objective assessment-based simulation training using animal organs. Surg. Endosc. **35**(8), 4399–4416 (2021). https://doi.org/10.1007/S00464-020-07940-7

21. Makowski, D., et al.: NeuroKit2: a python toolbox for neurophysiological signal processing. Behav. Res. Methods **53**(4), 1689–1696 (2021). https://doi.org/10.3758/S13428-020-01516-Y

22. Brookhuis, K.A., de Waard, D.: Monitoring drivers' mental workload in driving simulators using physiological measures. Accid. Anal. Prev. **42**(3), 898–903 (2010). https://doi.org/10.1016/J.AAP.2009.06.001

23. Taelman, J., Vandeput, S., Gligorijević, I., Spaepen, A., Van Huffel, S.: Time-frequency heart rate variability characteristics of young adults during physical, mental and combined stress in laboratory environment. In: Proceedings of the Annual International Conference of the IEEE Engineering in Medicine and Biology Society, EMBS, pp. 1973–1976 (2011). https://doi.org/10.1109/IEMBS.2011.6090556

24. Yurko, Y.Y., Scerbo, M.W., Prabhu, A.S., Acker, C.E., Stefanidis, D.: Higher mental workload is associated with poorer laparoscopic performance as measured by the NASA-TLX tool. Simul. Healthc. **5**(5), 267–271 (2010). https://doi.org/10.1097/SIH.0B013E3181E3F329

25. Zheng, B., Cassera, M.A., Martinec, D.V., Spaun, G.O., Swanström, L.L.: Measuring mental workload during the performance of advanced laparoscopic tasks. Surg. Endosc.Endosc. **24**(1), 45–50 (2010). https://doi.org/10.1007/S00464-009-0522-3

Collaborating with Agents in Architectural Design and Decision-Making Process: Top-Down and Bottom-Up Case Studies Using Reinforcement Learning

Ozan Yetkin[1]([✉]) [ID], Elif Surer[2] [ID], and Arzu Gönenç Sorguç[1] [ID]

[1] Department of Architecture, Graduate School of Natural and Applied Sciences, Middle East Technical University, 06800 Ankara, Turkey
oyetkin@metu.edu.tr
[2] Department of Modeling and Simulation, Graduate School of Informatics, Middle East Technical University, 06800 Ankara, Turkey

Abstract. This study focuses on how architectural designers, engineers, and academics can collaborate with computational intelligent agents in a design and decision-making process, which is a great challenge. Focusing on this idea, a novel approach is presented where designers can use intelligent agents to their advantage for exploring possibilities via data generation and data processing. The problem of collaboration is presented in two distinct approaches—top-down and bottom-up. In the top-down approach, a case is selected where the designer intends to solve a housing design problem starting from meeting the general requirements of total area and distribution of housing unit types. In the bottom-up approach, a case is selected where the designer plans for the very same problem by meeting the specific requirements of room area and relations. Both cases are based on a reinforcement learning (RL) approach in which the user is allowed to collaborate with the RL algorithm, and results are compared both with widely used algorithms for similar problems (genetic algorithms) and ground-truth (deterministic solutions by designer). Compared results of top-down and bottom-up approaches have shown that the reinforcement learning approach can be used as an intelligent data system to explore design space to find an optimal set of solutions within the objective space. Finally, both approaches are discussed from a broader perspective of how designers, engineers, and academics can collaborate with agents throughout the design and decision-making processes.

Keywords: Data Processing · Intelligent Decision Support · Intelligent Data Systems · Computational Design · Reinforcement Learning

1 Introduction

Formulating a problem in which a designer, engineer, or academic can collaborate with an intelligent agent throughout the design and decision-making process is a great challenge since there is still no end-to-end solution or algorithm approaching a design problem

P. J. Coelho et al. (Eds.): GOODTECHS 2023, LNICST 556, pp. 91–103, 2024.
https://doi.org/10.1007/978-3-031-52524-7_7

to provide a creative solution [1]. It is observed that most of the methods aiming to expand the solution space to provide freedom in design are probabilistic approaches [2, 3]. Nevertheless, studies that use probabilistic methods have limitations on narrowing the expanded solution space down to a set of optimal solutions. It is observed that methods aiming to narrow down the solution space to incorporate design knowledge are mainly formulated with deterministic approaches [4, 5]. Here, it should be noted that studies that use deterministic methods have restrictions on expanding the solution space to enable designers to explore a variety of different alternatives. To verify this gap, a survey is conducted in the game artificial intelligence (AI) domain, and it is observed that there are approaches that use data augmentation to balance the trade-off between exploration and exploitation using reinforcement learning (RL). The RL methods are formulated with the environment, agent, and interpreter triad—a common framework in reinforcement learning research. Some of the game AI studies in the RL literature mainly attack the exploration/exploitation problem (i.e., exploring new solutions versus rigorously following an already feasible solution) with a focus on procedural content generation. For example, in Khalifa et al. [6], the proposed method uses reinforcement learning to generate a level for a 2D game (Sokoban) that is playable by seeing the design problem as a sequential task and teaching agents how to take the next action so that the expected final level design quality is maximized. In another example [7], how creative machine learning techniques can be used to interpolate between actual levels from the same game (Super Mario) or even different games (Super Mario and Kid Icarus) to achieve a newly generated level is analyzed.

When similar studies in the literature focusing on the architectural design domain are examined, it is observed that studies are clustered in two main approaches: one group focuses on exploration while giving freedom to the user, but it lacks objectives to satisfy user needs (as ArchiGAN [8] by NVIDIA Research), and the other group focuses on exploitation that satisfies the objectives that user needs yet it lacks to allow freedom to the user (as Spacemaker [9] by Autodesk Research). Even though numerous studies in the architectural design domain focus on either two-dimensional plan layout generation or three-dimensional mass generation, the methods used in the machine learning domain, such as reinforcement learning, where an agent is set loose in an environment where it constantly acts and perceives and only occasionally receives feedback on its behavior in the form of rewards or punishments [10] are prone to define the state-of-the-art and remain unexplored.

This study aims to position itself between two approaches to propose a novel approach that balances the exploration-exploitation trade-off, which is still a gap in the literature. In light of the extensive literature review, the methodology is defined based on mapping reinforcement learning methods to the architectural design domain and acting as an intelligent decision support system. This study uses an approach that has been taken for an architectural design problem which is addressed in two main parts. The first one is an architectural design problem in which the designer starts with a three-dimensional mass study to primarily handle general requirements (such as total area, maximum height, and space distribution), and the second one is an architectural design problem in which the designer starts with a two-dimensional plan to primarily meet specific requirements (like room areas, partition wall locations, and space relations).

For the first case study, the top-down approach is formulated as a mass study where a designer is attempting to meet general requirements such as total floor plan area and count/distribution of plan types. This approach is acknowledged as a combinatorial optimization which consists of finding an optimal object from a finite set of objects, where the set of feasible solutions is discrete [11]—predefined sets of building plans in this case. Therefore, the proposed approach is formulated in a way that allows the designer to search for the design space (mathematical space that encapsulates all possible combinations) via intelligent computational agents to find the set of feasible combinations within the objective space (mathematical space that encapsulates all possible outcomes) using the inputs provided by the user. On the other hand, for the second case study, the bottom-up approach, the problem is formulated as a two-dimensional architectural plan layout generation where the designer is trying to meet specific requirements such as plan layouts, room areas, and spatial relations. The proposed case study is attacking the problem as a procedural layout generation given the boundary conditions, as often used within the game environments to generate different levels. Therefore, data processing and augmentation strategies used within the game design domain are harnessed to be implemented in the design domain to propose an intelligent decision support system.

2 Methods

The proposed methodology of both the top-down and bottom-up approach is mainly based on a reinforcement learning framework consisting of an environment, an agent, and an observer. For the top-down approach, defined as an architectural mass generation problem, the environment is defined as a generative building dataset consisting of available floor plans, area data, and the number of housing types; the agent is defined as a probabilistic combinator. It takes total area and distribution ratios corresponding to housing types input to select among the available set of floor plans with corresponding area data and type number data. The interpreter is defined as a combinatorial optimization algorithm that takes user input to generate rewards and states according to the environment (Fig. 1).

On the other hand, the bottom-up approach is basically a plan layout generation problem; the agent is defined as vectors responsible for determining the size and the geometry of the rooms, the environment is defined as boundary conditions of a building, and the interpreter is defined as the difference between the boundary conditions and the generated room. The proposed framework for the top-down approach is constructed to take the user input data consisting of the desired total area of the building and desired type distribution ratios to try different combinations of housing plans using the floor area and type numbers data iteratively.

This iterative process is projected to converge in order to satisfy both the intended area and type ratios given by the user. On the other hand, to simulate the framework of the bottom-up approach, the OpenAI Gym framework [12] is selected to be used as it has a simple source code that can be easily modified to be used in this context. Therefore, the OpenAI framework was adapted to combine housing plan layouts with different topologies and used as a main framework for generating new variations (Fig. 2).

The dataset that is used for the top-down approach is composed of 70 different three-dimensional (3D) housing plan models that are designed by the authors since available

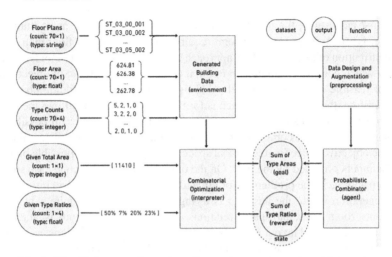

Fig. 1. The RL framework consists of an environment, agent, and interpreter.

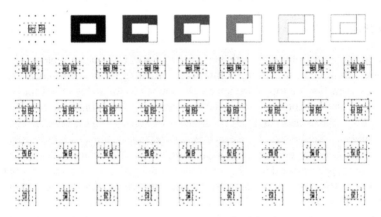

Fig. 2. Different plan layouts are used and combined for the top-down approach.

data for the architectural design domain is still lacking. Since the proposed machine learning method will be reinforcement learning and combinatorial optimization, related features/labels for each 3D housing plan were calculated using the Building Information Modeling (BIM) software and added to the dataset in correspondence. Features/labels that are used as input to calculate and satisfy the objective function consisting of the area of each housing plan and the number of housing types (i.e., 1+1, 2+1, 3+1, 4+1) in each plan. These features/labels are proposed to be used to calculate and satisfy the total area and ratio/distribution of housing types of the total building that the user demands. On the other hand, the data used for the bottom-up approach is derived from the GuessingGame-v0 environment of OpenAI, which aims to guess a number with a 1% deviation rate from the given range using 200-time steps (iterations), and it is modified in a way to adapt architectural plan layout generation for the predefined topology and the intended floor area of each room given by the user (Fig. 3). For the environment, the discrete action space is defined by: no guess submitted yet (0), guess is lower than the target (1), guess is equal to the target (2), guess is higher than the target (3), kept as the same. Yet, rewards changed to 0 if the agent's guess is outside of 5% of the target range and 1 if the agent's guess is inside 5% of the target range; since 1% of the original GuessingGame would increase the computational cost.

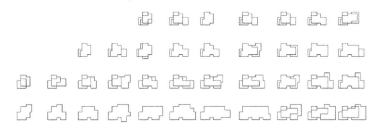

Fig. 3. Predefined housing plan layouts to be used in the bottom-up approach.

The implementation of the top-down approach is based on the reinforcement learning algorithms proposed by Bello et al. [13] for the famous 'traveling salesman problem'. The algorithm uses the TensorFlow framework, which is known to be one of the most robust frameworks within the machine learning domain. Yet, since it is implemented specifically on the traveling salesman problem, it requires further examination and adaptation to be implemented in the proposed problem. Accordingly, an alternative and simpler algorithm is employed, which is also used as a benchmark for the study [13]. The implemented algorithm is a knapsack solver, which is part of OR-Tools developed by Google AI. Even though the already implemented algorithm is not exactly a machine learning model but rather a more traditional artificial intelligence algorithm, it is still implemented to better understand the problem and observe the results. On the other hand, the implementation flow of the bottom-up approach (Fig. 4) is designed to have a graphics engine that is not available in the original GuessingGame environment, so that generated results can also be observed visually. For the graphical part, PyOpenGL is used, a Python binding of the commonly used OpenGL engine, to visualize room layouts generated by the agents. As a benchmark, the ground truth, which is the expected output of the algorithm, is also visualized in the background with a different color. Using the proposed flow, initial tests were conducted with tasks starting from the easiest to the most complex ones, such as guessing the area of a single square, guessing the dimensions of a single rectangle, guessing areas of multiple rectangles with a fixed ratio, and guessing both dimensions and positions of multiple rectangles.

Following the results obtained from the initial test of the framework, it is observed that data design and data augmentation processes are necessary both to transform the proposed framework into a reinforcement learning framework and increase the perfor-mance of the converged results (Fig. 5). Therefore, data design is conducted to transform the number of housing-type data derived from BIM into rewards that the agent can use within the reinforcement learning environment. To transfer the housing type numbers data into a reward mechanism, numbers are used to calculate the distribution ratios for

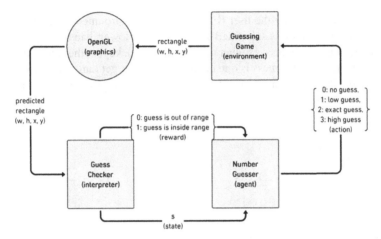

Fig. 4. Implementation workflow including graphics engine and adapted environment.

each plan, and then the absolute total differences between the ratios of each plan and the intended ratios that the user will give are calculated and scaled into a range between 0 and 10. Therefore, it is provided that the agent's probability of choosing a plan with a closer distribution of the intended housing types is aimed to increase since the interpreter will try to maximize the collected rewards. Furthermore, the dataset is augmented using a dataset multiplier calculated based on the ratio of the intended total area to the average area of each plan. This augmentation facilitates the agent's ability to utilize housing plans from the dataset multiple times as the total area increases. Such repetitive usage of suitable housing plans becomes essential, as attempting to find a viable solution by employing each unique plan in the dataset only once would be impractical.

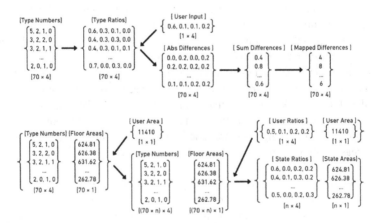

Fig. 5. Data design and data augmentation processes to increase performance.

3 Results and Discussion

Initial outcomes of the top-down approach algorithm are collected on ten different test cases. Initial results have shown a trade-off between total area and housing type ratios demanded by a user. Results show that the intended areas are approximated more precisely and yet often it fails to satisfy the type ratios requested by the user. It was observed that the size or variance of the dataset of 70 different floor plans might not be enough to find an instance that satisfies the type ratio and area objectives efficiently. However, after the integration of the data design and data augmentation process into the proposed workflow, performance is increased both in approximating ratios and the total area desired by the user.

Following the increase in the algorithm's performance, another implementation is also done to compare the proposed workflow with the common approaches in the current literature. Since the most common approach used in generative architectural design systems is genetic algorithms, a genetic algorithm written for a similar knapsack problem is implemented to the same dataset. The dataset is again subjected to the same data preprocessing (design and augmentation) to conform to the comparability of the algorithms and their results (*ceteris paribus* principle). The genetic algorithm is implemented using hyperparameters of crossover rate as 0.8, mutation rate as 0.4, solutions per population as 50, and the number of generations as 250. After the implementation, results are visualized in a line chart for area predictions and bar charts for ratio predictions to compare with the method proposed through the reinforcement learning framework (Fig. 6).

Results have shown that the proposed workflow performs better in finding combinations that have total area values closer to the intended total area by the user. Hence, the genetic algorithm approximated intended type ratios better than the reinforcement learning approach. Yet, not to compare the two methods just by intuition, commonly used regression performance metrics are calculated: mean absolute error (MAE) and root mean square error (RMSE). It is derived that the proposed approach of reinforcement learning outperforms the genetic algorithm in terms of approximating the area objective (with an MAE of 12.8 and an RMSE of 21.8 compared to an MAE of 99.6 and an RMSE of 111.7). In contrast, the genetic algorithm performs slightly better than reinforcement learning in terms of satisfying the ratio objective (with an MAE of 0.138 and RMSE of 0.105 compared to an MAE of 0.141 and RMSE of 0.115) (Table 1). The initial tests for the bottom-up approach are conducted on different levels, as mentioned in the previous section: a single square, a single rectangle, multiple rectangles with a fixed ratio, and multiple rectangles, then results are visualized. The first test conducted with a single square is executed with a single agent responsible for guessing the area of the square given by the user.

The results (Fig. 7) showed that the algorithm converged within 100 time steps when only integers were used in the action space without extensive computational resources. However, to optimize the performance for further tasks, the guessing range of the agent is modified not to include negative numbers since a negative number would not be possible for a floor area. Also, for the algorithm to work with multiple rectangles, the environment is modified to take the area value to be guessed as an input.

Further tests are conducted to implement the use of multiple intelligent agents since the dimensions (width, height) of any rectangle would affect the floor area, and therefore

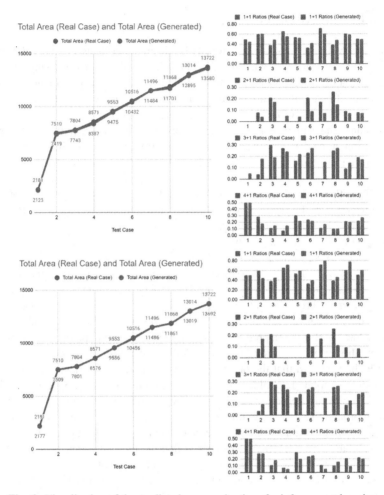

Fig. 6. Visualization of the predicted areas and ratios of reinforcement learning.

Table 1. Comparison of genetic algorithm and reinforcement learning with MAE and RMSE.

Genetic Algorithm		Reinforcement Learning	
Area MAE: 99.600	**Area RMSE:** 111.678	**Area MAE:** 12.800	**Area RMSE:** 21.758
1+1 MAE: 0.076	**1+1 RMSE:** 0.082	**1+1 MAE:** 0.105	**1+1 RMSE:** 0.108
2+1 MAE: 0.088	**2+1 RMSE:** 0.086	**2+1 MAE:** 0.133	**2+1 RMSE:** 0.128
3+1 MAE: 0.168	**3+1 RMSE:** 0.129	**3+1 MAE:** 0.098	**3+1 RMSE:** 0.089
4+1 MAE: 0.220	**4+1 RMSE:** 0.124	**4+1 MAE:** 0.230	**4+1 RMSE:** 0.137
Ratio MAE: 0.138	**Ratio RMSE:** 0.105	**Ratio MAE:** 0.141	**Ratio RMSE:** 0.115

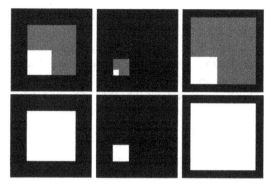

Fig. 7. Results of the first task with an agent (white) to guess an area of a square (pink).

both should be guessed by an agent to fit the common area objective. The second test, conducted after guessing the area of a square, is demonstrated on a simple rectangle where the width and height are tried to be guessed by different agents. Results showed that modifications in the previous test worked successfully in the second case, and the algorithm converged to the intended rectangle, further enhancing the decision-making process. Other tests, which are guessing areas of multiple rectangles with a fixed ratio and guessing both dimensions and positions of multiple rectangles conducted in a similar setting with the addition of more agents and algorithms, are again able to succeed in guessing the given plan layout (Fig. 8).

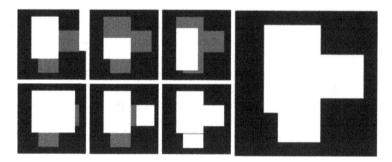

Fig. 8. Results of the complex task which has multiple agents to guess the plan geometry.

Hence, it is observed in this study that it is possible to generate different valid architectural plan layouts based on the relational and hierarchical information retrieved from the user. In addition, since the environment is set to boundary conditions of a building and a reward mechanism is proposed to control the difference between the generated layout and the feasible region of a valid architectural plan, the current study is proven to cover a reliable position between exploration and exploitation.

Both top-down and bottom-up approaches have shown that the reinforcement learning approach can be used to explore the design space to find optimal solutions within the objective space. In addition, to show its performance on extended cases that are not present in the test set, an automation algorithm is implemented to observe how successful the model is, given along with 4572 different inputs (each ratio ranging from 0.0 to 1.0 with an interval of 0.1 while providing a total of 1.0, and total area ranging from 2000 to 20000 with an interval of 1000) from the user. It is observed that the proposed method is still performing well with an MAE of 46.433 and an RMSE of 64.295 for the area objective, an MAE of 0.101, and an RMSE of 0.135 for the ratio objective. Similarly, another test is conducted on an extended dataset consisting of 8421 different housing plans in a different typology than the original dataset (Fig. 9). It is observed that the proposed framework can be adapted to different design problems.

There are also some limitations in the study regarding the following aspects. The first limitation is about the capabilities of the already implemented solver, which is declared to perform better over integers rather than floating numbers. However, since the real data consist of floating numbers for floor areas, it may cause a precision problem. The other limitation is the development process for working in BIM or other 3D environments, which requires further and interoperable development processes to visualize the result of the algorithms. Even though generating data from a correctly modeled 3D model is very easy, generating a model from predicted data back again is not. The last limitation is crucial and related to the problem itself, which is the NP-hardness (non-deterministic polynomial-time hardness) of the planning. Since the selected problem is often regarded as a very complex problem, the algorithm may not converge to a state that can be found manually with human cognition. As can be observed from the visualized results, even if the proposed method is successful in terms of satisfying the total area and the ratio distribution objectives, it fails to converge to compact results as found by human cognition by manual selection (Fig. 10).

However, the architectural design problem is often classified as an NP-hard problem that seems to be the case, considering the total process and subjective aspects. Nevertheless, it is also possible to see some parts, such as plan layout generation and combinatorial optimization of level stacking, as a straightforward engineering problem. Therefore, computational methods and state-of-the-art research in artificial intelligence can aid the architectural design process in that sense, as it has been aiding other disciplines. Hence, since the topologies of the housing plans are predetermined, the suggested approach can hardly be regarded as a creative approach that suggests a different housing plan than the ones already in the dataset. Yet as a future projection, the approach can be extended as a data augmentation and processing strategy, which is processed by agents taking action and passing the information after convergence to the other agent so that the algorithm cannot only guess the given condition with a predetermined topology but also offer different topologies having different relations between rooms.

In light of partial discussions throughout the paper, it can be observed that there is a whole lot more work to be done to achieve an AI agent that is really 'intelligent'. This idea is also clearly presented in the famous Chinese Room argument by Searle [14], which is formulated as a human in a room following a computer program to respond to Chinese characters slipped under the door where the human understands nothing, and yet, following the program for manipulating symbols and numerals, it sends appropriate strings of Chinese characters which leads those outside the door mistakenly suppose that there is a Chinese speaker in the room [15]. Therefore, this hypothesis relies on the idea that intelligence (whether it is human or machine intelligence) is more than just producing outputs that can fool the interrogator (human or machine), and the famous 'Imitation Game' proposed by Turing [16] is not enough to conclude that there is indeed an intelligent behavior. Yet, as machines can process, augment, and produce data that we can put to use as we intended, it provides great potential in collaboration for the future where humans design and machines execute.

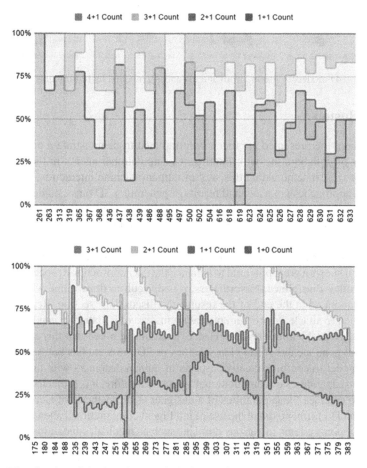

Fig. 9. Visualization of the first dataset of 70 plans and the extended dataset of 8421 plans.

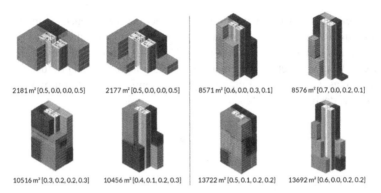

Fig. 10. 3D models of ground truth and instances generated by reinforcement learning.

4   Conclusion

In conclusion, the presented approach is formulated to demonstrate a novel and interactive way of collaborating with intelligent computational agents in the architectural design context. To demonstrate this way of human-machine interaction, top-down and bottom-up approaches are used, and results of generating 3D mass studies and 2D plan layouts are presented. The comparison results of RL algorithms with genetic algorithms and ground-truth solutions have shown that it is possible both to process and augment the domain-specific data with strategies from another domain which is game design and to use RL agents as a collaboration tool to explore possibilities in the design space. Therefore, it shows a great potential to enhance the decision-making processes in design, as well as other disciplines. Nevertheless, it is difficult to draw a line where creativity starts as elaborated at the end of the results and discussions section. Represented case studies aimed to attack the problem piecewise instead of holistically handling the architectural design problem in one shot. Hence, it should be noted that this approach is not presented to generate either 2D plan schemes or 3D mass studies but rather presented as a new model to combine creative aspects of human designers with the exploration-exploitation capabilities of computational agents. Therefore, it is projected that it has the potential to enhance the capabilities of a designer as a prosthesis of a creative mind in the future and to further expand the use of intelligent computational agents as intelligent decision support systems in various domains such as medical, educational, and societal challenges.

References

1. Dennett, D.C.: The Intentional Stance. MIT Press, Cambridge (1987)
2. Brown, N.C., Mueller, C.T.: Automated performance-based design space simplification for parametric structural design. In: Proceedings of IASS Annual Symposia, vol. 2017, no. 15, pp. 1–10. International Association for Shell and Spatial Structures (IASS) (2017)
3. Nagy, D., Villaggi, L., Zhao, D., Benjamin, D.: Beyond heuristics: a novel design space model for generative space planning in architecture. In: Proceedings of the 37th Annual Conference of the Association for Computer Aided Design in Architecture (ACADIA), pp. 436–445 (2017)

4. Pan, W., Turrin, M., Louter, C., Sariyildiz, S., Sun, Y.: Integrating multi-functional space and long-span structure in the early design stage of indoor sports arenas by using parametric modelling and multi-objective optimization. J. Build. Eng. **22**, 464–485 (2019)
5. Tsanas, A., Xifara, A.: Accurate quantitative estimation of energy performance of residential buildings using statistical machine learning tools. Energy Build. **49**, 560–567 (2012)
6. Khalifa, A., Bontrager, P., Earle, S., Togelius, J.: PCGRL: procedural content generation via reinforcement learning. In: Proceedings of the AAAI Conference on Artificial Intelligence and Interactive Digital Entertainment, vol. 16, no. 1, pp. 95–101 (2020)
7. Sarkar, A., Cooper, S.: Towards game design via creative machine learning (GDCML). In: 2020 IEEE Conference on Games (CoG), pp. 744–751. IEEE (2020)
8. ArchiGAN: a Generative Stack for Apartment Building Design. https://developer.nvidia.com/blog/archigan-generative-stack-apartment-building-design/. Accessed 18 Apr 2023
9. Spacemaker Software. https://www.autodesk.com/products/spacemaker/overview. Accessed 18 Apr 2023
10. Bringsjord, S., Govindarajulu, N.S.: Artificial Intelligence." Stanford Encyclopedia of Philosophy. Stanford University (2018). https://plato.stanford.edu/entries/artificial-intelligence/
11. Schrijver, A.: Combinatorial Optimization: Polyhedra and Efficiency, vol. 24. Springer, Berlin (2003)
12. Brockman, G., et al.: OpenAI Gym. arXiv preprint arXiv:1606.01540 (2016)
13. Bello, I., Pham, H., Le, Q.V., Norouzi, M., Bengio, S.: Neural combinatorial optimization with reinforcement learning. arXiv preprint arXiv:1611.09940 (2016)
14. Searle, J.R.: Minds, brains, and programs. Behav. Brain Sci. **3**(3), 417–424 (1980)
15. Cole, D.: The Chinese Room Argument. Stanford Encyclopedia of Philosophy. Stanford University (2020). https://plato.stanford.edu/entries/chinese-room/
16. Turing, A.M.: Computing machinery and intelligence. Mind **59**(236), 433–460 (1950)

Health Technology and Medicine

5G and IoT for Intelligent Healthcare: AI and Machine Learning Approaches— A Review

Hira Akhtar Butt[1], Abdul Ahad[1,2,3(✉)], Muhammad Wasim[1],
Filipe Madeira[4(✉)], and M. Kazem Chamran[5]

[1] Department of Computer Science, University of Management and Technology,
Sialkot 51040, Pakistan
{muhammad-wasim,abdul.ahad}@skt.umt.edu.pk
[2] School of Software, Northwestern Polytechnical University,
Xian 710072, Shaanxi, People's Republic of China
ahad9388@nwpu.edu.cn
[3] Department of Electronics and Communication Engineering, Istanbul Technical
University (ITU), 34467 İstanbul, Turkey
[4] Department of Informatics and Quantitative Methods, Research Centre for Arts
and Communication (CIAC)/Pole of Digital Literacy and Social Inclusion,
Polytechnic Institute of Santarém, 2001-904 Santarem, Portugal
filipe.madeira@esg.ipsantarem.pt
[5] Department of Information and Technology, City University, Menara City U,
No. 8, Jalan, 51A/223, Petaling Jaya, Malaysia
kazem.chamran@city.edu.my

Abstract. New opportunities for AI-powered healthcare systems have emerged thanks to the integration of 5G wireless technology, the Internet of Things (IoT), and AI. This article presents a comprehensive analysis of the current state and future prospects of artificial intelligence (AI) and machine learning (ML) applications in the healthcare sector, with a particular emphasis on their integration with 5G and IoT. Remote patient monitoring, telemedicine, and smart healthcare facilities are just some of the advantages of merging 5G with IoT in healthcare that we address. We also investigate how 5G and IoT-enabled intelligent healthcare systems might benefit from AI and machine learning. We take a look at how 5G and IoT may work together with AI and machine learning algorithms for real-time monitoring, data collection, and processing. Privacy and security worries, interoperability issues, and ethical considerations are only some of the obstacles and future approaches discussed in this study. This paper aims to analyze the existing literature on 5G and IoT applications in healthcare with the objective of identifying future research directions and providing insights into the current state of these technologies.

Keywords: 5G · Internet of Things · IoT · intelligent healthcare · artificial intelligence · AI · machine learning · remote patient monitoring · telemedicine · smart healthcare facilities

© ICST Institute for Computer Sciences, Social Informatics and Telecommunications Engineering 2024
Published by Springer Nature Switzerland AG 2024. All Rights Reserved
P. J. Coelho et al. (Eds.): GOODTECHS 2023, LNICST 556, pp. 107–123, 2024.
https://doi.org/10.1007/978-3-031-52524-7_8

1   Introduction

The advent of 5G (fifth-generation) wireless networks, the Internet of Things (IoT), and artificial intelligence (AI) in recent years has revolutionized many sectors, healthcare among them. Intelligent healthcare systems, which can transform patient care and boost healthcare outcomes, are now possible thanks to the convergence of these technologies [1]. When 5G and the Internet of Things (IoT) are combined in the healthcare industry, a large number of devices can easily exchange data in real-time [2]. To improve healthcare decision-making and enable predictive analytics, AI and machine learning (ML) approaches can effectively process the vast amount generated by IoT devices.

Remote patient monitoring, telemedicine, and smart healthcare facilities are just a few of the many possible applications of 5G and the IoT in the healthcare sector. Wearable gadgets and sensors are used for remote patient monitoring, which enables continuous health monitoring and proactive intervention [3]. 5G and IoT technologies are used in telemedicine and virtual healthcare to facilitate remote consultations, diagnostics, and even remote procedures, expanding access to medical treatment, especially for those living in rural areas [4]. Additionally, it should be noted that utilization of 5G and IoT in healthcare facilities paves the way for intelligent infrastructure and asset management, streamlines operations, and improves the patient experience.

Despite the exciting possibilities afforded by 5G, IoT, and AI in healthcare, it is essential to study how AI and ML intelligent healthcare systems can effectively interpret the vast amount of the available data, enabling streamlined predictive analytics and supported clinical decision-making processes [5]. Using AI and ML, intelligent healthcare systems can make sense of the mountains of data at their disposal, facilitate predictive analytics, and back up clinical decision-making procedures [6]. Additionally, Healthcare providers can ensure real-time monitoring and analysis for prompt interventions by integrating AI and ML algorithms with 5G and IoT.

Therefore, the purpose of this article is to present a high-level summary of the ways in which 5G and IoT might be used to improve healthcare, with an emphasis on AI and ML techniques. We also explore how AI and ML algorithms can be integrated with 5G and IoT for real-time monitoring of collected data. Privacy and security issues, as well as interoperability and ethical problems, are discussed in the article as well as the opportunities and possibilities for the future of this subject.

This paper aims to contribute to the understanding of the current state of 5G and IoT applications in healthcare by reviewing the existing literature, with the hope of shedding light on potential research directions for the integration of AI and ML approaches in the intelligent healthcare ecosystem.

1.1   5G Technology

With its unprecedented speed, capacity, and connection, fifth-generation (5G) mobile network technology is a major step forward in the telecommunications industry [7]. The 5G network as the successor to 4G, hold tremendous potential to transform various industry. It is advanced capabilities enable the development of previously impractical or even impossible applications and services, opening up new possibilities for the healthcare sector.

5G technology possesses several distinguishing characteristics that differentiate it from the previous generation. By utilising higher frequency bands like the millimetre-wave spectrum, 5G enabled significantly increased data transfer speeds and reduced latency [8].

Furthermore, 5G adoption in healthcare paves the way for smart hospitals and healthcare facilities, allowing for cutting-edge technologies like AR and VR for surgical training and remote surgeries. Improved patient care, increased efficiency, and new medical breakthroughs are all possible thanks to the power of 5G.

1.2   Role of IoT in Healthcare

The Connectivity of devices, sensors, and systems through the IoT facilitates efficient data gathering, monitoring, and decision-making, in modernizing healthcare. In the field of medicine, the (IoT) enables remote patient monitoring by letting doctors keep tabs on vital signs like a patient's heart rate, blood pressure, and glucose levels in real-time. Wearables and sensors connected to the Internet of Things will soon allow for the collection of vital patient data, paving the way for more individualized and preventative healthcare [9].

IoT-enabled healthcare uses smart devices and ambient intelligence to keep patients safer. Research has shown that these devices can be used for fall detection, medication monitoring and emergency alerts. For example, the implementation of IoT in healthcare improves the coordination of care and reduces medical errors. In Addition, IoT-enabled telemedicine services enabled remote consultations, eliminating the need for [10].

The growing use of IoT in healthcare has many potential benefits, but it also raises concerns about patient privacy, data integrity, and system compatibility. Sensitive patient data must be guarded using strong security protocols, encryption methods, and data governance frameworks. The smooth interchange and integration of data between IoT devices and systems depends on their interoperability.

1.3   Benefits of Combining 5G and IoT in Healthcare

In healthcare, 5G and IoT work together to improve real-time communication and data transfer across various devices, sensors, and systems [11]. Supporting remote consultations, telemedicine services, and remote diagnostics, 5G networks' ultra-low latency makes real-time transmission of important medical data possible. As a result, healthcare professionals, including doctors and nurses are able to make better faster and more informed decisions, which ultimately benefits the patient [12].

The combination of 5G and IoT makes it possible to monitor patients remotely, with real-time monitoring of vital signs and other health data [13]. With the help of connected wearable gadgets and sensors, doctors may monitor a patient's vital signs in real-time and gain significant insights for individualized care and early disease identification. Remote patient monitoring allows doctors to check in on their patients whenever they see fit and offer immediate feedback and advice.

Combining 5G and IoT in healthcare allows for secure data management and efficient data interchange [14]. Faster data transfer and more storage space are provided by 5G networks, allowing for the painless transfer of massive amounts of medical data. Secure data transmission from IoT devices to healthcare IT systems helps to maintain patient privacy and regulatory compliance. Better care coordination and efficiency might result from healthcare professionals' increased capacity to share data and work together [15].

Surgical training and remote procedures, for example, can benefit from the use of augmented reality (AR) and virtual reality (VR) thanks to the combination of 5G and IoT note that the use of such technologies has the potential to improve training and decrease geographical constraints for healthcare professionals by allowing them to cooperate, learn, and conduct procedures in virtual settings. Due to 5G high-resolution photos and videos may be transmitted in real-time, improving remote consultations and medical education [16].

Integrating 5G and IoT greatly improves healthcare accessibility, especially in underserved or rural areas. Eliminate the need for patients to travel long distances to see their doctors. This brings healthcare directly to them, which is particularly beneficial for those with limited mobility or who lie in remote areas [17].

1.4 Our Contribution

This paper will contribute by reviewing the use of AI and ML techniques in conjunction with 5G and the IoT to create intelligent healthcare. The potential for improved real-time communication, remote patient monitoring, data management, and access to healthcare services is highlighted, and the benefits and problems of combining 5G and IoT in healthcare settings are discussed. Our research not only lays the foundation for future research and innovation in intelligent healthcare but also provides valuable insights into the transformative impact of these technologies.

2   Literature Review

The potential of integrating 5G and IoT integration to revolutionize healthcare delivery and enhance patient outcomes has gained significant attention. In this paper, we examine the existing literature on the topic of 5G and IoT in intelligent healthcare with a special emphasis on AI and ML. Table 1 shows the existing reviews summary.

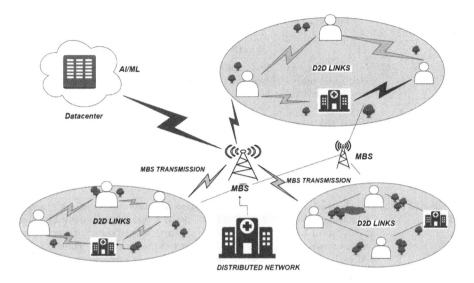

Fig. 1. General Architecture of Smart Healthcare Network based on 5G and IoT

The ability of 5G technology to facilitate real-time communication and data sharing in healthcare settings has been highlighted by a number of recent research. According to [18], 5G's low-latency and high-speed features allow for the smooth transmission of enormous amounts of medical data, which in turn enables telemedicine, remote consultations, and real-time diagnostics. In the event of an emergency or in a healthcare setting that is geographically dispersed, these requirements are essential for making timely and informed treatment decisions.

Figure 1 depicts the architecture of a smart healthcare network leveraging 5G and IoT. Central to this system is the AI/ML-powered data centre tasked with processing healthcare data. High-speed connections link the data centre to a Distributed Network of clusters, each populated with D2D links and represented by various symbols for healthcare facilities, patients, and providers. Peripheral MBS stations connect these clusters, enabling real-time data transfer across the 5G network, crucial for delivering efficient and reliable healthcare services. This architecture underscores the synergy between 5G's speed and IoT's connectivity in revolutionizing healthcare delivery.

In addition, 5G networks combined with IoT gadgets and sensors provide a robust Internet of Medical Things (IoMT) ecosystem. Continuous remote monitoring of patients and early detection of anomalies is made possible by this network's interconnected nodes. Healthcare practitioners can better monitor their patient's conditions and respond appropriately by analyzing data gathered in real-time through wearable devices and sensors both patient outcomes and hospital readmission rates can potentially benefit from the implementation of remote monitoring and individualized care at this level [19].

Table 1. Summary of the existing reviews

Ref.	Year	Title	Objectives
Devi et al. [20]	2023	5G technology in healthcare and wearable devices: a review	Investigate the function of wearable devices in enabling remote monitoring and individualized healthcare delivery, and present an overview of the uses and advantages of 5G technology in healthcare
Peralta-Ochoa et al. [1]	2023	Smart Healthcare Applications over 5G Networks: A Systematic Review	Examine the published research on 5G-enabled smart healthcare applications. The purpose of this article is to catalogue the many healthcare-related uses for 5G, to weigh their advantages and disadvantages, and to shed light on where the field could go from here in terms of research and development
Mazhar et al. [21]	2023	Analysis of Challenges and Solutions of IoT in Smart Grids Using AI and Machine Learning Techniques: A Review	IoT implementation difficulties in smart grids, and possible AI/ML-based solutions for overcoming them. The purpose of this article is to survey where smart grids stand in terms of the Internet of Things (IoT), highlight some of the biggest obstacles standing in the way of their widespread adoption, and suggest some novel solutions that make use of AI and Machine Learning to overcome those obstacles
Dash et al. [22]	2023	Fusion of Artificial Intelligence and 5G in Defining Future UAV Technologies-A Review	In the context of UAVs, investigate how well Artificial Intelligence (AI) and 5G technology work together. The purpose of this study is to examine the current status of artificial intelligence (AI) and fifth-generation (5G) integration in unmanned aerial vehicle (UAV) technologies, investigate their possible applications, and debate the difficulties and potential solutions associated with using this fusion to define the future of UAV technologies
Moglia et al. [23]	2022	5G in healthcare: from COVID-19 to future challenges	Investigate how 5G can help healthcare providers cope with the spread of the COVID-19 virus. The purpose of this article is to investigate the many uses of 5G in healthcare during the epidemic, to weigh its advantages and disadvantages, and to look ahead to the difficulties and possibilities that lie ahead for this technology in the healthcare sector
Abdul et al. [24]	2020	Technologies trend towards 5G network for smart health-care using IoT: A review	To look at how 5G network adoption is being pushed forward by recent technological developments for use in IoT-based smart healthcare applications. The purpose of this paper is to survey the state of the art in this area of research, examine how these technologies affect the field of smart healthcare, and propose new avenues for study
Abdul et al. [25]	2019	5G-based smart healthcare network: architecture, taxonomy, challenges and future research directions	To provide a detailed analysis of the structure and classification of 5G-based smart healthcare networks. This paper's objective is to catalogue and examine the problems that arise during the deployment of such networks, and to suggest avenues for further study in this area

Leveraging the data produced by IoT devices in healthcare relies heavily on the application of AI and ML techniques. Artificial intelligence AI algorithms can play a crucial role in early disease detection, predicting patient outcomes, and providing individualized therapy recommendations by analyzing data and identifying patterns. Healthcare providers can benefit from AI-powered predictive models in terms of both resource allocation and decision-making.

There are many opportunities presented by the integration of 5G and IoT in healthcare, but there are also certain obstacles that must be overcome. Patients' personal information is increasingly being communicated and kept in distributed databases, raising data security and privacy concerns. The lack of standardization and interoperability across IoT devices and systems hampers the smooth sharing of data.

The literature review concludes that combining 5G and IoT in intelligent healthcare with AI and Ml technologies has the potential to completely transform the healthcare system. The integration of these tools allows for real-time interaction, remote monitoring, and individualized treatment, all of which contribute to better health outcomes for patients. However, successfully implementing these technologies in healthcare settings depends on addressing issues such as data security, privacy, and interoperability.

3   AI and Machine Learning in Healthcare

By providing sophisticated methods for analyzing large amounts of medical data, predicting patient outcomes, and tailoring treatment strategies, AI (Artificial Intelligence) and machine learning are reshaping the healthcare sector [26].

The term "artificial intelligence" (AI) is used to describe the process of programming computers to carry out tasks that would otherwise need human intelligence. AI algorithms and systems aid clinical decision-making because they are programmed to mimic human cognition by collecting data, analyzing it, and drawing conclusions. Natural language processing, computer vision, expert systems, and knowledge representation are all examples of AI methods applied in healthcare today [27].

Machine learning (ML) is a subfield of artificial intelligence concerned with the study and creation of methods by which machines can learn from data without being explicitly programmed. In order to create predictions or carry out tasks, ML algorithms can automatically detect patterns and correlations within massive datasets. Medical data is used to train machine learning algorithms that can then identify trends, categorize diseases, forecast treatment outcomes, and make personalized recommendations [28].

AI and ML have produced important advances in the field of medical imaging and diagnosis. Medical imaging studies like X-rays, CT scans, and MRIs can be analyzed by computer vision algorithms to spot abnormalities, locate cancers, and aid radiologists in their diagnoses. In order to increase the accuracy and efficiency of disease detection, ML models can learn from large datasets of annotated medical images [29].

Artificial intelligence (AI) and machine learning (ML) methods are also applied to electronic health records (EHRs), genomic data, and other patient data to anticipate treatment outcomes, predict the course of diseases, and identify people at risk for developing specific diseases. Early warning indicators can be identified, patient management may be enhanced, and resource allocation can be optimized with the help of predictive models [30].

To enable customized medicine, in which treatment plans are individualized for each patient based on their specific traits, genetic makeup, and medical history, AI and ML play a vital role. Treatment alternatives, dose modifications, and individualized treatments can all be determined by using ML models to sift through massive volumes of patient data and medical literature [31].

Clinical decision support systems (CDSS): powered by AI and ML can help medical professionals make decisions based on the best available evidence by providing them with up-to-date information, treatment guidelines, and alarms as they occur. Diagnostic testing, treatment plans, and the avoidance of medication errors can all be improved with the help of such systems [32].

Continuous monitoring of a patient's vital signs, activity levels, and physiological data is now possible thanks to the Internet of Things (IoT) and wearable devices equipped with artificial intelligence (AI) and machine learning (ML) algorithms. Machine learning algorithms can assess data in real-time from wearable sensors to spot outliers, track chronic illnesses, and flag the onset of health decline [33].

Artificial intelligence (AI) and machine learning are increasingly being used in the medical field, which has great promise for improving diagnosis, therapy, patient care, and healthcare delivery as a whole.

4   Machine Learning Base Schemes and AI Base Schemes in Healthcare

4.1   Machine Learning Base Scheme

Yan et al. [34], provide a comprehensive analysis of machine-learning approaches for sepsis prediction and early detection using clinical text data. The objective of the paper is to review the existing literature and evaluate the performance of various machine learning models in this domain. The review emphasizes the significance of sensitivity, specificity, accuracy, AUC (Area under curve), and time to detection as performance measures for assessing the efficacy of the models. The paper highlights challenges such as variability in sepsis definitions, real-time implementation constraints, and generalizability to diverse healthcare settings. Overall, the review underscores the potential of machine learning in improving sepsis prediction and early detection, while suggesting further research areas for advancement in this field [34].

Wine et al. [38], delves into how machine learning could drastically alter the field of healthcare epidemiology. The article highlights the progress and uses of machine learning in the diagnosis, prognosis, and treatment of disease. In order to

Table 2. Summary of the existing reviews about ML base schemes

Ref.	Year	Title	Objectives	Performance Major	Limitations
yan et al. [34]	2022	Sepsis prediction, early detection, and identification using clinical text for machine learning: a systematic review	Discuss the use of machine learning in the early diagnosis of sepsis.	Sensitivity, specificity, accuracy, AUC, time to detection	Challenges in real-time implementation, transferability between settings, and the wide range of sepsis definitions
Rautela et al. [35]	2022	A Systematic Review on Breast Cancer Detection Using Deep Learning Techniques	Analyse the use of machine learning in digital mammography for the identification of breast cancer.	Sensitivity, specificity, accuracy, AUC, ROC curves	Lack of standardized datasets, potential biases in data collection, challenges in generalization
Benedetto et al. [36]	2022	Machine learning improves mortality risk prediction after cardiac surgery: systematic review and meta-analysis	Analyse the use of artificial intelligence in anticipating cardiac surgery complications	Sensitivity, specificity, accuracy, PPV, NPV, AUC	Need for large and diverse datasets, overfitting of models, challenges in real-time implementation
mahajan et al. [37]	2020	Machine learning for predicting readmission in patients with heart failure: A systematic review	Analyse the state of the art in machine learning for heart failure readmission prediction.	Accuracy, precision, recall, F1 score, AUC	The requirement for massive datasets, the indeterminacy of model performance, and the difficulty of interpreting complicated models
wine et al. [38]	2019	Machine learning for healthcare: on the verge of a major shift in healthcare epidemiology	Highlight the potential of machine learning in healthcare epidemiology	Accuracy, sensitivity, specificity, AUC	Ethical considerations, model interpretability, and the need for high-quality data

evaluate the effectiveness of machine learning models in healthcare, the research stresses the significance of accuracy, sensitivity, specificity, and AUC. It also addresses the issues of data quality, model interpretability, and ethical concerns that must be resolved before machine learning can be successfully implemented in healthcare. The paper concludes that machine learning has the potential to significantly enhance healthcare outcomes, and it urges greater study and collaboration in this area [38].

Mahajan et al. [37], offer a thorough investigation of ML models developed for this purpose. The goal of this research is to assess the effectiveness of various machine learning algorithms by reviewing the relevant literature. In order to evaluate the prediction capacities of the models, the review emphasises the significance of accuracy, precision, recall, F1 score, and area under the curve (AUC). While acknowledging the importance of huge datasets, the article also highlights the difficulties associated with interpreting complicated models and addressing performance variations across healthcare settings. The review highlights the promise of machine learning to enhance readmission prediction for heart failure patients and identifies avenues for future study in this field [37].

The research paper "A Systematic Review on Breast Cancer Detection Using Deep Learning Techniques" examines the use of deep learning methods for this purpose in great detail. The purpose of this research is to conduct a literature review and assess the effectiveness of several deep learning algorithms in this setting. To evaluate the effectiveness of deep learning models, the paper highlights the significance of sensitivity, specificity, accuracy, AUC, and ROC curves. The limitations of the article are acknowledged, including the lack of standardised datasets, the possibility of bias in data, and the ability to generalise to different populations. To conclude, the review demonstrates the promise of deep learning for better breast cancer diagnosis and suggests where to go from here to investigate more [35].

The paper "Machine Learning for the Prediction of surgical complications in patients undergoing cardiac surgery: A Review" provides a comprehensive analysis of the application of machine learning in this area. The objective is a review of the relevant literature and an assessment of the effectiveness of various machine learning models in this context. To emphasise the importance of assessing the predictive capabilities of models the review highlights performance metrics sensitivity, specificity, accuracy, PPV, NPV, and AUC. The requirement for big and diverse datasets, the possibility of overfitting, and the difficulty of implementation in real-time contexts are all acknowledged in the paper. In sum, the review demonstrates the promise of machine learning in enhancing the prediction of surgical complications and points to avenues for future research.

4.2   AI Base Scheme

Accordingly Alloghani et al. [39], the absence of standardised datasets, difficulties in actual implementation, and ethical concerns are discussed as three of the most pressing problems in the field of artificial intelligence today. The authors

Table 3. Summary of the existing reviews about AI base Scheme

Ref.	Year	Title	Objectives	Performance Measures	Limitations
Yousaf et al. [40]	2023	Artificial intelligence-based decision support systems in complex medical domains: Review, examples, and future trends	Overview of AI-based decision support systems in complex medical domains	Sensitivity, specificity, accuracy, precision, F1 score	Need for large and diverse datasets, model interpretability, ethical considerations
loh, et al. [41]	2022	Application of explainable artificial intelligence for healthcare: A systematic review of the last decade (2011–2022)	Comprehensive review of AI applications in healthcare	Accuracy, sensitivity, specificity, AUC, precision	Lack of standardized protocols, transparency of AI algorithms, integration challenges
Montani et al. [42]	2019	Machine learning and artificial intelligence in clinical decision support systems: A focused literature review	Review of machine learning and AI in clinical decision support systems	Accuracy, sensitivity, specificity, precision, F1 score	High-quality data, integration challenges, potential biases
Alloghani et al. [39]	2019	The application of artificial intelligence technology in healthcare: a systematic review	Systematic review of AI applications in healthcare	Sensitivity, specificity, accuracy, AUC, F1 score	Lack of standardized datasets, real-world implementation challenges, ethical considerations
Miotto [27]	2018	Deep learning for healthcare: review, opportunities and challenges	Review of deep learning techniques in healthcare	Sensitivity, specificity, accuracy, AUC, precision	Large annotated datasets, interpretability, algorithm robustness

stress the need to use standard datasets to compare various AI models and algorithms fairly and accurately. They also bring to light issues like data collecting, system integration, and user acceptance that arise during the deployment of AI systems in the real world. Privacy issues, algorithmic prejudice, and unforeseen repercussions are only some of the ethical ramifications of AI that are discussed in this study. The authors insist that these issues must be resolved for the safe and effective implementation of AI [39].

In a systematic literature review, Montani, & Striani et al. [42], focus on the use of machine learning and AI in clinical decision support systems (CDSS). The benefits of utilising ML and AI algorithms to aid healthcare workers in making precise and fast clinical choices are highlighted [42]. Deep learning, support vector machines, and random forests are just some of the ML methods they investigate, along with their use in CDSS. Review topics include data quality, interpretability, and regulatory issues as barriers to ML and AI use in healthcare. The authors stress the need for ongoing studies to guarantee the efficient and secure implementation of ML and AI in CDSS.

Miotto et al. [27], presented a thorough analysis of the current state of deep learning applications in medicine. Disease diagnosis, treatment prediction, and medical imaging analysis are just some of the areas where scientists believe deep learning might make a difference in healthcare. Large, high-quality datasets, interpretability of models, and ethical considerations are only some of the issues they bring up in relation to utilising deep learning in healthcare. While the research emphasises the revolutionary potential of deep learning in healthcare, it also stresses the importance of rigorous validation, regulatory frameworks, and collaboration between clinicians and data scientists.

Yousaf et al. [40], in their article, provides an in-depth analysis of how AI has been used in the medical field. Machine learning, NLP, and computer vision are only a few of the artificial intelligence methods discussed by the writers. Disease diagnosis, individualised treatment plans, and continuous patient monitoring are just a few examples of AI's potential applications brought to light. Data privacy, algorithm openness, and legal barriers are just a few of the issues that are discussed in this overview of the difficulties of implementing AI. To realise the full potential of AI in healthcare, the authors stress the need for cross-disciplinary cooperation, ethical issues, and continuous research.

This comprehensive overview looks at how AI has been used in healthcare over the past decade. The authors assess the effectiveness of AI methods in improving the explainability and openness of AI healthcare models. They feature the many ways in which AI has been put to use in the medical field, including in fields like clinical decision support, medical imaging, and patient monitoring. Ultimately, the review's goal of increasing trust and understanding between AI systems and healthcare professionals through their integration into healthcare systems highlights the necessity for ongoing research and development of AI technologies.

5   Possible Solutions

Here are some possible solutions after examining the limitations of the previous papers:

- Many options exist for dealing with the problems listed in the Table 2 and 3. Coordination across healthcare organisations is essential to address the requirement for big and diverse datasets and guarantee model interpretability. Through proper anonymization and security measures, this partnership can incorporate data sharing without compromising patient privacy. To further improve the quality and diversity of AI model training, synthetic data creation techniques can be used to supplement scarce datasets.
- Establishing industry-wide standards and guidelines is crucial to addressing the lack of standardised protocols and transparency of AI algorithms. These guidelines can be used as a basis for consistent and reproducible data collection, annotation, and evaluation. By making AI algorithms publicly available, academics and practitioners will have a better chance of trusting and collaborating on the underlying models.

- Working together, AI researchers and medical professionals can overcome integration obstacles. Integration problems can be sorted out with the help of end-users who are brought into the design process early on and whose needs and processes are taken into account. Integration of AI technologies into the current healthcare infrastructure relies heavily on the widespread adoption of interoperability standards.
- Various approaches can be adopted to improve the fairness of AI systems and reduce the biases that may arise from using high-quality data. This encompasses methods for identifying and correcting biases in both data and algorithms. Biases in deployed AI systems can be uncovered and corrected by continuous monitoring and review.
- Finally, ethical considerations should be built in at every stage of the AI creation process. This necessitates following predetermined moral norms during data gathering, model development, and rollout. Guidelines and laws tailored to AI in healthcare can also protect patients' privacy and keep their faith in these technologies intact.

  If these problems are addressed, it may be possible to integrate and deploy AI technology in the healthcare sector and overcome the obstacles that have hampered their use thus far.

6   Challenges and Future Research Directions

6.1   Challenges

There are many obstacles that must be overcome before 5G, the Internet of Things, artificial intelligence, and machine learning can be successfully implemented in the healthcare sector. In order to pave the road for future directions in this subject, an appreciation of these obstacles is essential.

- Patient data is generated in large quantities due to the interconnected nature of 5G, IoT, AI, and ML in healthcare, which raises concerns about data security and privacy. Maintaining patient trust and meeting legal standards necessitate the implementation of stringent data security and privacy protection procedures. Protecting sensitive patient data requires the use of cutting-edge encryption methods, safe data storage, and rigorous authentication procedures.
- Data formats, communication protocols, and interfaces need to be standardized to allow for the seamless integration of different technologies. It is crucial to facilitate efficient data interchange, cooperation, and integration across diverse healthcare devices, systems, and platforms by achieving seamless interoperability. The efficient sharing of data between healthcare facilities is dependent on the development of standardized protocols that allow for interoperability between those facilities.
- Ethical Considerations: Concerns about algorithm bias, transparency, and responsibility arise when using AI and Machine Learning algorithms. If we don't want to see unfair healthcare inequities and biased decisions, we need

to make sure that AI algorithms are fair, transparent, and interpretable. The proper application of AI in healthcare calls for the establishment of ethical frameworks, norms, and regulatory frameworks.

- To integrate 5G, IoT, AI, and ML in healthcare, a substantial investment in infrastructure is required. This includes things like 5G network coverage, dependable connectivity, and enough computing resources. There may be monetary difficulties associated with investing in new healthcare technology and upgrading old facilities. To guarantee widespread adoption and accessibility, these technologies need to have their infrastructure and costs addressed.

- Integration of cutting-edge healthcare technologies calls for a trained staff with the requisite expertise. Effective use of AI and data analytics in clinical practice requires training for healthcare personnel. The full potential of these technologies can only be realized if healthcare practitioners' skill gaps are closed through training programs and educational activities.

6.2   Future Research Direction

When thinking about where healthcare technology is headed, it is clear that more study and experimentation are required to fully realize the potential of technologies like 5G, IoT, AI, and ML. Some examples are:

- Research should be directed toward creating more advanced AI algorithms and Machine Learning models that can deal with complex healthcare data, enhance accuracy, and permit real-time decision-making. In order to further expand AI's potential in healthcare, it is important to investigate cutting-edge approaches like deep learning, reinforcement learning, and federated learning.

- Exploring the intersection of 5G, IoT, AI, and ML with other emerging technologies like blockchain, edge computing, and VR can lead to exciting new developments in healthcare. These connections have the potential to strengthen data privacy, facilitate distributed data administration, and enrich interactive healthcare environments.

- Patient-centered approaches should be prioritized in future healthcare innovations to encourage greater patient engagement. Patient monitoring, information access, and treatment plan participation are all facilitated through the creation of user-friendly mobile applications, wearable devices, and individualized health management systems.

- Governments and regulatory organizations need to craft policies and regulations to safeguard patients' rights and privacy while promoting the ethical application of new technologies in healthcare. The establishment of a complete regulatory framework requires the combined efforts of lawmakers, healthcare providers, and technology developers.

- Implementing these technologies after thorough review and validation is essential for ensuring their efficacy, safety, and impact on patient outcomes. Evidence for the widespread adoption and integration of these technologies in healthcare can be gathered by conducting rigorous clinical trials, real-world research, and outcome assessments.

7   Conclusion

The potential for a dramatic improvement in healthcare delivery and patient outcomes is created by the combination of 5G, the IoT, AI, and ML. Remote monitoring of patients, telemedicine, cutting-edge diagnostics, predictive analytics, and individualized healthcare are all made possible by the convergence of these technologies. Better patient care and results are possible because to real-time data gathering, analysis, and decision-making by healthcare providers.

However, there are obstacles to overcome in the healthcare industry when implementing these technologies. There are considerable obstacles that must be surmounted, such as data security and privacy concerns, interoperability issues, ethical considerations, infrastructure needs, and a lack of skilled workers. To overcome these obstacles, the healthcare community, technology industry, legislators, and regulators will need to work together.

Further improvement in AI and Machine Learning algorithms, integration with emerging technologies, patient-centric approaches, policy and regulatory framework creation, and evidence-based validation and implementation are all potential next steps for the discipline. By moving into these areas, healthcare systems may make better use of 5G, IoT, AI, and Machine Learning to provide faster, easier-to-use, and more individualized treatment for their patients.

The introduction of 5G, IoT, AI, and ML into healthcare marks a major paradigm change that has the potential to completely transform healthcare delivery around the globe. For these innovations to improve healthcare outcomes and patients' quality of life, it is essential that all relevant parties embrace them, face the obstacles they pose, and work together to ensure their widespread adoption.

Acknowledgment. This work is funded by national funds through FCT - Foundation for Science and Technology, I.P., under project UIDP/04019/2020.

References

1. Peralta-Ochoa, A.M., Chaca-Asmal, P.A., Guerrero-Vásquez, L.F., Ordoñez-Ordóñez, J.O., Coronel-González, E.J.: Smart healthcare applications over 5G networks: a systematic review. Appl. Sci. **13**(3), 1469 (2023)
2. Poncha, L.J., Abdelhamid, S., Alturjman, S., Ever, E., Al-Turjman, F.: 5G in a convergent internet of things era: an overview. In: 2018 IEEE International Conference on Communications Workshops (ICC Workshops), pp. 1–6. IEEE (2018)
3. Ahad, A., et al.: A comprehensive review on 5G-based smart healthcare network security: taxonomy, issues, solutions and future research directions. Array 100290 (2023)
4. Ahad, A., Tahir, M.: Perspective-6G and IoT for intelligent healthcare: challenges and future research directions. ECS Sens. Plus **2**(1), 011601 (2023)
5. Butt, H.A., et al.: Federated machine learning in 5G smart healthcare: a security perspective review. Procedia Comput. Sci. **224**, 580–586 (2023)
6. Deo, R.C.: Machine learning in medicine. Circulation **132**(20), 1920–1930 (2015)
7. Mughees, A., Tahir, M., Sheikh, M.A., Ahad, A.: Energy-efficient ultra-dense 5G networks: recent advances, taxonomy and future research directions. IEEE Access **9**, 147692–147716 (2021)

8. Qureshi, H.N., Manalastas, M., Ijaz, A., Imran, A., Liu, Y., Al Kalaa, M.O.: Communication requirements in 5G-enabled healthcare applications: review and considerations. In: Healthcare, vol. 10, p. 293. MDPI (2022)

9. Ahad, A., Al Faisal, S., Ali, F., Jan, B., Ullah, N., et al.: Design and performance analysis of DSS (dual sink based scheme) protocol for WBASNs. Adv. Remote Sens. 6(04), 245 (2017)

10. Islam, S.R., Kwak, D., Kabir, M.H., Hossain, M., Kwak, K.-S.: The internet of things for health care: a comprehensive survey. IEEE Access 3, 678–708 (2015)

11. Varga, P., et al.: 5G support for industrial IoT applications-challenges, solutions, and research gaps. Sensors 20(3), 828 (2020)

12. Ahad, A., Tahir, M., Sheikh, M.A.S., Hassan, N., Ahmed, K.I., Mughees, A.: A game theory based clustering scheme (GCS) for 5G-based smart healthcare. In: 2020 IEEE 5th International Symposium on Telecommunication Technologies (ISTT), pp. 157–161. IEEE (2020)

13. Asghari, P., Rahmani, A.M., Javadi, H.H.S.: Internet of things applications: a systematic review. Comput. Netw. 148, 241–261 (2019)

14. Chen, Z., et al.: Machine learning-enabled IoT security: open issues and challenges under advanced persistent threats. ACM Comput. Surv. 55(5), 1–37 (2022)

15. Ahad, A., Tahir, M., Sheikh, M.A., Ahmed, K.I., Mughees, A.: An intelligent clustering-based routing protocol (CRP-GR) for 5G-based smart healthcare using game theory and reinforcement learning. Appl. Sci. 11(21), 9993 (2021)

16. Palmaccio, M., Dicuonzo, G., Belyaeva, Z.S.: The internet of things and corporate business models: a systematic literature review. J. Bus. Res. 131, 610–618 (2021)

17. Ahad, A., Tahir, M., Sheikh, M.A.S., Mughees, A., Ahmed, K.I.: Optimal route selection in 5G-based smart health-care network: a reinforcement learning approach. In: 2021 26th IEEE Asia-Pacific Conference on Communications (APCC), pp. 248–253. IEEE (2021)

18. Lasi, H., Fettke, P., Kemper, H.-G., Feld, T., Hoffmann, M.: Industry 4.0. Bus. Inf. Syst. Eng. 6, 239–242 (2014)

19. Aghdam, Z.N., Rahmani, A.M., Hosseinzadeh, M.: The role of the internet of things in healthcare: future trends and challenges. Comput. Methods Programs Biomed. 199, 105903 (2021)

20. Devi, D.H., et al.: 5G technology in healthcare and wearable devices: a review. Sensors 23(5), 2519 (2023)

21. Mazhar, T., et al.: Analysis of challenges and solutions of IoT in smart grids using AI and machine learning techniques: a review. Electronics 12(1), 242 (2023)

22. Dash, B., Ansari, M.F., Swayamsiddha, S.: Fusion of artificial intelligence and 5G in defining future UAV technologies-a review. In: 2023 International Conference on Device Intelligence, Computing and Communication Technologies, (DICCT), pp. 312–316. IEEE (2023)

23. Moglia, A., et al.: 5G in healthcare: from Covid-19 to future challenges. IEEE J. Biomed. Health Inform. 26(8), 4187–4196 (2022)

24. Ahad, A., Tahir, M., Aman Sheikh, M., Ahmed, K.I., Mughees, A., Numani, A.: Technologies trend towards 5G network for smart health-care using IoT: a review. Sensors 20(14), 4047 (2020)

25. Ahad, A., Tahir, M., Yau, K.-L.A.: 5G-based smart healthcare network: architecture, taxonomy, challenges and future research directions. IEEE Access 7, 100747–100762 (2019)

26. Topol, E.J.: High-performance medicine: the convergence of human and artificial intelligence. Nat. Med. 25(1), 44–56 (2019)

27. Miotto, R., Wang, F., Wang, S., Jiang, X., Dudley, J.T.: Deep learning for healthcare: review, opportunities and challenges. Brief. Bioinform. **19**(6), 1236–1246 (2018)
28. Esteva, A., et al.: Dermatologist-level classification of skin cancer with deep neural networks. Nature **542**(7639), 115–118 (2017)
29. Shen, D., Wu, G., Suk, H.-I.: Deep learning in medical image analysis. Annu. Rev. Biomed. Eng. **19**, 221–248 (2017)
30. Obermeyer, Z., Emanuel, E.J.: Predicting the future-big data, machine learning, and clinical medicine. N. Engl. J. Med. **375**(13), 1216 (2016)
31. Uppamma, P., Bhattacharya, S., et al.: Deep learning and medical image processing techniques for diabetic retinopathy: a survey of applications, challenges, and future trends. J. Healthcare Eng. **2023** (2023)
32. Sittig, D.F., Singh, H.: A new sociotechnical model for studying health information technology in complex adaptive healthcare systems. BMJ Qual. Saf. **19**(Suppl. 3), 68–74 (2010)
33. Pavel, M., et al.: The role of technology and engineering models in transforming healthcare. IEEE Rev. Biomed. Eng. **6**, 156–177 (2013)
34. Yan, M.Y., Gustad, L.T., Nytrø, Ø.: Sepsis prediction, early detection, and identification using clinical text for machine learning: a systematic review. J. Am. Med. Inform. Assoc. **29**(3), 559–575 (2022)
35. Rautela, K., Kumar, D., Kumar, V.: A systematic review on breast cancer detection using deep learning techniques. Arch. Comput. Methods Eng. **29**(7), 4599–4629 (2022)
36. Benedetto, U., et al.: Machine learning improves mortality risk prediction after cardiac surgery: systematic review and meta-analysis. J. Thorac. Cardiovasc. Surg. **163**(6), 2075–2087 (2022)
37. Mahajan, S.M., Heidenreich, P., Abbott, B., Newton, A., Ward, D.: Predictive models for identifying risk of readmission after index hospitalization for heart failure: a systematic review. Eur. J. Cardiovasc. Nurs. **17**(8), 675–689 (2018)
38. Wiens, J., Shenoy, E.S.: Machine learning for healthcare: on the verge of a major shift in healthcare epidemiology. Clin. Infect. Dis. **66**(1), 149–153 (2018)
39. Alloghani, M., Al-Jumeily, D., Aljaaf, A.J., Khalaf, M., Mustafina, J., Tan, S.Y.: The application of artificial intelligence technology in healthcare: a systematic review. In: Khalaf, M.I., Al-Jumeily, D., Lisitsa, A. (eds.) ACRIT 2019. CCIS, vol. 1174, pp. 248–261. Springer, Cham (2020). https://doi.org/10.1007/978-3-030-38752-5_20
40. Yousaf, A., Kayvanfar, V., Mazzoni, A., Elomri, A.: Artificial intelligence-based decision support systems in smart agriculture: bibliometric analysis for operational insights and future directions. Front. Sustain. Food Syst. **6**, 1053921 (2023)
41. Loh, H.W., Ooi, C.P., Seoni, S., Barua, P.D., Molinari, F., Acharya, U.R.: Application of explainable artificial intelligence for healthcare: a systematic review of the last decade (2011–2022). Comput. Methods Programs Biomed. 107161 (2022)
42. Montani, S., Striani, M.: Artificial intelligence in clinical decision support: a focused literature survey. Yearb. Med. Inform. **28**(01), 120–127 (2019)

Experience of Visually-Impaired Children in the Enjoyment of Cartoons

Marina Buzzi[1], Daniele Di Bella[2], Cristiano Gazzarrini[2], and Barbara Leporini[3]([⊠])

[1] IIT-CNR, via Moruzzi 1, 56124 Pisa, Italy
`marina.buzzi@iit.cnr.it`
[2] Audiocartoon, Prato, Italy
[3] ISTI-CNR, via Moruzzi 1, 56124 Pisa, Italy
`barbara.leporini@isti.cnr.it`

Abstract. Accessing video media by people with visual impairments is still a challenge. Audio descriptions are used as a tool to describe images that cannot be perceived by those who cannot see and cannot be understood from dialogues. The creation of audio descriptions involves (1) modifying the videos in terms of additional audio tracks with the use of tools that require specific skills, and (2) the need to alter the original video, unless the same is directly inserted by the producers. In addition, the structure and language used for audio descriptions are often adult-oriented and less designed for children with visual impairments. In this paper, we propose a solution to provide audio descriptions without editing the original videos. A pilot test with 4 children with visual impairment allowed us to evaluate the audio descriptions prepared for a series of episodes of a cartoon popular among children, and the use of the proposed system.

Keywords: Cartoons · audio-descriptions · blind children · accessibility

1 Introduction

The usage of videos is popular across a variety of disciplines and learning contexts (e.g. leisure time, school, higher education, and work). Videos can contribute to the promotion of an inclusive society through the multimodal presentation of information. However, it is important to note that the usage of videos can also exclude citizens if they are not designed to be accessible (Wilkens et al. 2021).

Cartoons are one of the most famous kinds of entertainment for children and adolescents. They can be very important for delivering educational content such as science, math, history, etc. since they are usually very attractive to children. Often younger children have far fewer accessible tools for entertainment unless they are specifically for education (Buzzi et al. 2015). For children with disabilities, cartoons may have a therapeutic value in terms of learning skills and behaviors (Anwar et al. 2020). Therefore it is very important that cartoons are accessible to all, including visually impaired children.

AudioCartoon (https://audiocartoon.com/) is a project that aims to fill this kind of gap by addressing accessibility in the enjoyment of cartoons which are usually available

P. J. Coelho et al. (Eds.): GOODTECHS 2023, LNICST 556, pp. 124–135, 2024.
https://doi.org/10.1007/978-3-031-52524-7_9

to sighted children. Thus, the multimedia content considered in this paper is related to cartoons for children with visual impairment.

Our solution for delivering accessible cartoons to children with visual impairments is based on audio descriptions (ADs), which are widely used to make videos usable by people with visual disabilities (Snyder 2020). Our approach synchronizes audio descriptions with the audio cartoon while avoiding video editing usually applied to add ADs. Specifically, in our study we focus on:

a) How to narrate images for visually-impaired children;
b) How to associate narration with the videos and to enjoy them by the children.

The proposed solution was applied to 26 episodes of a popular cartoon. A preliminary study was carried out to obtain a first evaluation of the proposed accessibility features of the audio cartoons with the synchronized external ADs.

The paper is organized into 6 sections. Section 2 briefly discusses the relevant literature, and Sect. 3 introduces the method. Section 4 presents the proposed solution. Section 5 describes the pilot test conducted with 2 visually-impaired and 2 totally blind children. Conclusions end the paper.

2 Related Work

Blind people can miss important information and communication when this is only or predominantly delivered in visual form. Audio description is a narrative technique which enables blind and visually impaired people to have full access to multimedia videos such as movies, talks, shows, theatre performances, museum and gallery exhibitions (Zabrocka 2018). Audio descriptions are useful not only to overcome multimedia obstacles experienced by people due to their vision impairment but also as of integration tool for people with disabilities (Wilkens et al. 2021). Furthermore, the study in (Hättich and Schweizer 2020) confirms that audio description is a useful tool for sightless people to immerse themselves and enjoy films as much as sighted people do.

Audio can affect or influence people's feeling and mood (Shadiqin Binti Firdus 2012). Zabrocka (2021) analyzes the potential of ADs also in terms of psycho-social development, considering the importance of accessing videos, cartoons and movies by children and adolescents. Visual elements in fact can favor conversation, enabling the acquisition of communication skills and new knowledge. Important opportunities in terms of child and adolescent social and personal development. This author also offers guidelines for AD creators to increase the effectiveness of their descriptions.

Audio descriptions are a practice now widely used to tell the images and scenes of videos to those who cannot see them (Schmeidler and Kirchner 2001). Audio Description (AD) allows persons with visual impairments to hear what cannot be seen at theatre performances, on film and video, in museum exhibitions—in a wide range of human endeavors. Viewers through a secondary audio channel can hear the regular program audio accompanied by the descriptions, precisely timed to occur only during the lapses between dialogue (Snyder 2020). To find videos that are accessible, or understandable without additional description of the visual content, in Liu et al. (2021) people with vision impairments involved in the studies reported that they used a time-consuming trial-and-error approach: clicking on a video, watching a portion, leaving the video, and repeating the process. Unfortunately, ADs need to be prepared by a human and added to the video. Most audio descriptions have been proposed for films, documentaries and videos for adults (Holsanova 2016; Fryer 2016; Ramos 2015). A wide range of examples – from film to multimedia events and touch tours in theatre, along with comments throughout from audio description users are discussed in (Fryer 2016).

The AD audience is diverse in terms of sight experience and circumstances. Visually impaired children have needs different from the general public, as they are more likely to have delayed language than other children because of the gaps in their experience (López 2010).

Generally speaking, a small number of existing studies indicate that cartoons are not fully accessible and suggest how to increase the effectiveness of audio descriptions (Janier et al. 2013). There are many studies in the literature on how to deal with audio descriptions in education (Diaz Garcia et al. 2017), or how to generate them even automatically (Campos et al. 2020) or in real time through the use of the Text-To-Speak (TTS) (Kurihara et al. 2019). Other works investigate accessible tools to reproduce accessible multimedia contents, such as (González et al. 2015). However, these studies assume that the content is not for children and that the audio descriptions are embedded directly in the multimedia videos. Therefore, further studies are needed to investigate the issue of accessibility of cartoons and especially how to provide audio descriptions for children. For successfully accessing cartoons, it becomes crucial to understand how non visual content can be delivered with an equivalent expressive meaning and comprehensible for blind children. Our study tries to put a little step ahead in this direction.

3 Method

Our study aims to investigate audio descriptions suitable for children with visual impairments and then how to play them while watching videos. Specifically, we focus on (1) a system for playing audio descriptions synchronized with the original videos of the episodes of the cartoon 'Masha and Bear' and (2) the level of verbosity of the narration used to describe the images to children with visual impairment.

We propose a solution for playing ADs synchronized with the videos without having to alter the source video file. Three narrative verbosity levels have been evaluated with a pilot user test conducted with 4 children with visual impairment. One questionnaire - for children - was used to collect qualitative information.

A team of experts was set up to set up and conduct the user test. The team was composed of a typhlology educator, a psychologist (blind), an expert in assembling and editing videos, an expert in preparing audio descriptions, and two researchers with expertise in HCI and accessibility. The team meetings were focused on defining (1) the aspects to be evaluated, (2) the characteristics of the episodes to be included in the evaluation, and (3) the qualitative data to be collected with the questionnaire. After analyzing the qualitative results collected with the questionnaire, a further meeting was held with the educators to better analyze and discuss some of the collected answers.

4   The Proposed Solution

Usually, audio descriptions are added to a second channel or track of the video being audio described. This procedure implies a modification of the source file, resulting in a new, modified video file as output. This requires specific digital skills to use the proper tools to process audio tracks of videos. This might limit the dissemination of audio descriptions that could otherwise be made by more people, even if specific skills in editing ADs are important (Fryer 2016). An audio track has to be added so that such a track runs parallel to the audio of the video and such that it is played synchronously, i.e., at the right time and avoiding overlapping with the original dialogues of the video. As a result, Ad services may require skills, time and costs. So, the producers of movies, shows and other TV programs view AD as a costly service with no revenue potential (Plaza 2017). Such a process implies that the original video needs to be modified by adding one or more audio tracks. This means that permissions need to be sought from the producers of the videos (movies, documentaries, cartoons, etc.), and there might be some copyright issues. This can take time and resources, and scalability is not assured.

The solution we propose is to run an audio track with ADs synchronized with the original video, avoiding overlapping of ADs with dialogues (as indicated for the generation of audio descriptions). To verify the feasibility of the proposed solution, audio descriptions have been produced for 26 episodes of the 'Masha and bear' cartoon, published on the official 'Audiocartoon' YouTube channel. Next, to evaluate its pros and cons, a pilot test has been carried out with four children.

Practically, a single audio track containing the whole episode narration is started together with the original episode. The audio track only shows a static black window with the details of the episode (Fig. 1). It is automatically synchronized using a link on the page which activates the video of the original episode in a new tab that receives the system focus (Fig. 2).

Fig. 1. Episode 7: Playing the audio track.

4.1   The Procedure

The solution we propose does not require any manipulation of the original videos, simplifying and facilitating the whole process. Specifically, it is based on:

a) Prepare a single audio track with the audio descriptions;
b) Upload the audio track to an online server;

Fig. 2. Episode 7: Playing the original video.

c) Play the two files (original video and AD audio track) simultaneously so that the audio contents are synchronized with the original video.

Point a) can be developed in different ways and tools. The solution we propose is independent of how the audio descriptions are produced. In the 'Audio cartoon' project, for example, experts and volunteers use software called 'ADauthor' (http://www.audiod escription.info) designed specifically to support the audio descriptor in preparing narrative content. However, this does not directly impact the solution we propose. Therefore, we take into account the audio track coming out from step a).

4.2 How to Use the Audio Descriptions

The user can listen to the audio descriptions synchronized to the original 'Masha and Bear' video thanks to two YouTube pages opened simultaneously.

The user, after accessing the YouTube channel 'Audiocartoon', chooses and clicks on the desired episode. The first tab opens the track related to the audio description of the chosen episode. The link to the original episode is also available on the page. When the link to the original episode is clicked, a second tab opens and the video is played. To ensure synchronization, it is important to click on the link to the original video at a specific time. The time at which to open the link is provided by the instructions given verbally at the beginning of the audio description giving a countdown to the actual click. Accordingly, a second tab opens and the original video is played. A specific tutorial is available that explains in more detail how to listen to the audio descriptions in a way that is synchronized with the playback of the original video. The tutorial also describes how to proceed in case of loss of synchronization between the audio description and the original episode.

In our study we started to evaluate three different levels of verbosity. Three audio descriptions delivering three different levels of detail of information to the user were associated with three different episodes: from having more details, such as character descriptions, to minimal information to describe the bare minimum. A more in-depth study needs to be conducted, but in the meantime in this study we started to analyze the acceptance of different levels of narration by the visually impaired child.

5 The Pilot Test

In this section, we describe the user experiences of blind and visually-impaired children when playing audio cartoons through the proposed solution (i.e. with synchronized external ADs). A pilot test has been carried out to have a preliminary assessment of the proposed solution, specifically to collect an early feedback about the verbosity of ADs. For this purpose, we used episodes with different verbosity.

A laptop equipped with Windows 10, Google Chrome and the Jaws for Windows screen reader was used to listen to the episodes. External audio speakers were connected to the computer to play the videos with clearer audio.

Three audio cartoons episodes with different verbosity levels have been used for the pilot test:

a) Detailed ADs with character descriptions (verbose ADs)
b) Detailed ADs without character descriptions (intermediate ADs)
c) Small ADs without charactes descriptions (small ADs)

The test was included among a set of activities planned as part of a summer boot camp for blind and visually impaired children organized by the I.Ri.Fo.R. Two educators supported the children during the test: an expert in typhlo-didactics (special education for the blind) and a psychologist (also blind) with experience on visual impairment.

Before the test, the educators described the scope and activities to be performed to the children's parents and asked them to sign the consent form. Next, demographic data were collected for the users participating in the test. Data about the participants and the evaluation was collected via digital questionnaires completed by the educator.

5.1 Tasks

Three episodes of the 'Masha and Bear' audio cartoons were proposed to participants in the following order:

1) episode N. 1 - "First Meeting", with verbose ADs;
2) episode N. 7 "Spring Comes for the Bear" intermediate ADs;
3) episode N. 18 - "laundry day" with small ADs.

The episodes were activated by the educators. All participants in a semi-circle were able to see and/or listen the selected cartoon.

5.2 Questionnaire

An online questionnaire was drawn up to investigate preferences and feedback with regard to the experience in playing audio cartoons by both blind and visually impaired children. The questionnaire is composed of 21 questions grouped into three sections:

I. user demographic data (five questions);
II. Information on audio descriptions (six questions);
III. System Usability Scale (SUS) simplified for the child (10 questions). Simplified SUS has been successfully applied to children in recent studies (Putnam et al. 2020; Ahmetovic et al. 2022).

In the 'Information on audio descriptions' section, two questions were asked for each episode:

- Were the audio descriptions understandable by the child?
- Did the child like the audio descriptions?

The audio descriptions had a different level of verbosity for each episode proposed, in order to understand the participants' appreciation and enjoyment related to different kinds of ADs. A 5-based Likert scale (1 = strongly agree, 2 = agree, 3 = neutral, 4 = disagree, and 5 = strongly disagree) was used to collect preferences about comprehension and enjoyment.

The questionnaire for each child was filled out by the educator after watching the episode, interviewing the child. The language of the questions was adapted to the participant age. A simple language was used and the questions were formulated to make them easy to remember in association with the Likert scale. The questionnaire was made available in Italian language as a web-based form using the Google Docs suite.

5.3 Participants

Four children: 2 totally blind and 2 visually impaired were recruited by the Institute for Research, Training and Rehabilitation (I.Ri.Fo.R.), which is a body managed by the Italian Association for the Blind and Visually Impaired People (UICI). The children were recruited to play the audio cartoons as part of a recreative time. Table 1 shows the Participants' demographic data. The participants' group is gender-balanced: 2 females and 2 males, 2 visually impaired and 2 totally blind.

Participants' ages ranged from 8 to 13 years as shown in Fig. 3. One is adolescent since it is difficult to recruit totally blind children. However, this participant could evaluate the audio descriptions from the point of view of a sightless person and provide useful feedback. The two visually impaired participants (50%) previously have never enjoyed cartoons or other videos with audio descriptions, while 2 (totally blind) have occasionally played this kind of audio enriched videos. Overall, 3 users usually exploit a smartphone (iPhone/Android) while 1 participant prefers a Tablet - (iPad/Android).

Table 1. Participants' demographic data.

PID	SEX	AGE	Visual Condition	Playing videos with ADs	Preferred Device
P1	F	8	Low vision	Never	Smartphone
P2	M	8	Low vision	Never	Smartphone
P3	M	10	Blind	Sometimes	Smartphone
P4	F	13	Blind	Sometimes	Tablet

5.4 Results

As mentioned before, three episodes with different levels of verbosity have been proposed to participants. All questions of the child questionnaire propose a 5-item Likert scale, thus in all graphs the X-axis reflects this scale (1..5, i.e. from strongly disagree to strongly agree).

As shown in Fig. 3 episodes 7 and 18 were very comprehensible for all participants and episode 1 was very comprehensible by 3 participants, and comprehensible by 1 participant. All episodes were very liked by 3 out 4 participants and liked by 1 out 4 (Fig. 4). However, the comprehension and liking of episodes could depend on many factors: including ADs verbosity, the content of the episode, and knowledge of the characters.

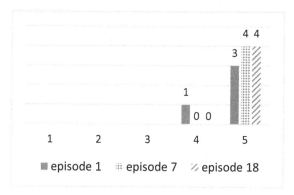

Fig. 3. Comprehension of episode 1, 7 and 18. X axis:: 5-item Likert scale.

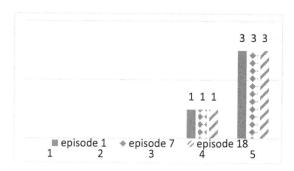

Fig. 4. Liking of episodes 1, 7 and 18. X axis:: 5-item Likert scale

In the SUS section, the focus was on usability and detected issues. The SUS scale alternates between positive and negative phrases to account for biases due to a lack of attention while filling it (Peres et al. 2013). Overall, ten questions (shown in Table 2) were proposed for cross-validation. On the right side of Table 2 sum and average for each question are reported.

To make the comparison easy, related questions were grouped in the discussion to make easier their comparison. Figure 5 shows the SUS results, aggregated by Likert values (from 1 strongly disagree to 5 strongly agree). It can be observed that the consistency of the answers: positive evaluation (Q1, Q3, Q5, Q7, Q9) varies from 4.25 to 4.75, confirming the effectiveness and usability of the proposed approach.

Table 2. Participants' survey questions and answers rating.

QID	Questions	Sum	Average
Q1	I would like to watch cartoons like this again	17	4,25
Q2	It was complicated to watch cartoons like this	7	1,75
Q3	It was easy to follow the cartoons	18	4,5
Q4	I could use some help to be able to watch audio cartoons	11	2,75
Q5	I understood the cartoon descriptions well	19	4,75
Q6	Some things in the cartoon didn't make sense	9	2,25
Q7	I think my friends would like these cartoons	17	4,25
Q8	Some things that were said in the cartoon were strange	7	1,75
Q9	I enjoyed watching the cartoon	19	4,75
Q10	Descriptions should be improved	6	1,5

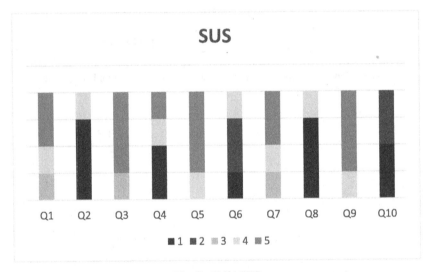

Fig. 5. Child SUS

Concerning ease of watching/following the cartoon (Q3), three participants (75%) strongly agree it was easy and 1 (25%) believe that it is neutral (neither easy nor complicated). However, in the opposite question (Q2 - It was complicated to watch cartoons like this), one participant believe that this is a little bit complicated while more than half of the participants (3, i.e. 75%) believe that It was not at all complicated to watch cartoons of this kind. Concerning the need to have some help to be able to watch cartoons of this type (Q4), 2 participants (50%) strongly disagree (believe they do not need help), while 1 (25) agree (need some help) and 1 (14.3%) strongly agree (absolutely need support).

Another group of questions is composed of Q5, Q6, Q8 and Q10 which are related to the ADs and their overall comprehension. Three participants (75%) strongly agree and 1 agrees that they understood ADs very well. Concerning the opposite question, "some things in the cartoon didn't make sense" one participant agree (25%) while 2 disagree (50%) and 1 strongly disagree (25%) respectively. Some things that were said in the cartoon were a little bit strange for 1 (25%) of the participants while 3 of the participants (75%) strongly disagree. The descriptions should be improved 2 (50%) participants disagree and 2 strongly disagree (50%) respectively.

The last group of questions, concerning the pleasantness of the audio-cartoon episodes, and includes questions: Q7, Q9, Q1. Two participants (50%) strongly agree they would like to watch cartoons of this kind again, 1 (25%) agreed while 1 selected the neutral option (the older female blind participants). Three participants (75%) strongly agree they enjoyed a lot watching the cartoons and 1 (25%) agree.

Concerning the question "I think my friends would like these cartoons" 2 participants (50%) strongly agree and 1 agree while 1 (25%) expressed the neutral option. In the last two questions, we have to consider the episodes were more suitable for children while one of the participants is a totally blind adolescent.

6 Discussion

The preliminary evaluation of the system and the audio descriptions was positive, by both the children and the educators. All episodes were evaluated as very comprehensible (score 5), except for 1 user who evaluated episode 1 (the higher level of verbosity) as comprehensible (score 4). All episodes were liked by 1 participant and very liked by 3 out of 4 (score 5). The SUS confirmed these results showing a high degree of usability of the system. Children believe that is not necessary to improve ADs. However, some critical points emerged from the in-depth discussion with the educators who supported the children during the test.

Concerning educators, they can offer valuable feedback. What surprised the educators was how few children had experience with audio descriptions. This confirms how ADs are really few used in the community of young children. The children enjoyed the system and the audio descriptions but expressed comments that highlighted the difficulty of the system in actual use.

The educators noted how much the children enjoyed this activity, thanks to the audio cartoons described to discuss all together. Thus, the activity was considered very positive since it fosters group sociability. The educators also noted that audio descriptions - if appropriately narrated - could be a valuable aid in enriching the language of young children.

7 Conclusion

In this paper, we have presented a way to play audio descriptions synchronised with a video, without actually embedding them in the video itself. Usually, audio descriptions are included in the video requiring specific skills and the need to have the rights to add and edit the audio tracks. The proposed solution offers a general method for distributing audio descriptions without the need to use specific and possibly paid-for software for editing videos. The idea is based on the use of audio tracks prepared with commonly used tools and synchronised using the YouTube channel.

In our study, we targeted children with visual impairments, as the younger community is the one that suffers most from the lack of amusing and entertaining material, such as cartoons. The proposed solution was applied to 26 episodes of the first series of the 'Masha and Bear' cartoon, which is the result of the 'Audiocartoon Italia' project developed in collaboration with the Italian Association for the Blind and Visually Impaired.

We perform a preliminary test of three different levels of verbosity of the audio descriptions used in the different episodes. Although the ADs subject needs to be further investigated via a specific study, the preliminary test, conducted with 2 blind and 2 visually impaired children, allowed us to gain initial feedback on the type of audio descriptions and their usefulness in the educational field for visually-impaired children.

The proposed system was not practical for young children. The difficulty is related to opening two pages simultaneously so that the respective audios are synchronized. In addition, observations and comments of the educators leading the pilot test suggest the need to have at least two levels of verbosity and the ability of the user to activate the type of audio description to listen to, more or less verbose. These are the aspects we will consider in future work.

Acknowledgement. The authors would like to thank Elisabetta Franchi, Elena Ferroni and all the operators who contributed with their valuable support to the study. Thanks also go to I.ri.Fo.R. Toscana and to all the children and families who made this study possible.

References

Anwar, A.I., Zulkifli, A., Syafar, M., Jafar, N.: Effectiveness of counseling with cartoon animation audio-visual methods in increasing tooth brushing knowledge children ages 10–12 years. Enfermeria Clinica **30**, 285–288 (2020)

Putnam, C., Puthenmadom, M., Cuerdo, M.A., Wang, W., Paul, N.: Adaptation of the system usability scale for user testing with children. In: Extended Abstracts of the 2020 CHI Conference on Human Factors in Computing Systems, pp. 1–7 (2020)

Ahmetovic, D., Bernareggi, C., Leporini, B., Mascetti, S.: WordMelodies: supporting the acquisition of literacy skills by children with visual impairment through a mobile app. Trans. Accessible Comput. **16**, 1–19 (2022)

Buzzi, M.C., Buzzi, M., Leporini, B., Senette, C.: Playing with geometry: a multimodal Android app for blind children. In: Proceedings of the 11th Biannual Conference on Italian SIGCHI Chapter, pp. 134–137 (2015)

Campos, V.P., de Araújo, T.M., de Souza Filho, G.L., Gonçalves, L.M.: CineAD: a system for automated audio description script generation for the visually impaired. Univ. Access Inf. Soc. **19**, 99–111 (2020)

Diaz Garcia, D.F., Marín Marín, J.S., Herrón Garcia, D.: The cartoons museum: a didactic sequence to work on descriptive texts (2017)

Fryer, L.: An Introduction to Audio Description: A Practical Guide. Routledge (2016)

González, M., Moreno, L., Martínez, P.: Approach design of an accessible media player. Univ. Access Inf. Soc. **14**, 45–55 (2015)

Hättich, A., Schweizer, M.: I hear what you see: effects of audio description used in a cinema on immersion and enjoyment in blind and visually impaired people. Br. J. Vis. Impair. **38**(3), 284–298 (2020)

Holsanova, J.: A cognitive approach to audio description. In: Researching Audio Description, pp. 49–73. Palgrave Macmillan, London (2016)

Janier, J.B., Ahmad, W.F.W., Firdus, S.B.: Representing visual content of movie cartoons through narration for the visually impaired. In: 2013 International Conference on Computer Applications Technology (ICCAT), pp. 1–6. IEEE (2013)

Kurihara, K., et al.: Automatic generation of audio descriptions for sports programs. SMPTE Motion Imaging J **128**(1), 41–47 (2019)

Liu, X., Carrington, P., Chen, X.A., Pavel, A.: What makes videos accessible to blind and visually impaired people? In: Proceedings of the 2021 CHI Conference on Human Factors in Computing Systems, pp. 1–14 (2021)

López, A.P.: The benefits of audio description for blind children. In: New Insights into Audiovisual Translation and Media Accessibility, pp. 213–225. Brill (2010)

Peres, S.C., Pham, T., Phillips, R.: Validation of the system usability scale (SUS) SUS in the wild. In: Proceedings of the Human Factors and Ergonomics Society Annual Meeting, vol. 57, no. 1, pp. 192–196. SAGE Publications, Sage (2013)

Plaza, M.: Cost-effectiveness of audio description production process: comparative analysis of outsourcing and 'in-house' methods. Int. J. Prod. Res. **55**(12), 3480–3496 (2017)

Ramos, M.: The emotional experience of films: does audio description make a difference? Translator **21**(1), 68–94 (2015)

Schmeidler, E., Kirchner, C.: Adding audio description: does it make a difference? J. Vis. Impair. Blindness **95**(4), 197–212 (2001)

Shadiqin Binti Firdus, S.: Exploring the Use of Narration for Audio Description in Enhancing Blind and Visually Impaired Children's Visualization of Video Movie Films (2012)

Snyder, J.: The Visual Made Verbal: A Comprehensive Training Manual and Guide to the History and Applications of Audio Description. Academic Publishing (2020)

Wilkens, L., Heitplatz, V.N., Bühler, C.: Designing accessible videos for people with disabilities. In: Antona, M., Stephanidis, C. (eds.) HCII 2021. LNCS, vol. 12769, pp. 328–344. Springer, Cham (2021). https://doi.org/10.1007/978-3-030-78095-1_24

Zabrocka, M.: Rhymed and traditional audio description according to the blind and partially sighted audience: results of a pilot study on creative audio description. J. Specialised Transl. **29**, 212–236 (2018)

Zabrocka, M.: Audio description accompanying video content as a compensatory tool in socialization and cognitive-linguistic development of children with visual impairment: the search for theory for alternative AD application. Educ. Dev. Psychol. **38**(2), 215–226 (2021)

A Review of Wearable Sensor Patches for Patient Monitoring

Sónia Santos[1], Maria Pedro Guarino[2], Sandra Neves[3], and Nuno Vieira Lopes[4($\boxtimes$)]

[1] ciTechCare - Center for Innovative Care and Health Technology, Polytechnic University of Leiria, Leiria, Portugal
[2] ciTechCare, School of Health Sciences, Polytechnic University of Leiria, Leiria, Portugal
[3] LIDA - Research Laboratory in Design and Arts, School of Arts and Design, Polytechnic University of Leiria, Caldas da Rainha, Portugal
[4] ciTechCare, School of Technology and Management, Polytechnic University of Leiria, Leiria, Portugal
nuno.lopes@ipleiria.pt

Abstract. Wearable sensor patches are potent tools for patient monitoring in hospital care, with a particular focus on the Emergency Department waiting areas. They can enhance patient safety by alerting healthcare professionals to abnormal changes in vital physiological signals. Wearable sensors have been shown to be useful in monitoring patients' vital signs continuously and in real-time in emergency rooms. However, there are still some challenges that need to be addressed before they can be widely adopted in emergency rooms. Some of these challenges include sensor stability with minimized signal drift, on-body sensor reusability, and long-term continuous health monitoring. This paper reviews wearable sensor patches that have the potential for use in hospital patient monitoring, considering the key variables monitored in emergency rooms. Eligible patches must be wearable, present at least one approval (CE or FDA), and measure more than one physiological parameter.

Keywords: Vital signals · monitoring · wearable · patch

1 Introduction

Healthcare professionals are the most important and critical part of a hospital. They are assigned to perform a wide range of functions such as diagnosis, supervision, cooperation, training, or conflict resolution, always seeking to respond to all needs, even if unforeseen [1].

An emergency room (ER) in a public hospital must always be prepared to provide medical, surgical, or psychiatric care to any patient. It includes an initial evaluation, diagnosis, and subsequent treatment that requires higher active cooperation between these health professionals, compared to others assigned to a different hospital service [2].

P. J. Coelho et al. (Eds.): GOODTECHS 2023, LNICST 556, pp. 136–148, 2024.
https://doi.org/10.1007/978-3-031-52524-7_10

The number of patients who are admitted to the ER can be very high, and the workload on these healthcare professionals, who try to act quickly and effectively, becomes difficult to calculate, however easy to imagine [3].

At the hospital level, the continuous monitoring of patients is critical and allows health professionals to verify and evaluate the physiological condition of the patients more quickly, check the evolution of the clinical status, validate the results of the applied therapies, and prevent and detect critical situations that may endanger the patient. On the other hand, patients with monitoring devices feel safer and more confident when they are in the ER. However, due to the limitations of human and physical resources in hospitals, it is only possible to monitor some patients. With electronic miniaturization, advances in data processing, battery technology, and wireless protocols, several small and light wearable monitoring devices have emerged, which can be placed on patients without causing movement restrictions.

Different types of wearable devices are available in the market, such as watches, wristbands, and patches. Watches are convenient, they are often multifunctional and can perform various tasks, such as monitoring heart rate, blood oxygenation, sleep quality, and physical activity. Also, they can provide notifications for calls, messages, and emails. However, they have limited battery life, and, in general, they are expensive and not waterproof. Wristbands are thin, comfortable, and often more affordable than watches. Typically they have longer battery life than watches, and many wristbands are water-resistant, which makes them suitable for hospital sterilization. Wearable devices like wristbands may have limited features and perform fewer tasks than watches.

Watches and wristbands are readily available in the market, and there are many brands and models to choose from, making them accessible. Several research studies involving the use of watches and wristbands for healthcare can be found in the literature [4–7]. According to these studies, these devices should only be used as a self-control tool and rigorous research on their use in clinical settings is still needed. Also, from the health professionals' point of view, the wrist should be kept free as it provides rapid and easy vascular access.

In [7] six medical patches were reviewed, however three of them were discontinued. Wearable devices like skin patches are discreet and can be worn under clothing. They are comfortable to wear and do not cause discomfort or movement restrictions. Typically they are often more affordable than wristbands. Also, they could be placed in several body locations to continuously monitor health parameters, leaving the wrists and arms free. Some patch devices are fully disposable, but in some cases, the core hub can be detached, sterilized, and reusable. For these reasons, using skin patch monitoring devices to verify and evaluate the physiological condition of ER patients could be a valuable help for patients and health professionals. Patches have become increasingly popular, and many companies are developing novel products. SAFETRACK is a multidisciplinary project that involves academia experts in health, informatics, electronic engineering and design, and companies dedicated to medical devices development and commercialization to explore how emergency departments in hospital can better respond to patient safety during hospitalization and deliver a prototype solution [8].

Within this scope this paper aims to review the wearable sensor patches, already available in the market, that could be used for patient monitoring in a hospital emergency room.

2   Wearable Sensor Patches

In this section, vital signs monitoring devices with adhesive surfaces commonly defined as patches will be described. Devices were excluded if they measure just one vital sign, if they are not wearable and wireless and if they had no formal approval as a medical device through the Conformité Européenne (CE) mark or Food and Drug Administration (FDA) clearance or both.

2.1   Biobeat Chest Monitor

The Biobeat chest monitor is both CE and FDA certified (Fig. 1) [9]. According to the manufacturer, one of the main features of the Biobeat chest monitor is its ability to continuously monitor a wide range of vital signs, including heart rate (HR), respiratory rate (RR), blood oxygen saturation (SpO_2), heart rate variability (HRV), blood pressure (BP), stroke volume (SV), cardiac output (CO), cardiac index (CI), pulse pressure (PP), one lead electrocardiogram (ECG), sweat level, and skin temperature (ST). A non rechargeable battery lasts for up to 7 days, at the end of which the sensor is disposed of. It also features a simple smartphone app, that collects data via Bluetooth, and allows users to track their vital signs, set personalized alerts, and view detailed health reports over time [10].

Recent peer reviewed publications can be found in the literature. This patch was used to evaluate continuous BP measurements in 10 patients after a cardiac surgery [11]. Results were compared with an arterial line transducer, and this device has shown high accuracy. In [12] it was used to evaluate the influence of sex, skin tone, or Body Mass Index (BMI) in PPG-based BP measurements. 1057 participants were used in the experiment and the device have provided valid results. This device was also used in 160 participants to identify physiological changes following COVID-19 vaccine administration [13]. According to this study, almost all vital parameters exhibited significant changes following vaccine administration in both symptomatic and asymptomatic participants. These changes were more pronounced at night, especially in younger participants and those who had received the second vaccine dose. In [14], a continuous monitoring of ECG, respiratory rate, systolic and diastolic blood pressure, pulse rate, cardiac output, and cardiac index was performed on 15 patients (median age of 52.8 years) after a coronary intervention. The patch have showed high satisfaction rates among the nursing staff. The Biobeat chest monitor was also used in a study with 521 participants to perform multi-parameter measurements to assess clinical deterioration [15]. High correlation RR values were obtained in a validation study presented in [16]. A patient deterioration detection tool was implemented in [17] and [18] with encouraging results.

Fig. 1. Biobeat Chest Monitor.

2.2 Sensium Patch

Sensium Patch (Fig. 2) is also CE and FDA certified. It utilises radio frequency (RF) technology to wirelessly communicate physiological information such as HR, RR and axillary temperature, providing data every two minutes. It is easy to apply and remove, and can be worn comfortably on the skin for up to 6 days. The patch transmits the information to a bridge module that allows seamless transition of patch data to nursing stations, desktop or mobile apps. Healthcare professionals can quickly and accurately assess a patient's condition and make informed treatment decisions [19].

In [23] a validation study measuring RR, HR and temperature on 51 patients recovering from a major surgery is presented. In this study the differences between manual and patch measurements for all three measurements were outside of acceptable limits. Authors justify such differences due to artefacts in the continuous signal, errors during manual measurement and concerning the temperature, the skin temperature measured by the patch not accurately reflect the tympanic temperature measured by the nursing staff. This wearable device was successfully used in several studies to evaluate the feasibility, patient and surgical stuff acceptability, and clinical outcomes of using continuous remote monitoring [20–22]. An economical analysis is presented in [24]. The study involved monitoring post-operative patients in two hospital wards for 30 days. The authors concluded that the use of this patch could be a cost-saving strategy, as it has the potential to reduce the length of post-operative hospital stays, readmission rates, and associated costs in post-operative patients.

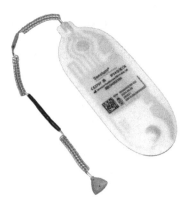

Fig. 2. Sensium Patch.

2.3   VitalPatch RTM

The VitalPatch Real-Time Monitoring (RTM) is a fully disposable wireless wearable device that allows continuous real-time monitoring of ECG, HR, RR, ST, HRV, activity (including step count), posture and fall detection (Fig. 3). It is manufactured by VitalConnect, a company based in California and it is both CE and FDA certified. Bluetooth Low Energy connectivity allows for continuous data transmission to a central monitoring station or a mobile device. According to the manufacturer, the patch weights 13g and is powered by a non-rechargeable battery that lasts up to 7 days. Also, a proprietary third-party artificial intelligence software continuously analyzes the transmitted data to detect 21 unique cardiac arrhythmias [25].

Validation studies concerning the accuracy of HR, RR and temperature measurements can be found in [26–28]. Another validation study, considering 29 participants performing different movements and controlled hypoxia [29], the VitalPatch has demonstrated to be safely used and accurate throughout both the movement and hypoxia phases, except for RR during the sit-to-stand and turning page movements.

In a comparative study [30], the patch performance was assessed against 2 other weareable sensors (Everion and Fitbit Charge 3) and 2 reference devices (Oxycon Mobile and iButton). Using a total of 20 volunteers performing various daily life activities, authors have conclude the accuracy of all sensors decreased with physical activity, however, the VitalPatch was found to be the most accurate.

2.4   Philips Biosensor BX100

The BX100 is a dual-certified wireless wearable device that can be attached to a patient's chest using an adhesive patch (Fig. 4). The device is equipped with sensors that measure the patient's HR, RR, activity level and posture.

Fig. 3. VitalPatch RTM.

The device sends data over Bluetooth Low Energy (BLE), is also lightweight and comfortable to wear, making it an ideal solution for patients who require long-term monitoring. It is designed to work with the IntelliVue Guardian Software to assist in the early identification of clinical deterioration, leading to early intervention [31].

[32] presents a respiratory rate validation study against values derived from capnography via nasal cannula that suggests the Philips Biosensor can provide comparable respiratory rates. Comparing the data from the Biosensor with a reference monitor, (General Electric Carescape B650), in severely obese patients during and after bariatric surgery, it was concluded the sensor had performed accordingly for HR monitoring, but not for RR [33]. 44 adult patients receiving care in an ER have wore the patch and they reported that it was comfortable and no serious adverse reactions were observed [35]. A remote ECG monitoring system with real time diagnosis was implemented in [34].

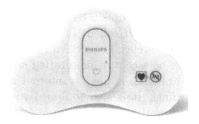

Fig. 4. Philips Biosensor BX100.

2.5   BodyGuardian Heart

The BodyGuardian Heart sensor, illustrated in Fig. 5 is a wearable wireless device that continuous monitors patients' vital signs such as ECG, HR, RR and physical activity. Preventice Solutions manufacture it with CE and FDA approval. It is a small, discreet device that can be placed in the user's chest via a disposable strip with medical-grade adhesive and electrode gel. Bluetooth connectivity allows continuous data transmission to a mobile phone which acts as a gateway to a remote station. The company also offers a service that provides remote cardiac diagnostic monitoring. Patients' results are then sent and interpreted by doctors [36].

A pilot study assessing ECG quality in remote monitoring is presented in [37]. The patch is capable of acquiring and transmitting high quality diagnostic ECG data. It is relevant to note that some authors may have a financial interest in the technology.In [38] the BodyGuardian Heart sensor was successfully used to detect HR changes after amphetamine administration, and in [39], the patch was used to describe and validate a platform for ECG interpretation named BeatLogic developed by the same company.

Fig. 5. BodyGuardian Heart.

2.6   1AX Biosensor

The 1AX biosensor, manufactured by LifeSignals, is a wearable wireless device with both FDA and CE marking approvals (Fig. 6). This single-use patch can continuously acquire ECG, HR, RR, skin temperature, and posture status. The company also offers another patch called the 1AXe Biosensor solely for ECG and HR measurements. The wireless connectivity allows continuous data transmission to a mobile device or a central monitoring station. When the wireless connection is lost or unavailable, it has an internal memory cache that supports up to 16 h of recordings. It is also equipped with a Lithium-Manganese dioxide (Li-MnO$_2$) battery that can last up to 5 days [40]. The company has announced an upgraded version of this patch that includes SpO$_2$ measurement but has yet to be available in the market. No validation studies with comparison to gold-standard methodologies or peer reviewed publications were found in the literature.

2.7   Multi-vital ECG

The Multi-Vital ECG patch developed by Vivalink can capture ECG, HR, RR, ST, step count and posture status on a single device and stream data to a mobile or the cloud (Fig. 7). The device is FDA cleared for ECG and HR, and CE cleared for ECG, HR and RR. According to the manufacturer, using a rechargeable battery, it transmits data over BLE and can work continuously up to 14 days. In network failure, it can record data up to 30 days in its internal memory and then

Fig. 6. 1AX Biosensor.

automatically synchronize it once network connection is established [41]. It has a fully disposable adhesive band, but the hub can be reusable, safely sanitized, and recharged using the provided charger. No peer reviewed studies concerning this sensor were found in the scientific literature.

Fig. 7. Multi-Vital ECG.

3   Discussion

Wearable sensor patches are small, unnoticeable devices that can be attached directly to a person's skin. They can be used for monitoring health conditions such as heart rate and blood pressure. First generation wearable patches were lightweight and flexible and consisted of several coatings, including an electronic circuitry, a protective cover and an attaching system. Some first-generation patches use microscopic needles as minimally invasive techniques to support biosensors or to deliver medications. Regarding the presented patches, it is possible to observe that, compared to the previous generation of patches, they are smaller, lighter, and can be worn under clothing. They are placed on the patient's chest and do not introduce movement restrictions. The chest positioning allows better heart electrical activity and thoracic impedance measurements.

Analysing the technical specifications, all the presented patches can provide two significant clinical parameters: HR and RR. Some are equipped with a temperature sensor to measure superficial skin temperature and an accelerometer or an inertial measurement unit to measure activity level, body posture, or steps.

The BioBeat Chest Monitor, the VitalPatch RTM and the Multi-Vital ECG can provide a wide range of parameters.

Due to energy limitations, the preferred wireless technology is Bluetooth except the 1AX Biosensor that uses Wi-Fi and the Sensium Patch that uses a proprietary RF protocol. Two devices (BodyGuardian Heart and Multi-Vital ECG) are partially reusable since their core can be detached from the disposable adhesive strip. They can be adequately cleaned and have a proper charger to recharge their batteries. The remaining patches are fully disposable.

Concerning battery life no information was found about the BodyGuardian Heart but the Multi-Vital ECG announces a lifespan of 14 days, a significantly longer duration compared to the other patches. Based on this, it is reasonable to assume that all patches can be adopted in emergency rooms.

Sensium Patch, Biosensor BX100, 1AX Biosensor, and Multi-Vital ECG patches have internal memory to save data when the wireless connection between the companion device is lost. Once again, the Multi-Vital ECG states a significantly higher cache capacity, but no further information was found about how they achieve it. Table 1 presents a summary of the devices' main characteristics.

Finally, it is important to note that the BodyGuardian Heart, VitalPatch RTM, and Multi-Vital ECG were designed to monitor heart activity continuously, and they have a support analysis platform with advanced algorithms to process the sensor data and detect risk situations such as cardiac arrhythmias or sudden cardiac arrest.

In scientific publications, numerous cases evaluating the use of the BioBeat Chest Monitor and the Sensium Patch in various clinical scenarios, including validation tests, clinical trials, patient outcomes, and perspectives from both patients and healthcare professionals can be found. Multiple validation studies are also available concerning the VitalPatch RTM and the Philips Biosensor BX100. However, it should be noted that a significant number of these papers were written and published by individuals related to the companies that produce such devices.

On the other hand, no peer-reviewed publications were found for both the 1AX Biosensor and Multi-Vital ECG, which may be explained by their recent introduction to the market, lack of knowledge on the part of the scientific community or company strategy.

Since it is an emergent technology, it faces several challenges. These challenges are critical to address for the successful integration and adoption of these devices in clinical practice. Some of these challenges are:

- Informed Consent and Ethical Considerations: Patients must be informed about the purpose of monitoring, the data collected, and how it will be used. Ethical considerations also involve ensuring that patients' rights, autonomy, and privacy are respected throughout the monitoring process.
- Patient Engagement: Engaging patients in their own care and encouraging compliance with biosensor patch usage is a challenge. Healthcare providers should educate patients about the benefits of continuous monitoring and help them understand the importance of adhering to monitoring protocols.

- Health Professionals' Acceptance: Healthcare professionals, including doctors, nurses, and technicians, must be willing to incorporate biosensor patch data into their clinical practice. Proper training and education are necessary to ensure that healthcare providers understand the values and limitations of the technology.
- Definition of New Hospital Staff Workflows: The introduction of biosensor patches may require the development of new workflows within healthcare facilities. This includes protocols for data monitoring, response to alerts, and coordination among healthcare teams.
- Data Privacy and Security: As biosensor patches collect sensitive health data, maintaining privacy and data security is mandatory. Robust encryption, secure data transmission, and strict access controls are necessary to protect patient information from unauthorized access or breaches.
- Integration with the Hospital Information System (HIS): Integrating biosensor patch data with the hospital's existing information systems can be complex. Seamless integration allows healthcare providers to access and utilize the data efficiently.
- Cost and Reimbursement: The cost of implementing biosensor patch technology, including device acquisition, maintenance, and data management, may pose financial challenges for healthcare institutions. Ensuring appropriate reimbursement models is crucial to support the adoption of these technologies.

Table 1. Device main characteristics.

Device Name	Vital Signs	Other Parameters	Wireless Technology	Internal Memory	Battery Life	Weight	Reusable
BioBeat Chest Monitor	HR, RR, SpO$_2$, BP, ECG	HRV, SV, CO, CI PP sweat level	Bluetooth	No	5 days	23g	No
Sensium Patch	HR, RR, ST	None	RF	3h (max)	6 days	15g	No
VitalPatch RTM	HR, RR, ECG, ST	HRV, steps, posture fall detection activity	Bluetooth	No	7 days	13g	No
Biosensor BX100	HR, RR, ST	Activity, posture	Bluetooth	4h (max)	5 days	10g	No
BodyGuardian Heart	HR, RR	Activity	Bluetooth	No	N/D	35g	Partial
1AX Biosensor	HR, RR, ST	Posture	Wi-Fi	16h (max)	5 days	28g	No
Multi-Vital ECG	HR, RR, ECG, ST	HRV, steps activity	Bluetooth	30 days (up to)	14 days	7.5g	Partial

4   Conclusions

Wearable sensor patches have revolutionized healthcare by providing continuous monitoring of vital signs through a small and discreet device, without introducing movement restrictions to the patients and alerting healthcare professionals if any physiological abnormality is detected. Like all medical devices it is mandatory that healthcare professionals carefully understand their clinical procedures, applications, limitations and challenges when using a wearable sensor patch on their patients.

Despite their benefits, wearable sensor patches present some limitations and challenges. They lack autonomy since they require wireless connectivity to a companion device or a remote station to receive, monitor and process the data. In general, the devices that are entirely disposable have a life period of about one week, after that, they are useless or require periodic battery recharging. For patients with certain skin conditions, the adhesive band can cause skin irritation, particularly for long time monitoring.

In the literature, there is also an observed lack of unbiased peer-reviewed publications, as some studies are performed in close collaboration with the manufacturers. This emphasizes the need for more independent research in the field.

Also, there are some challenges to be addressed such as ethical considerations, data privacy and security, patients and professionals' acceptance, HIS integration and economic viability. Addressing these challenges is essential for the successful integration of biosensor patches into healthcare providers.

This work aimed to present technical information, relevant research studies, limitations, and challenges about multi-parameter biosensor patches. However, as technology continues to advance, it is expected to see even more innovative wearable sensor patches in the near future.

Acknowledgements. Funded by SafeTrack - CENTRO-01-0247-FEDER-070111. Supported by Fundação para a Ciência e a Tecnologia (FCT) (UIDB/05468/2020), Laboratório de Investigação em Design e Artes (LIDA), (UI/05704/2020), Center for Innovative Care and Health Technology (ciTechCare).

References

1. Brazão, M. da Luz, Nóbrega, S., Bebiano, G., Carvalho, E.: Atividade dos Serviços de Urgência Hospitalares. Medicina Interna **23**(3), 8–14 (2016)
2. Definition of Emergency Medicine: Ann. Emerg. Med. **52**(2), 189–190 (2008)
3. Gedmintas, A., Bost, N., Keijzers, G., Green, D., Lind, J.: Emergency care workload units: a novel tool to compare emergency department activity. EMA - Emerg. Med. Australas. **22**(5), 442–448 (2010)
4. Lu, T.C., Fu, C.M., Ma, M.H., Fang, C.C., Turner, A.M.: Healthcare applications of smart watches. A Syst. Rev. Appl. Clin. Inf. **7**(3), 850–869 (2016)
5. Reeder, B., David, A.: Health at hand: a systematic review of smart watch uses for health and wellness. J. Biomed. Inform. **63**, 269–276 (2016)
6. Jachymek, M., et al.: Wristbands in home-based rehabilitation-validation of heart rate measurement. Sensors **22**(1) (2021)

7. Soon, S., Svavarsdottir, H., Downey, C., Jayne, D.: Wearable devices for remote vital signs monitoring in the outpatient setting: an overview of the field. BMJ Innov. **6**, 55–71 (2020)
8. Neves, S., Oliveira, V., Guarino, M.: Using co-design methods to develop a patient monitoring system in hospital emergency care to support patient safety. In: 13th International Conference on Applied Human Factors and Ergonomics (AHFE 2022). AHFE International, New York (2022)
9. BioBeat Product Homepage. https://www.bio-beat.com/products. Accessed 1 Apr 2023
10. BioBeat Platform User Guide. https://www.mindtecstore.com/mediafiles/Sonstiges/Shop/Biobeat/Biobeat_User_Manual_July2020.pdf. Accessed 1 Apr 2023
11. Kachel, E., et al.: A pilot study of blood pressure monitoring after cardiac surgery using a wearable, non-invasive sensor. Front. Med. **8**, 693926 (2021)
12. Nachman, D., et al.: Influence of sex, BMI, and skin color on the accuracy of non-invasive cuffless photoplethysmography-based blood pressure measurements. Front. Physiol. **13**, 911544 (2022)
13. Gepner, Y., et al.: Utilizing wearable sensors for continuous and highly-sensitive monitoring of reactions to the BNT162b2 mRNA COVID-19 vaccine. Commun. Med. **2**, 27 (2022)
14. Sharabi, I., et al.: Assessing the use of a noninvasive monitoring system providing multiple cardio-pulmonary parameters following revascularization in STEMI patients. Digit. Health **9** (2023)
15. Eisenkraft, A., et al.: Developing a real-time detection tool and an early warning score using a continuous wearable multi-parameter monitor. Front. Physiol. **14**, 519 (2023)
16. Eisenkraft, A., et al.: Clinical validation of a wearable respiratory rate device: a brief report. Chronic Respir. Disease **20** (2023)
17. Eisenkraft, A., et al.: Developing a real-time detection tool and an early warning score using a continuous wearable multi-parameter monitor. Front. Physiol. **14** (2023)
18. Itelman, E., et al.: Assessing the usability of a novel wearable remote patient monitoring device for the early detection of in-hospital patient deterioration: observational study. JMIR Formative Res. **6**(6), e36066 (2022)
19. Sensium System Webpage. https://www.tsc-group.com/connected-care/products/sensium/. Accessed 1 Apr 2023
20. Downey, C.L., et al.: Trial of remote continuous versus intermittent NEWS monitoring after major surgery (TRaCINg): a feasibility randomised controlled trial. Pilot Feasibility Stud. **6**(1), 183 (2020)
21. Joshi, M., et al.: Perceptions on the use of wearable sensors and continuous monitoring in surgical patients: interview study among surgical staff. JMIR Formative Res. **6**(2), e27866 (2022)
22. Joshi, M., et al.: Short-term wearable sensors for in-hospital medical and surgical patients: mixed methods analysis of patient perspectives. JMIR Perioperative Med. **4**(1), e18836 (2021)
23. Downey, C., Ng, S., Jayne, D., Wong, D.: Reliability of a wearable wireless patch for continuous remote monitoring of vital signs in patients recovering from major surgery: a clinical validation study from the TRaCINg trial. BMJ Open **9**(8), e031150 (2019)

24. Javanbakht, M., et al.: Cost utility analysis of continuous and intermittent versus intermittent vital signs monitoring in patients admitted to surgical wards. J. Med. Econ. **23**(7), 728–736 (2020)
25. VitalConnect Homepage. https://vitalconnect.com/. Accessed 1 Apr 2023
26. Selvaraj, N., Nallathambi, G., Moghadam, R., Aga, A.: Disposable wireless patch sensor for continuous remote patient monitoring. In: Annual International Conference of the IEEE Engineering in Medicine and Biology Society. IEEE Engineering in Medicine and Biology Society, pp. 1632–1635 (2018)
27. Rajbhandary, P. L., Nallathambi, G.: Feasibility of continuous monitoring of core body temperature using chest-worn patch sensor. In: Annual International Conference of the IEEE Engineering in Medicine and Biology Society. IEEE Engineering in Medicine and Biology Society, pp. 4652–4655 (2020)
28. Selvaraj, N., Nallathambi, G., Kettle, P.: A novel synthetic simulation platform for validation of breathing rate measurement. In: 40th Annual International Conference of the IEEE Engineering in Medicine and Biology Society (EMBC), Honolulu, pp. 1177–1180 (2018)
29. Morgado Areia, C., et al.: A chest patch for continuous vital sign monitoring: clinical validation study during movement and controlled hypoxia. J. Med. Internet Res. **23**(9), e27547 (2021)
30. Haveman, M.E., et al.: Continuous monitoring of vital signs with wearable sensors during daily life activities: validation study. JMIR Formative Res. **6**(1), e30863 (2022)
31. Biosensor BX100 Product Page. https://www.philips.ca/healthcare/product/HC989803203011/biosensor-bx100-wearable-remote-measurement-device. Accessed 1 Apr 2023
32. Li, T., Divatia, S., McKittrick, J., Moss, J., Hijnen, N.M., Becker, L.B.: A pilot study of respiratory rate derived from a wearable biosensor compared with capnography in emergency department patients. Open Access Emer. Med. **11**, 103–108 (2019)
33. Kant, N., et al.: Continuous vital sign monitoring using a wearable patch sensor in obese patients: a validation study in a clinical setting. J. Clin. Monit. Comput. **36**(5), 1449–1459 (2022)
34. Bhattarai, A., Peng, D., Payne, J., Sharif, H.: Adaptive partition of ECG diagnosis between cloud and wearable sensor net using open-loop and closed-loop switch mode. IEEE Access **10**, 63684–63697 (2022)
35. Miller, K., et al.: Deployment of a wearable biosensor system in the emergency department: a technical feasibility study. In: Proceedings of the Annual Hawaii International Conference on System Sciences, pp. 3567–3572 (2021)
36. Preventice Solutions Home Page. https://www.preventicesolutions.com/us/en/home.html. Accessed 10 Apr 2023
37. Bruce, C.J., et al.: Remote electrocardiograph monitoring using a novel adhesive strip sensor: a pilot study. World J. Cardiol. **8**(10), 559–565 (2016)
38. Izmailova, E.S., et al.: Continuous monitoring using a wearable device detects activity-induced heart rate changes after administration of amphetamine. Clin. Transl. Sci. **12**(6), 677–686 (2019)
39. Teplitzky, B.A., McRoberts, M., Ghanbari, H.: Deep learning for comprehensive ECG annotation. Heart Rhythm **17**(5 Pt B), 881–888 (2020)
40. 1AX Biosensor Product Page. https://lifesignals.com/wearable-biosensors/1ax-biosensor/. Accessed 10 Apr 2023
41. Multi-Vital ECG Sensor Product Page. https://www.vivalink.com/wearable-ecg-monitor. Accessed 10 Apr 2023

Enhancing Student Well-Being: The Impact of a Mindfulness-Based Program (Mind7 +) on Stress, Anxiety, Sleep Quality, and Social Interactions in a Sample of Portuguese University Students

Paula Pinto[1,2,3](✉) ⓘ, Susana Franco[2,4] ⓘ, Susana Alves[2,4] ⓘ, Patrícia Januário[5], and Isabel Barroso[5] ⓘ

[1] Agriculture School, Polytechnic University of Santarém, 2001-904 Santarem, Portugal
paula.pinto@esa.ipsantarem.pt
[2] Life Quality Research Centre (CIEQV), 2040-413 Rio Maior, Portugal
[3] Research Centre for Natural Resources, Environment and Society (CERNAS), 3045-601 Coimbra, Portugal
[4] Sports Science School of Rio Maior, Polytechnic University of Santarém, 2040-413 Rio Maior, Portugal
[5] Polytechnic University of Santarém, Social Services, 2001-904 Santarem, Portugal

Abstract. There is an urgent need to promote mental health strategies in university students, and mindfulness-based interventions provide alternative and complementary approaches. The present study aimed to investigate the impact of a mindfulness-based program (Mind7 +) on Portuguese students from the Polytechnic University of Santarem, focusing on stress levels, depression, anxiety, and sleep quality. The intervention consisted of a 8 week mindfulness-based program, with six presential sessions and two online sessions. The participants completed self-filled validated questionnaires before and after intervention. The study revealed that Mind7 + program not only positively influenced stress levels, anxiety, and sleep quality among university students but also had a positive impact on their social interactions. A correlation between sleep quality and frequency of individual practices was observed. The observed medium effect size underscores the practical relevance of Mind7 + program and the potential of mindfulness-based interventions in higher education to enhance both individual well-being and social connections. Next steps will be to adapt the mindfulness-based program for a mobile device and test with a wider intervention group, as well as an active control group.

Keywords: Mindfulness · Sleep quality · Stress · Anxiety · Digital self-help

1 Introduction

The rise in mental health problems is a general trend in our world, especially among young people. Underlying causes include climate anxiety, a highly competitive society, the uncertainty of working life, and a massive flood of information [1]. This trend was

P. J. Coelho et al. (Eds.): GOODTECHS 2023, LNICST 556, pp. 149–158, 2024.
https://doi.org/10.1007/978-3-031-52524-7_11

worsened by COVID-19 pandemic, which has led to about 25% increase of depression and anxiety disorders, with a higher incidence in people with ages of 20 to 24 years old [1]. Thus, there is an urgent need to promote mental health strategies to reverse this trend, and mindfulness-based interventions provide alternative and complementary approaches to traditional clinical practices. Recent scientific evidence shows that mindfulness meditation interventions have successfully reduced depression in emerging adults [2, 3].

University students must cope with various stressful situations: adapting to new environments, economic difficulties, making new friends, time management, workload pressures, and exams. This can lead to increased anxiety and decreased motivation to study and research. To achieve their goals and reach their potential, university students must be able to self-regulate and maintain psychological well-being. There is recent scientific evidence that integrating mindfulness in higher education leads to diverse positive outcomes such as: reduction of stress, anxiety, depression and better emotional regulation [2–4], increased well-being, higher engagement and life meaning [5], increased focus, concentration and organization [4], increased efficiency at work, better handling of interpersonal interactions, work more effectively with other members, better handling of research setbacks, and higher satisfaction with research work in PhD students [6].

In Portugal, the research of mindfulness in higher education is scarce. One study has assessed the effect of a mindfulness-based program in university students, showing significant improvement in stress, emotion regulation, mindfulness, positive solitude, and optimism [7]. Thus, we aimed to gather more information on the impact of these types of interventions in Portuguese higher education. This pilot study developed and applied a 8-week structured program, based on strategies of Mindfulness, to Portuguese students enrolled at Polythecnic Institute of Santarem (IPSantarem). As primary outcomes, we assessed subjective well-being, anxiety, stress, depression, and sleep quality. Secondary outcomes were healthy food habits, and socialization.

2 Methodology

2.1 Study Design and Ethics

This was a non-controlled experimental study, approved by the Ethics Commission of IPSantarem (Parecer Nº27-ESAS), developed according to the principles of Helsinki Declaration and the European Data Protection Regulation. The intervention Mind7 + consisted of a 8 week program, with one 4h session per week (six presential sessions and two online sessions, from October to December, 2022). Inclusion criteria were (1) adults $\geq$ 18 years old; (2) Portuguese speakers, (3) being a student in IPSantarem. No selection criterion was applied in terms of gender, educational level, health condition or social and cultural background. For enrolment, the program was advertised at the start of the semester in the institutional website, through institutional email, and face to face contact with the researchers involved in the study. The participants enrolled in the program through an online form. All participants signed an informed consent in the first session of the program and were given a code to insert on the questionnaires for data collection (pseudo anonymization of data). Participation was voluntary, and unpaid.

Questionnaires were self-filled at the first and the last week of the intervention, assuring confidentiality.

2.2 Data Collection and Analysis

The following validated scales for Portuguese language were used:; IPAQ (International Physical Activity Questionnaire), short version, to assess physical activity [8]; PSQI (Pittsburg Sleep Quality Index), short version to assess sleep quality [9]; EADS-21 (Scale of Anxiety, Depression and Stress) to assess anxiety, depression and stress [10]; 14-MEDAS (Mediterranean Diet Adherence Screener) to assess adherence to Mediterranean Diet [11]. An online questionnaire was constructed on Google forms including a section for information about the study, authorization for the use of collected data and a question for the individual code insertion; a section for demographic and health data; a section for the 14-MEDAS; and a section for the IPAQ. The two other questionnaires (EADS-21 and PSQI) were filled on paper. All questionnaires were filled in at the beginning of the first session and at the end of the last session.

Statistical analyses were performed using the Statistical Package for the Social Sciences (SPSS) version 28.0 statistical package for Windows (SPSS, Inc., Chicago, IL, USA). Continuous variables were tested for normality with Shapiro-Wilk test (recommended for samples with $n < 50$). To assess differences between pre and post intervention, parametric paired t-tests were used for normal variables, and non-parametric related samples Wilcoxon Signed Rank Tests were used for non-normal variables with acceptable skewness (-1 to 1 values). Effect sizes were determined by Cohen's D test for paired T-tests and by Z value divided by the square root of N for Wilcoxon Tests. Effect sizes were classified as small (0.2 to 0.5), moderate (0.5 to 0.8) or large (>0.8) [12]. Scale variables are presented using the mean ± standard deviation (SD). Percentages are used to represent ordinal or nominal variables. All statistical tests were based on two-sided tests (bilateral significance) with a significance level of 5% ($\alpha = 0.05$).

Non-parametric partial Spearman correlation coefficients (ρ) adjusted for confounding variables were used to investigate the potential association between variables. Data are presented as the Spearman's partial correlation values with their corresponding p-values. Correlation coeficients were classified as weak (<0.3), moderate (0.3 to 0.7) and strong (>0.7) [13].

2.3 Intervention

The program consisted of 8 sessions, based on Jon Kabat Zin MBSR (mindfulness based stress reduction) program, with the following topics: 1) concept of Mindfulness; formal and non-formal practices, diaphragmatic breathing; 2) the 9 Mindfulness attitudes; body scan; 3) dealing with stress and anxiety; scientific evidence of mindfulness effects; guided meditation; 4) flipping limiting thoughts to empowering thoughts; 10 Yoga movements and relaxing the body; guided meditation; 5) goal setting; anchoring tranquility and focus; walking meditation; 6) Yoga class; sitting meditation; values; 7) neurologic levels; loving-kindness meditation; 8) personal impact statement; mindfulness state meditation. Sessions 3 and 6 were online; all other sessions were presential. At the end of each session, the participants were introduced to the daily practices for the week (10 to 15 min in the first two weeks, 15 to 30 min the following four weeks, and 30 to 45 min the last two weeks). All course materials were available for the participants at the institutional e-learning platform (https://eraizes.ipsantarem.pt/moodle/course/view.php?id=941). All the research team was involved in the design and organization of the program.

3 Results

3.1 Sample Characterization

Forty students enrolled in the program between 9th of September and 7th of October 2022. Before the beginning of the program, 10 students cancelled their registration. At the first session (19th October), 24 participants attended the session and filled in the starting questionnaires. Two other participants joined the second session but did not fill in the starting questionnaires. Before the end of the program seven participants dropped out and did not fill in the ending questionnaires (appointed reasons for dropout were disease and lack of time due to academic workload). More than half of the participants (53.9%) attended from 5 to 8 sessions out of 8. At the end, 18 pre and post intervention questionnaires were available for paired statistical analysis. Table 1 presents the characteristics of the sample. Most were healthy, with an active lifestyle (87.5% with MET-min per week > 600) and moderate adherence to Mediterranean diet (62.5% with MEDAS score between 6 and 9). Regarding contact with nature and friends, most participants reported to be occasionally or sometimes in nature (73.1%) and with friends (69.2%).

Table 1. Characteristics of the initial sample (N = 24)

Gender (% Female)	84.6
Age (mean ± SD)	22.8 ± 6.1
BMI (% normal weight; BMI < 25 kg/m^2	61.6
Smoker (%)	19
Diagnosed pathology (%)	26.9
Physical Activity (mean MET-min/week ± SD)	2197 ± 1850
Adherence to MD (mean MEDAS ± SD)	6.3 ± 1.6

3.2 Effect of the Intervention on Depression, Anxiety, Stress, Sleep Quality and Lifestyle

Depression, anxiety, and stress are the three domains assessed by the EADS validated scale, with 7 items evaluated from 0 (best condition) to 3 (worst condition) in each domain. The items in each domain were: depression - no positive feelings, difficulty to take initiative, nothing to expect from future, feeling discouraged and melancholic, no enthusiasm, no value as a person, no meaning in life; anxiety - dry mouth, difficulty to breathe, tremors, worry, almost in panic, changes in heart rate without physical exercise, frightened without reason; stress - difficulty in self-calming, overreact, nervous energy, feeling agitated, difficulty in relaxing, being intolerant, feeling to sensitive. Stress levels were higher than depression or anxiety, both at the start and end of the intervention (Table 2). A significant decrease was observed in anxiety and stress levels after the intervention, with medium effect sizes.

Sleep quality was calculated according to the PSQI instructions, in a scale from 0 (best condition) to 15 (worst condition). A significant decrease was observed in the calculated PSQI, indicating an improvement with a moderate effect size (Table 2).

Table 2. Values before (Pre) and after (Pos) the intervention for depression, anxiety, stress and sleep quality.

Domain (scale) Items of each domain	Pre (mean ± sd)	Pos (mean ± sd)	P-value[a,b]	Effect size[a,b]
Depression (EADS)	1.1 ± 0.8	0.9 ± 0.9	0.198[a]	0.307[a]
Anxiety (EADS)	1.1 ± 0.8	0.6 ± 1.3	**0.031[a]**	0.589[a]
Stress (EADS)	1.6 ± 0.7	1.1 ± 0.8	**0.014[b]**	0.646[b]
Sleep Quality (PSQI)	4.9 ± 3.5	3.0 ± 2.1	**0.027[b]**	0.611[b]

EADS (Scale of Anxiety, Depression and Stress), scale from 0 (best condition) to 3 (worst condition); PSQI (Pittsburg Sleep Quality Index), scale from 0 (best condition) to 15 (worst condition). Differences between pre and post intervention were tested by parametric paired t-tests for normal variables, with Cohen's D effect size (a), and non-parametric related samples Wilcoxon Signed Rank Tests for non-normal variables with acceptable skewness (-1 to 1 values) and effect sizes calculated by Z values divided by the square root of N (b); N = 18. Significant differences in bold (p-values < 0.05). Effect sizes: no effect < 0.2; small effect 0.2 to 0.5; moderate effect 0.5 to 0.8; large effect > 0.8.

Secondary outcomes were related to some lifestyle habits, in particular food habits, assessed as adherence to Mediterranean diet by (MEDAS score), physical activity, assessed in MET-min/week, frequency of contact with nature and frequency of contact with friends (Table 3). The only variable with a significant change was frequency of contact with friends, which increased (pre, occasionally or sometimes: 69.2%, frequently or most of the times: 23%; post, occasionally or sometimes: 38.4%, frequently or most of the times: 38.5%; Wilcoxon Rank Test p = 0.008; moderate effect size = 0.628).

For the participants who filled in pre and post questionnaires, 70% attended from 5 to 8 sessions. Regarding frequency of home practices, half the participants (50%) reported that they practiced sometimes but not every week, 40% reported practices 3 to 4 times per week; the other 10% divided themselves between practices once or twice a week (5%) or no practices (5%). Independently of the frequency of practices, most participants reported practicing 5 to 10 min (70%) and 30% reported spending 15 to 30 min in their practices. Favorite practices included focus on breathing, guided meditations, and yoga exercises. We further explored if the observed improvements in sleep quality, anxiety

Table 3. Values before (Pre) and after (Pos) the intervention for Mediterranean Diet Adherence (MEDAS score), Physical Activity, frequency of contact with nature and with friends.

Variable	Pre	Pos	P-value[a]	Effect size[a]
Mediterranen Diet Adherence (MEDAS; mean ± sd)	6.3 ± 1.6	6.4 ± 1.9	0.935	0.02
Physical Activity (MET-min/week; mean ± sd)	1.1 ± 0.8	0.6 ± 1.3	0.609	0.123
Frequency of contact with nature (%)				
Never	0.0	15.0	0.218	0.275
Occasionally	37.5	20.0		
Sometimes	41.7	20.0		
Frequently	20.8	40.0		
Most of the times	0.0	5.0		
Frequency of contact with friends (%)				
Never	0.0	0.0	**0.008**	0.590
Occasionally	29.2	5.0		
Sometimes	45.8	45.0		
Frequently	12.5	30.0		
Most of the times	12.5	20.0		

MEDAS, Mediterranean Diet Adherence Screener, score from 0 (worse) to 14 (best) [11]. MET-min per week calculated according to IPAQ (International Physical Activity Questionnaire) [8]. a) Differences between pre and post intervention were tested non-parametric related samples Wilcoxon Signed Rank Tests for non-normal variables with acceptable skewness (−1 to 1 values) and effect sizes calculated by Z values divided by the square root of N. Significant differences in bold (p-values < 0.05). Effect sizes: no effect < 0.2; small effect 0.2 to 0.5; moderate effect 0.5 to 0.8; large effect > 0.8.

and stress were associated with the number of sessions attended or the frequency of the mindfulness practices at home. None of the variables that improved (sleep quality, anxiety and stress) showed any correlation with the number of sessions attended (Pearson p-value > 0.05). Regarding frequency of practices, a significant correlation was observed only for sleep quality (Pearson p-value = 0.039), with a moderate positive association (Pearson r = 0.538). This correlation was maintained after adjusting for the number of presences (Pearson p = 0.045; r = 0.507). No association was observed between number of presences and frequency of practices.

4   Discussion

The present study aimed to investigate the impact of a mindfulness-based program on Portuguese students from IPSantarem, focusing on stress levels, depression, anxiety, and sleep quality. The findings revealed noteworthy insights into the effectiveness of the intervention, shedding light on the potential benefits of mindfulness practices in the context of Portuguese higher education. In the current study stress levels were found to be consistently higher than depression or anxiety levels, both at the start and end of the mindfulness-based intervention. The results emphasize the need for targeted interventions to address stress-related challenges in the university setting.

Interestingly, the mindfulness-based program demonstrated a significant positive impact on anxiety and stress levels. This finding suggests that the program effectively contributed to reducing participants' feelings of anxiety and stress, aligning with the program's core principles of cultivating present-moment awareness and non-judgmental acceptance. These results are consistent with a growing body of research that supports the efficacy of mindfulness interventions in mitigating anxiety and stress symptoms in university students. In fact, a meta-analysis that compared the effect of mindfulness-based interventions on students mental health, with passive (no intervention) and active controls (for example, muscle relaxation, or cognitive restructuring) has shown a significant improvement in anxiety levels in the students that were subjected to the mindfulness-based intervention [14]. Also, some studies highlight that mindfulness is negatively correlated with stress in university students [15, 16].

Furthermore, the study evaluated sleep quality using the Pittsburgh Sleep Quality Index (PSQI), a widely used instrument for assessing sleep disturbances. The significant decrease in the calculated PSQI scores indicates a positive impact of the mindfulness-based program on sleep quality. Improved sleep quality is a notable outcome, as poor sleep patterns are often intertwined with stress, anxiety, and depressive symptoms. The observed moderate effect size underscores the practical relevance of this improvement in sleep quality, suggesting that the mindfulness practices employed in the intervention may have facilitated better sleep hygiene and regulation among the participants. The observed results are in line with other studies which reported that mindfulness has a mediating effect in sleep quality through lower levels of anxiety, stress, and depression [15–17]. Perceived social support along with mindfulness has also been shown to improve sleep quality in university students [18]. This is aligned with results observed for one of the secondary outcomes of the present study, which was an increase in the frequency of contact with friends, as indicated by a shift from occasional or sometimes interactions to more frequent engagements.

The results of this study contribute to the literature by highlighting the potential of mindfulness-based interventions to address multiple dimensions of well-being among university students.

When examining participants' engagement with the mindfulness-based program, it was observed that 70% of those who completed both pre and post questionnaires attended between 5 and 8 sessions. This level of participation suggests a relatively high level of program engagement among the participants. Additionally, home practice frequency was diverse, with 50% reporting occasional practice, 40% engaging 3 to 4 times per week, and the remainder practicing with varying frequencies. Most participants reported dedicating 5 to 10 min to their mindfulness practices, with a smaller percentage investing 15 to 30 min. The wide range of practice approaches reflects the adaptability of mindfulness techniques to individuals' schedules and preferences.

Regarding the correlation between program engagement and outcomes, the observed improvements in stress and anxiety levels were not significantly associated with the frequency of individual practices. This result underscores the potential accessibility and effectiveness of mindfulness interventions even when engaged with varying levels of commitment. However, an interesting finding emerged when examining the relationship between frequency of mindfulness practice and sleep quality. A moderate positive correlation was observed, indicating that participants who engaged in mindfulness practices more frequently at home reported better sleep quality. This correlation remained significant even after accounting for the number of program sessions attended, suggesting that the frequency of home practices exerted a distinct influence on sleep quality beyond program engagement.

While the present study provides valuable insights into the effects of the mindfulness-based program, certain limitations warrant consideration. The absence of a control group and the reliance on self-reported measures could introduce biases and limit causal inferences. Furthermore, the narrow range of lifestyle habits examined may not capture the full spectrum of potential changes influenced by the intervention. Future research should explore a broader range of lifestyle habits and employ more rigorous experimental designs to further validate the findings of the present study and test its potential adaptability as a digital self-help option. With the emergence of digital technologies, it is important to address the potential use of mindfulness-based programs as digital therapeutics. Some results suggest that the efficacy of instructor-led programs and self-help programs have similar effects [14]. A meta-analysis explored the effect of mindfulness meditation intervention implemented using mobile devices, showing an improvement in stress and anxiety levels of university students [19]. Sleep quality has also been reported to improve in adults with insomnia through a self-help mindfulness-based smartphone app with guided meditations [20].

5 Conclusion

The present study revealed that a mindfulness-based program not only positively influenced stress levels, anxiety, and sleep quality among university students but also had an impact on their social interactions, as evidenced by an increase in the frequency of contact with friends. The study also highlighted the role of home practice frequency in improving sleep quality. These findings underscore the multifaceted benefits of mindfulness interventions in higher education, suggesting their potential to enhance both individual well-being and social connections. Next steps will be to adapt the mindfulness-based program for a mobile device and test with a wider intervention group, as well as an active control group.

Funding . Research Centre for Natural Resources, Environment and Society (CERNAS), funded by the Portuguese Foundation for Science and Technology, I.P., Grant/Award Number UIDP/00681/2020 (https://doi.org/10.54499/UIDP/00681/2020). Life Quality Research Centre (CIEQV), funded by the Portuguese Foundation for Science and Technology, I.P., Grant/Award Number UIDP/04748/2020

References

1. WHO. Mental Health and COVID-19: Early evidence of the pandemic's impact, p. 13 (2022). https://www.who.int/publications/i/item/WHO-2019-nCoV-Sci_Brief-Mental_health-2022.1. Accessed 12 Oct 2022

2. Lampe, L.C., Müller-Hilke, B.: Mindfulness-based intervention helps preclinical medical students to contain stress, maintain mindfulness and improve academic success. BMC Med. Educ. **21**(1), 1–8 (2021). https://doi.org/10.1186/s12909-021-02578-y

3. Reangsing, C., Abdullahi, S.G., Schneider, J.K.: Effects of online mindfulness-based interventions on depressive symptoms in college and university students: a systematic review and meta-analysis. J. Integr. Complement. Med. **29**(5), 292–302 (2023). https://doi.org/10.1089/jicm.2022.0606

4. Bamber, M., Schneider, J.: College students' perceptions of mindfulness-based interventions: a narrative review of the qualitative research. Curr. Psychol. **41**(2), 667–680 (2022). https://doi.org/10.1007/s12144-019-00592-4

5. Wingert, J.R., Jones, J.C., Swoap, R.A., Wingert, H.M.: Mindfulness-based strengths practice improves well-being and retention in undergraduates: a preliminary randomized controlled trial. J. Am. Coll. Health **70**(3), 783–790 (2022). https://doi.org/10.1080/07448481.2020.1764005

6. Crone, W.C., Kesebir, P., Hays, B., Mirgain, S.A., Davidson, R.J., Hagness, S.C.: Cultivating well-being in engineering graduate students through mindfulness training. PLoS ONE **18**(3), e0281994 (2023). https://doi.org/10.1371/journal.pone.0281994

7. Chiodelli, R., de Jesus, S.N., de Mello, L.T.N., Andretta, I., Oliveira, D.F., Costa, M.E.S., et al.: Effects of the interculturality and mindfulness program (PIM) on university students: a quasi-experimental study. Eur. J. Invest. Health Psychol. Educ. **12**(10), 1500–1515 (2022). https://doi.org/10.3390/ejihpe12100104

8. Craig, C.L., Marshall, A.L., Sjöström, M., Bauman, A.E., Booth, M.L., Ainsworth, B.E., et al.: International physical activity questionnaire: 12-country reliability and validity. Med. Sci. Sports Exerc. **35**(8), 1381–1395 (2003). https://doi.org/10.1249/01.MSS.0000078924.61453.FB

9. Buysse, D.J., Reynolds, C.F., Monk, T.H., Berman, S.R., Kupfer, D.J.: The Pittsburgh sleep quality index: a new instrument for psychiatric practice and research. Psychiatry Res. **28**(2), 193–213 (1989). https://doi.org/10.1016/0165-1781(89)90047-4

10. Ribeiro, J.L.P., Honrado, A.A.J.D., Leal, I.P.: Contribuição para o estudo da adaptação portuguesa das escalas de ansiedade, depressão e stress (EADS) de 21 itens de Lovibond e Lovibond, pp. 229–239. Psicologia, Saúde & Doenças, Portugal (2004)

11. García-Conesa, M.T., Philippou, E., Pafilas, C., Massaro, M., Quarta, S., Andrade, V., et al.: Exploring the validity of the 14-item Mediterranean diet adherence screener (MEDAS): a cross-national study in seven European countries around the Mediterranean region. Nutrients **12**(10), 2960 (2020). https://doi.org/10.3390/nu12102960

12. Marôco, J.: Análise estatística com o SPSS Statistics, 6 ed. Pêro Pinheiro (2014)

13. Akoglu, H.: User's guide to correlation coefficients. Turk. J. Emer. Med. **18**(3), 91–93 (2018). https://doi.org/10.1016/j.tjem.2018.08.001

14. Dawson, A.F., Anderson, J., Jones, P.B., Galante, J., Brown, W.W., Datta, B., et al.: Mindfulness-based interventions for university students: a systematic review and meta-analysis of randomised controlled trials. Appl. Psychol.-Health Well Being **12**(2), 384–410 (2020). https://doi.org/10.1111/aphw.12188

15. Roberts, K.C., Danoff-Burg, S.: Mindfulness and health behaviors: is paying attention good for you? J. Am. Coll. Health **59**(3), 165–173 (2011). https://doi.org/10.1080/07448481.2010.484452

16. Simione, L., Raffone, A., Mirolli, M.: Stress as the missing link between mindfulness, sleep quality, and well-being: a cross-sectional study. Mindfulness **11**(2), 439–451 (2020). https://doi.org/10.1007/s12671-019-01255-y

17. Bogusch, L.M., Fekete, E.M., Skinta, M.D.: Anxiety and depressive symptoms as mediators of trait mindfulness and sleep quality in emerging adults. Mindfulness **7**(4), 962–970 (2016). https://doi.org/10.1007/s12671-016-0535-7

18. Chen, H.Y.: Roles of mindfulness and perceived social support in mediating the effect of psychological distress on sleep quality of college students. Neuroquantology. **16**(4), 93–100 (2018). https://doi.org/10.14704/nq.2018.16.4.1213

19. Chen, B., Yang, T., Xiao, L., Xu, C., Zhu, C.: Effects of mobile mindfulness meditation on the mental health of university students: systematic review and meta-analysis. J. Med. Internet Res. **25**(1), e39128 (2023). https://doi.org/10.2196/39128

20. Low, T., Conduit, R., Varma, P., Meaklim, H., Jackson, M.L.: Treating subclinical and clinical symptoms of insomnia with a mindfulness-based smartphone application: a pilot study. Internet Interv. Appl. Inf. Technol. Mental Behav. Health **21**, 100335 (2020). https://doi.org/10.1016/j.invent.2020.100335

Algorithm for Diagnosis of Metabolic Syndrome and Heart Failure Using CPET Biosignals via SVM and Wavelet Transforms

Rafael Fernandes Pinheiro[1]([✉]) [ID] and Rui Fonseca-Pinto[1,2] [ID]

[1] Center for Innovative Care and Health Technology (ciTechCare), Polytechnic of Leiria, Rua de Santo André - 66-68, 2415-736 Leiria, Portugal
{rafael.f.pinheiro,rui.pinto}@ipleiria.pt
[2] School of Health Sciences (ESSLei), Polytechnic of Leiria, Campus 2 - Morro do Lena, Alto do Vieiro - Apartado 4137, 2411-901 Leiria, Portugal

Abstract. Early diagnosis of diseases is essential to avoid health complications and costs to the health system. For this purpose, algorithms have been widely used in the medical field to assist in the diagnosis of diseases. This work proposes an algorithm with a new approach to analyze biosignals from cardiopulmonary exercise testing (CPET) to identify metabolic syndrome (MS) and heart failure (HF). The algorithm uses the support vector machine (SVM) as a classification technique and wavelet transforms for extraction of the features. For training, CPET data from 30 volunteers were used, of which 15 are diagnosed with MS and 15 with HF. The SVM-L-W approach, which uses wavelet transforms, has been shown to have better accuracy (93%) compared to some other approaches found in the literature. In addition, the SVM-L-W algorithm can be applied to identify other diseases, and is also adaptable to modifications in order to obtain better performance, as suggested in future work to continue this research.

Keywords: Classification algorithms · Biosignals · CPET · Metabolic diseases · Heart diseases · Wavelet transforms

1 Introduction

Both metabolic syndrome (MS) and heart failure (HF) are public health issues of major global relevance. MS involves several metabolic risk factors, such as obesity and type 2 diabetes, increasing the risk of cardiovascular disease. More than 15 years ago, studies [1] already showed that the prevalence of MS was between 20% and 25% worldwide and was already considered one of the most

This work was funded by Portuguese national funds provided by Fundação para a Ciência e Tecnologia (FCT) in the scope of the research project 2 ARTs - Acessing Autonomic Control in Cardiac Rehabilitation (PTDC/EMD-EMD/6588/2020).

P. J. Coelho et al. (Eds.): GOODTECHS 2023, LNICST 556, pp. 159–171, 2024.
https://doi.org/10.1007/978-3-031-52524-7_12

common chronic diseases, ranking fourth in the list of leading causes of death worldwide. On the other hand, HF is when the heart does not pump enough blood to fulfil the body's needs, causing severe symptoms. Heart failure is increasing in prevalence, with approximately 26 million patients affected worldwide [5]. Prevention, early diagnosis and appropriate treatment are key to mitigating the impact of these conditions on society.

Cardiopulmonary Exercise Testing (CPET) is a test that assesses the body's response to exercise by combining cardiovascular, respiratory and metabolic analysis. It provides important information for diagnosis, prognosis and therapeutic planning in various medical conditions, including cardiac [17], metabolic [16] and pulmonary [14]. The interpretation of the data is done by health professionals and helps in the assessment of cardiorespiratory capacity, diagnosis of diseases and optimization of physical training.

In contrast, the interpretation of CPET data is based on a thorough analysis of the variables recorded during the test. Currently, interpretation follows guidelines and criteria established by medical and exercise physiology societies, as well as by scientific studies that provide references for understanding the results (basically the flowchart is used - see [13] and [10]). In this line, it is understood that the interpretation of CPET data for diagnosis is not yet a closed subject, and with the improvement of artificial intelligence techniques, new methods and algorithms have emerged to help doctors provide more accurate diagnoses and therapeutic plans.

In the field of artificial intelligence, classification algorithms have been used for the development of diagnostic algorithms, the most common are in the areas of machine learning and artificial neural networks. In the area of machine learning, for a training dataset of approximately 70 CPET files for each disease, [12] shows that the support vector machine (SVM) technique is an excellent tool for classifying diseases such as heart failure and chronic obstructive pulmonary disease, reaching accuracy levels of 100%. In the area of artificial neural networks, the work of Brown et al. [6] can be highlighted, which develops hybrid models using convolutional neural networks (CNN) and autoencoders (AE) with principal component analysis (PCA) and logistic regression (LR) for the classification of heart failure and metabolic syndrome with a set of 15 CPET files for each disease. The methodologies of these works are very different, however, both show very effective results, especially the one that uses a very small dataset.

In this paper, it is presented an algorithm for diagnosis of MS and HF, based on supervised learning, with two new approaches for analyzing CPET data. Diagnostic algorithms are of great value to medicine because they can prevent severe health damage and death. The training of this algorithm is performed using the same dataset of [6]. The simplest approach uses SVM classificator with kernel linear, the features being the means and variances of the CPET data (algorithm called SVM-L). The second version is a linear kernel SVM classifier algorithm that employs a different methodology to obtain the features and uses the means and variances of the coefficients of the Daubechies wavelets of order 2 with 3 levels (algorithm called SVM-L-W).

The main contributions of this paper are highlighted below:

- According to the literature search conducted by the authors, there are no previous works dealing with the development of algorithms for disease diagnosis from CPET data that combine the use of SVM with wavelets.
- The use of wavelet transforms to prepare the data and obtain the features from the CPET data is presented in this work as a very efficient alternative to reduce the computational cost. This technique allows to drastically reduce the dimension of the features used in the classification algorithms for analyzing CPET data. The authors believe that this approach is the greatest contribution of the work, presenting an efficient algorithm with low computational cost compared to [12] and [6].
- The work presents an algorithm with better accuracy compared to other algorithms that use CNN, PCA, LR and flowchart, proving to be able to compete with the AE+LR technique of [6]. In this sense, future work is proposed, which aims to train the SVM-L-W algorithm with artificial data for its improvement and with more features extracted from the CPET variables. This future work may show that SVM-L-W surpasses AE+LR in accuracy.
- Since the feature dimension reduction technique is essential for biosignals from the brain (e.g. electroencephalography data), due to the huge amount of information, it is understood that the SVM-L-W algorithm can be effectively used in the diagnosis of neurological and psychiatric diseases.

Figure 1 shows the illustrative design that covers all phases of the process, from data collection by the CPET to diagnosis after processing the patient data by the SVM-L-W algorithm. In the figure, the interrogation signs represent the authors' intention to continue with this investigation to design a more comprehensive algorithm that provides diagnostics in several other diseases from the CPET data collection.

The rest of the paper is developed as follows: in the Sect. 2, the main theoretical bases for the development of the algorithms are presented; in the Sect. 3, information about the data and the creation of the features are brought; the Sect. 4, deals with the construction of the algorithms; the results regarding the performance of the algorithm are presented in the Sect. 5; finally, the work ends with the conclusions, Sect. 6, where a summary of the findings is made and future work is proposed.

2   Theoretical Basis

This section presents the main theoretical basis for the development of the algorithm.

2.1   Support Vector Machine

Support Vector Machine (SVM), proposed by Vladimir Vapnik [4], is a supervised machine learning method of classification and regression that seeks to find

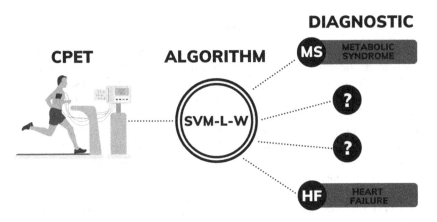

Fig. 1. Illustration of the diagnostic system from CPET data.

the optimal hyperplane in multidimensional spaces to separate two classes of data. Its effectiveness stems from the process of maximizing the margin between the support vectors, which are the closest points to the decision boundaries. This approach allows for robust generalization even in complex, high-dimensional datasets, making it a prominent choice in various data analysis and pattern recognition applications. Its variants, what is called the SVM kernel, include linear, polynomial, sigmoidal and RBF. Linear SVM is used to separate linearly separable classes, while polynomial and sigmoidal SVM are applied to non-linearly separable datasets using transformations. RBF SVM is highly powerful, mapping the data to a high-dimensional space to separate complex classes.

2.2   Wavelet Transforms

Wavelet transforms are a powerful mathematical tool widely used in signal and image analysis. Unlike traditional transforms, wavelets offer a multiresolution approach, allowing to capture both local and global signal information efficiently. Wavelets have stood out as a promising approach in classification algorithms [9,18]. By applying the wavelet technique in data analysis, it is possible to extract relevant features from different scales and frequencies, allowing a richer representation of the patterns present in the datasets. This ability to identify discriminative information at multiple resolutions has led to the development of more accurate and robust classification models in several areas, such as pattern recognition, image processing and medical diagnostics.

When applying a wavelet transform, the signal is decomposed into levels (d_1, d_2, d_3, etc.) representing details at different frequencies. The coefficients in these decompositions reflect the contributions of each level in the overall representation of the original signal. These wavelet coefficients allow a detailed analysis of the signal at various resolutions. In this work, it was used the Daubechies wavelet of order 2 with 3 levels (d_1, d_2, d_3,) and an approximation, both for the CPET variables under consideration presented in the next section.

2.3   Validation Process

For the validation of the algorithm, the cross validation k-fold was used (see more in [21]). The cross validation k-fold is a technique used in machine learning that is very useful when you have small datasets, which is the case of this work. The technique involves dividing the dataset into k subsets (folds) of approximately equal sizes. The model is trained k times, where, in each iteration, one of the subsets is used as a test set and the remaining $k-1$ subsets are used for training. At the end of the k iterations, the results are combined to produce a single metric for evaluating model performance. This allows for a more accurate and robust assessment of model performance, using all available data efficiently and avoiding biases in the assessment.

3   Dataset

In this section, it was presented the origin of the data used and the methodology for creating the features for use in the diagnostic algorithm, as well as the labels.

3.1   Data Source

The CPET dataset used to create the algorithm was obtained from a public database[1] which has been used in several other works [2,3,6–8,11,15]. The data on MS come from a study supported by the National Institute of Health/National Heart Lung and Blood Institute (NIH/NHLBI), "Exercise dose and metformin for vascular health in adults with metabolic syndrome" and the HF data came from patient studies supported by the American Heart Association, "Personalized Approach to Cardiac Resynchronization Therapy Using High Dimensional Immunophenotyping," as well as the NIH/NHLBI, "MRI of Mechanical Activation and Scar for Optimal Cardiac Resynchronization Therapy Implementation." In the data, a total of 30 individuals were sampled, 15 of them with a diagnosis of MS and another 15 with HF.

CPET provides a wide variety of information extracted from the patient during the test. In this work, for the creation of the features, the CPET variables were used according to Table 1.

3.2   Features and Labels

Features are the information taken from the data for training the classification algorithms. Labels are the classifications (names) given to a set of features. For example, consider the heart rate (HH) and respiratory rate (RR) data of a given patient. You can use the variables themselves (HH and RR) as features, this usually gives a large dataset. However, for computational gain, one can extract parameters from these variables, for example the mean. Thus, the features for this patient will be the mean HH and RR. On the other hand, the labels are the

---

[1] https://github.com/suchethassharma/CPET.

Table 1. Variables for the creation of features.

Description	Feature
Metabolic equivalents	$METS$
Heart Rate	HR
Peak oxygen consumption	$\dot{V}O_2(L/min)$
Volume of carbon dioxide released	$\dot{V}CO_2(L/min)$
Respiratory exchange ratio	RER
Ventilation	$VE(L/min)$
Expiratory tidal volume (expiratory time)	$Vtex(L)$
Inspiratory tidal volume (inhale time)	$Vtin(L)$

classifications given to the patient connected to their features, for example, if it is a non-diabetic patient, it is given the label 0 and if it is a diabetic patient it is given label 1. Therefore, a set of data from several patients is the information used to train the algorithm. The greater the number of patients for training, the better the algorithm's ability to determine a disease. More content on feature extraction can be found at [19, 22].

For this work, the features were obtained from the CPET variables presented in the previous subsection. Two sets of features were used. The first set, called X, consists of the mean and variance of each variable in Table 1, with the first 15 lines corresponding to data from patients with HF and the other 15 lines with data from patients with MS. The X feature was constructed by organizing the data using Excel software functions where the means and variances were also extracted. Table 2 shows how the data are presented to the algorithm. The table shows that the matrix X has a dimension of 30 rows with 16 columns.

Table 2. Features with mean and variance.

	METS		HR		...	Vtin	
	Mean	Var	Mean	Var	...	Mean	Var
1	2.639	0.285	113.68	193.79	$\cdots$	1.079	0.187
2	4.075	0.704	102.613	81.259	$\cdots$	1.778	0.128
3	2.647	0.264	124.911	130.344	$\cdots$	1.716	0.125
$\vdots$	$\vdots$	$\vdots$	$\vdots$	$\vdots$	$\ddots$	$\vdots$	$\vdots$
30	5.074	1.708	131.645	439.237	$\cdots$	1.643	0.13

The second set of features, called W, contains the mean and variance of the wavelet transform coefficients at three levels (d_1, d_2 and d_3) obtained from the CPET variables. The algorithm presented in the next section is implemented to obtain the matrix of features W, with the first 15 rows corresponding to data from patients with HF and the other 15 rows with data from patients with MS. Figure 2 shows the structure of the matrix W returned by the algorithm. It can be seen from the figure that the matrix W has a dimension of 30 rows with 64 columns.

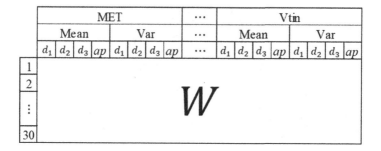

Fig. 2. Features using wavelets provided by the algorithm.

On the label, the value 0 (zero) was used to represent HF and the value 1 (one) to represent MS. These values were inserted in a vector, called Y, of dimension 30, with the first 15 elements of values 0 and the other 15 of values 1.

4   The Algorithm

Diagnostic algorithms have been widely used in the medical field to support the diagnosis of diseases. These types of algorithms generally use artificial intelligence techniques and are built using a database for training. Considering a supervised learning algorithm, it is trained with a database that provides the data of people with a certain disease, and this disease receives a type of classification. Thus, when the model is ready, i.e., after training, the algorithm is able to identify the type of disease when a new patient's data is presented.

The algorithm for diagnosis developed in this work uses Matlab functions specific to machine learning projects, and its training is done using the database presented in the previous section. Two approaches were used to obtain the results. In both cases, the Matlab reference code [20] was used to construct the confusion matrices.

The first development approach, called SVM-L, which is simpler, receives the feature X and labels Y, performs the classification via SVM, cross-validates and prints the confusion matrix. The second approach, called SVM-L-W, differs from the first in the creation of the feature. This version receives the data from the CPET variables (Table 1) and creates the W feature, i.e., it applies the wavelet transforms and obtains their coefficients, and then obtains the mean and variance creating the W matrix.

Figure 3 illustrates the methodology for the development of the algorithm with the two approaches and presents the Matlab functions used. It can be observed that in the SVM-L-W approach, it is necessary to create only the SVM with Linear kernel, since the results of the first approach showed that the SVM classifier with linear kernel has better accuracy (see next section).

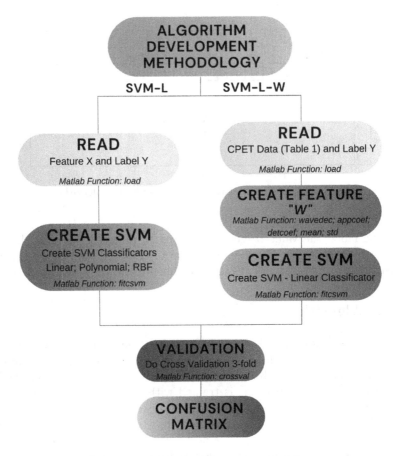

Fig. 3. Algorithm development methodology.

5   Results

In this section, the performance results of the algorithm for the SVM-L and SVM-L-W approaches are presented. Then, comparisons are made with some existing results in the literature.

In this type of work, some evaluation metrics are used to validate the algorithms, the most common are: accuracy, precision, recall and F1-score. The formula for each metric is obtained from the confusion matrix (see Fig. 4). In this paper, only the accuracy metric is taken into account. Accuracy shows the overall performance of the model, indicating, among all diagnostics, how many the model indicated correctly.

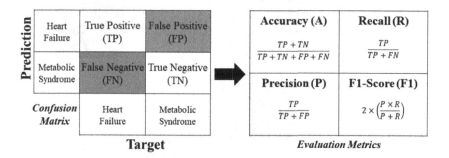

Fig. 4. Formulas of the evaluation metrics.

5.1 SVM-L Algorithm

This version of the algorithm uses the X feature with linear kernel SVM. Figure 5 shows the confusion matrix for each classifier. With emphasis on accuracy, it is observed that the linear classifier performs better.

5.2 SVM-L-W Algorithm

This second version of the algorithm uses the W feature with the linear kernel SVM model that showed better accuracy in the previous version. It should be noted that the W feature is constructed by the algorithm from the means and variances of the wavelet transform coefficients with the biosignal data provided by CPET (Table 1). Figure 6 shows the confusion matrix for the SVM-linear classifier with wavelet transforms.

5.3 Comparisons

The basic method used to interpret CPET results is a flowchart. According to [6], flowcharts have been used to interpret CPET results for more than 30 years. Here, the guidelines FRIEND [13] and of Hansen, et al. [10] were used. In addition to the flowchart method, the results of this work were compared with those obtained from Brown, et al. [6] who propose methods that utilize neuralnetwork

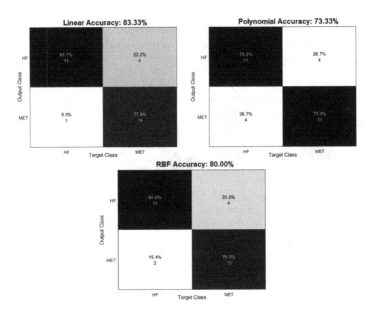

Fig. 5. Confusion matrices.

techniques (AE and CNN), PCA and LR. Table 3 shows the accuracy obtained in each of the methods.

Table 3. Comparisons with other methods.

Method	Accuracy (%)
AE + LR [6]	97
SVM-L-W	93
CNN [6]	90
PCA + LR [6]	90
SVM-L	83
Flowchart [13]	77
Flowchart [10]	70

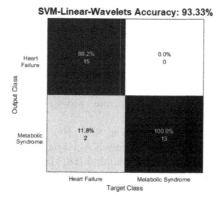

Fig. 6. Confusion matrix of the approach SVM-L-W.

6 Conclusion

This work presented a new approach to build an algorithm that uses CPET data for diagnosis of metabolic syndrome and heart failure. The algorithm, called SVM-L-W, presented an accuracy of 93%, ranking better than some other algorithms found in the literature. However, in this first investigation, SVM-L-W presented lower accuracy compared to AE+LR of [6], in this case, one believes that in the future, the SVM-L-W could overcome AE+LR with some adaptations in terms the use of more features and artificial data for training. It is also considered that the SVM-L-W algorithm can be applied to determine other types of pathologies that may be related to biosignals from CPET, given proper training with an adequate database.

For future works, it is suggested to use this algorithm to analyze electroencelography signals to assist in the diagnosis of neurological and psychiatric diseases. Also, one intends to continue the development of the algorithm by investigating the use of artificial data for training and a larger number of features, in order to improve its accuracy, as well as designing it to provide diagnostics of a larger number of diseases.

References

1. Alberti, K.G.M.M., Zimmet, P., Shaw, J.: Metabolic syndrome-a new world-wide definition: a consensus statement from the international diabetes federation. Diab. Med. **23**(5), 469–480 (2006)
2. Auger, D.A., et al.: Reproducibility of global and segmental myocardial strain using cine dense at 3t: a multicenter cardiovascular magnetic resonance study in healthy subjects and patients with heart disease. J. Cardiovasc. Magn. Reson. **24**(1), 1–12 (2022)
3. Bilchick, K.C., et al.: CMR dense and the seattle heart failure model inform survival and arrhythmia risk after CRT. Cardiovasc. Imaging **13**(4), 924–936 (2020)

4. Boser, B.E., Guyon, I.M., Vapnik, V.N.: A training algorithm for optimal margin classifiers. In: Proceedings of the Fifth Annual Workshop on Computational Learning Theory, pp. 144–152 (1992)

5. Bowen, R.E., Graetz, T.J., Emmert, D.A., Avidan, M.S.: Statistics of heart failure and mechanical circulatory support in 2020. Ann. Transl. Med. **8**(13) (2020)

6. Brown, D.E., Sharma, S., Jablonski, J.A., Weltman, A.: Neural network methods for diagnosing patient conditions from cardiopulmonary exercise testing data. BioData Mining **15**(1), 16 (2022)

7. Gaitán, J.M., Eichner, N.Z., Gilbertson, N.M., Heiston, E.M., Weltman, A., Malin, S.K.: Two weeks of interval training enhances fat oxidation during exercise in obese adults with prediabetes. J. Sports Sci. Med. **18**(4), 636 (2019)

8. Gao, X., et al.: Cardiac magnetic resonance assessment of response to cardiac resynchronization therapy and programming strategies. Cardiovasc. Imaging **14**(12), 2369–2383 (2021)

9. Guo, T., Zhang, T., Lim, E., Lopez-Benitez, M., Ma, F., Yu, L.: A review of wavelet analysis and its applications: challenges and opportunities. IEEE Access **10**, 58869–58903 (2022)

10. Hansen, D., et al.: Exercise training intensity determination in cardiovascular rehabilitation: should the guidelines be reconsidered? Eur. J. Prev. Cardiol. **26**(18), 1921–1928 (2019)

11. Heiston, E.M., et al.: Two weeks of exercise training intensity on appetite regulation in obese adults with prediabetes. J. Appl. Physiol. **126**(3), 746–754 (2019)

12. Inbar, O., Inbar, O., Reuveny, R., Segel, M.J., Greenspan, H., Scheinowitz, M.: A machine learning approach to the interpretation of cardiopulmonary exercise tests: development and validation. Pulmonary Med. **2021**, 1–9 (2021)

13. Kaminsky, L.A., Imboden, M.T., Arena, R., Myers, J.: Reference standards for cardiorespiratory fitness measured with cardiopulmonary exercise testing using cycle ergometry: data from the fitness registry and the importance of exercise national database (friend) registry. In: Mayo Clinic Proceedings, vol. 92, pp. 228–233. Elsevier (2017)

14. Luo, Q., et al.: The value of cardiopulmonary exercise testing in the diagnosis of pulmonary hypertension. J. Thorac. Dis. **13**(1), 178 (2021)

15. Malin, S.K., Gilbertson, N.M., Eichner, N.Z., Heiston, E., Miller, S., Weltman, A., et al.: Impact of short-term continuous and interval exercise training on endothelial function and glucose metabolism in prediabetes. J. Diab. Res. **2019** (2019)

16. Rodriguez, J.C., Peterman, J.E., Fleenor, B.S., Whaley, M.H., Kaminsky, L.A., Harber, M.P.: Cardiopulmonary exercise responses in individuals with metabolic syndrome: the ball state adult fitness longitudinal lifestyle study. Metab. Syndr. Relat. Disord. **20**(7), 414–420 (2022)

17. Saito, Y., et al.: Diagnostic value of expired gas analysis in heart failure with preserved ejection fraction. Sci. Rep. **13**(1), 4355 (2023)

18. Serhal, H., Abdallah, N., Marion, J.M., Chauvet, P., Oueidat, M., Humeau-Heurtier, A.: Overview on prediction, detection, and classification of atrial fibrillation using wavelets and AI on ECG. Comput. Biol. Med. **142**, 105168 (2022)

19. Subasi, A.: EEG signal classification using wavelet feature extraction and a mixture of expert model. Expert Syst. Appl. **32**(4), 1084–1093 (2007)

20. Tshitoyan, V.: Plot confusion matrix (2023). https://github.com/vtshitoyan/plotConfMat. Accessed 27 July 2023

21. Wong, T.T., Yeh, P.Y.: Reliable accuracy estimates from k-fold cross validation. IEEE Trans. Knowl. Data Eng. **32**(8), 1586–1594 (2019)
22. Xing, Z., Pei, J., Yu, P.S., Wang, K.: Extracting interpretable features for early classification on time series. In: Proceedings of the 2011 SIAM International Conference on Data Mining, pp. 247–258. SIAM (2011)

Meal Suggestions for Caregivers and Indecisive Individuals Without a Set Food Plan

Carlos A. S. Cunha[(✉)], Tiago R. Cardoso, and Rui P. Duarte

Polytechnic Institute of Viseu, Viseu, Portugal
{cacunha,tcardoso,pduarte}@estgv.ipv.pt

Abstract. Recommendation systems have played a crucial role in assisting users with decision-making across various domains. In nutrition, these systems can provide valuable assistance by offering alternatives to inflexible food plans that often result in abandonment due to personal food preferences or the temporary unavailability of certain ingredients. Moreover, they can aid caregivers in selecting the most suitable food options for dependent individuals based on their specific daily goals. In this article, we develop a data-driven model using a multilayer perceptron (MLP) network to assist individuals in making informed meal choices that align with their preferences and daily goals. Our study focuses on predicting complete meals rather than solely on predicting individual food items since food choices are often influenced by specific combinations of ingredients that work harmoniously together. Based on our evaluation of a comprehensive dataset, the results of our study demonstrate that the model achieves a prediction accuracy of over 60% for an individual complete meal.

Keywords: food recommendation · deep learning · autonomous nutrition

1 Introduction

Nutrition is a concern in modern societies that has to deal with old challenges and new problems to people's health. The leading challenges include the population's lack of domain knowledge and the particularities of individuals, such as their nutrition goals and food preferences [7]. Thus, people need assistance choosing their food to meet their nutritional goals.

Recommendation systems use historical data records to predict users' preferences. They have been widely adopted to recommend e-commerce products, movies, and music [4,15,16]. The importance of food preferences justifies the use of recommendation systems to support the food choices of one person during the

National Funds fund this work through the FCT—Foundation for Science and Technology, I.P., within the scope of the project Ref. UIDB/05583/2020. Furthermore, we thank the Research Centre in Digital Services (CISeD), under project Ref. PIDI/CISeD/2022/009, and the Polytechnic of Viseu for their support.

© ICST Institute for Computer Sciences, Social Informatics and Telecommunications Engineering 2024
Published by Springer Nature Switzerland AG 2024. All Rights Reserved
P. J. Coelho et al. (Eds.): GOODTECHS 2023, LNICST 556, pp. 172–183, 2024.
https://doi.org/10.1007/978-3-031-52524-7_13

day. Choices are made by the person directly or by an informal caregiver, as is the case of the elderly, particularly those suffering from some level of dementia.

This study addresses the problem of recommending food to people according to their preferences. Its relevance is described by the support of users or their caregivers deciding on meals adjusted to their energy objectives. Previous work on this topic addresses generic health and fitness support [5,11,14], and the recommendation of specific diets for specific target groups (e.g., diabetics) [12]. We explore deep-learning techniques for food recommendation based on the person's target daily calories and preferences to answer the following research questions:

- RQ1. How do we predict food combinations meeting the individual's preferences and the energetic and nutrient goals specified in the food plan designed by a nutritionist?
- RQ2. Which features are relevant for determining food preferences?
- RQ3. Which data preprocessing techniques are relevant to improve prediction accuracy?

The remainder of this article is structured as follows. Section 2 presents the related work. Section 3 describes the problem addressed in this article. Section 4 describes the data gathering and preprocessing methodology. Section 5 analyses behavioral patterns from the data. Finally, Sect. 6 presents the conclusion.

2 Related Work

The current body of research on food recommendation encompasses various objectives, ranging from providing general food recommendations to catering to specific groups, such as individuals with specific medical conditions or dietary needs.

2.1 Generic Recommendation

Food recommendation systems for general public addresses are designed for people that want to make food and lifestyle choices for better health and fitness. The context-aware food recommendation system presented in [11] is based on the user's profile, physiological signals, and environmental information to recommend food from Korean menus. Results have shown that integrating three contexts makes predicting approximately 95% of user intentions possible.

In [14], a food recommendation system based on user preferences and ingredients is presented. For food content-based recommendations, the authors explore graph clustering, food deep embedding, food similarity calculation, food clustering, and food-based rating prediction. They used deep-learning techniques and user similarity calculation, generation of the trusted network, graph representation of users, user clustering, and user-based rating prediction. The solution was evaluated using a dataset created by crawling the Allrecipes.com website. The results have outperformed other state-of-the-art approaches.

In [5] the authors created a food recommendation system using graph convolutional networks (FGCNs). They model several food-related relations: ingredient-ingredient, ingredient-recipe, and recipe-user. A real-world dataset collected from Allrecipes.com was used for model evaluation. The authors concluded that the presented solution outperforms four state-of-the-art works on recall and normalized discounted cumulative gain (NDCG) metrics.

A food recommendation approach based on many-objective optimization, given the user preferences, nutritional values, dietary diversity, and user diet patterns, is presented in [17]. A MyFitnessPal dataset was used for evaluation. The Positive Point-wise Mutual Information (PPMI) determines the correlation between food items and the evaluation of food preferences. The Simpson index is used as the diversity metric to promote food diversity, while Dynamic Time Wrapping (DTW) measures changes in diet patterns over time. Results show that PEA2+SDE Many-objective optimization algorithms exhibit the best results.

2.2 Specific Diets

In [12] it is proposed a food recommender system for diabetic patients. A Self-Organizing Map and K-mean algorithms support food clustering to provide food substitution within food groups. Clustering is established on the similarity of eight significant nutrients for diabetic patients. Food is categorized into 22 groups based on food characteristics (e.g., rice, juice) and three additional groups based on the impact on diabetics (i.e., normal, limited, and avoidable). Questionnaires addressed to users have shown an overall score of the solution of 3.64 on a scale of 0–5.

A diabetes self-care recommendation system for American Indians is presented in [1]. Food intake and physical workouts based on ontological profiles with general clinical diabetes guidelines are recommended utilizing users' smartphones. The profile is build-up from biological, cultural, socioeconomic, and environmental factors, encoded with professional guidelines as a rule set, which a forward chaining-based reasoner interprets to provide recommendations. Evaluation results by experts have shown accuracy levels between 90% and 100%.

In [2], a food recommendation approach for chronic kidney disease patients is presented. Selection of food for recommendation using the Naïve Bayes, Support Vector Machines, and Random Forest algorithms according to the blood potassium level of people was performed with accuracy levels close to 100%.

Contrasting with previous work, we consider the recommendation of complete meals based on their sequence during the day and the maximum calorie intake specified for that person. The combination of ingredients in a meal obeys cultural, diet type, and individual rules, which makes the meal the recommendation granularity.

3 Problem Statement

Food plans are built upon an energy amount the nutritionist determines for a specified individual based on their goals, physical condition, and clinical status. Energy is further broken down into macronutrients (i.e., carbohydrates, fat, or protein). Each macronutrient contributes a percentage of the total energy amount (Eq. 1). Several times, alcohol (ethanol) is forgotten in the decomposition of macronutrients, but it contributes to the amount of energy consumed by an individual.

$$energy = carbo + fat + protein + alcohol \qquad (1)$$

Micronutrient values may be incorporated into the food plan. Still, their control is difficult when the person resorts to food equivalents frequently due to their appetite or availability of the recommended food.

Our work is bound to analyze macronutrients since they are frequently the main elements of the food plan for generic diets based on caloric intake. By contrast, some diseases need control of some micronutrients– e.g., potassium for chronic kidney disease [2]. However, we added the daily limit of sodium and sugar, as they are specified in most food plans due to their direct relation with obesity [8,10].

Food granularity represents another design decision for our solution. The recommended food granularity can be: (1) the meal; or (2) the food associated with the meal. We decided on (1) because several food combinations are commonly chosen (e.g., hamburgers, french fries, and coke are commonly eaten together).

Food preferences are not only individual but also culture-dependent. That means that meal prediction can be performed based on the preferences of a person or a community. The articulation between preference granularities can be complex since they involve variables such as the number of individual records available for personalized preference learning or the cohesion of food preferences in a specific community. Our work focuses on community preferences to predict the preferences of one individual based on the nutrients specified for their food plan.

Based on the aforementioned assumptions, the problem can be defined as follows: given the individual goals regarding nutrients G, the meal's day sequence s, the proper combination C of food for a specific meal, and the food nutrients N_G, the temporal context T, the model should predict the most appropriate food combination F for that person.

4   Model Building Methodology

We follow a traditional model-building methodology, starting with a data selection activity (Fig. 1). Data preprocessing, transformation, model training, and evaluation activities follow.

4.1   Dataset

To validate the effectiveness of our approach, we utilized a dataset sourced from MyFitnessPal [6]. This dataset comprises 587,187 days of food diary records

Fig. 1. Data preparation methodology

logged by approximately 9.9K MyFitnessPal users from September 2014 to April 2015.

The dataset includes the person's daily goals for calories and macronutrients (protein, carbs, and fat) and micronutrients (sodium and sugar). Each dataset record contains a list of food chosen by the person for one meal, their goals, and a sequence representing the meal order – i.e., the first meal of the day is represented as one, and the following meals increment this value.

4.2   Data Selection and Preprocessing

Data preparation is required to select, preprocess, and transform raw data stored in the original dataset. One important goal of data preparation is to filter outliers and provide the learning process with data in the appropriate form.

We reduced the dataset by considering users whose number of samples is above the 5th percentile to exclude outliers. A similar lower 5th percentile filter was applied to foods with few samples (Fig. 2).

	date	food_ids	goal_calories	goal_carbs	goal_fat	goal_protein	goal_sodium	goal_sugar	sequence	...
0	15/09/2014	{1,2,3,4,4}	1572	196	52	79	2300	59	1	...
1	16/09/2014	{5,1,2,3,6,7}	1832	229	61	92	2300	69	1	...
2	17/09/2014	{1,2,3,6,8,9,10}	1685	210	56	85	2300	63	1	...
3	18/09/2014	{1,6,2,3,11,12}	1597	199	53	80	2300	60	1	...
4	19/09/2014	{1,7,13,12,2,3,12,12}	1589	198	53	80	2300	60	1	...

Fig. 2. Table after preprocessing

Data preprocessing involved feature normalization and transformation of their representation. Normalization is performed according to the maximum and minimum values of each feature (Eq. 2). This technique gets all the scaled data in the range (0, 1).

$$x'_{i,n} = \frac{x_{i,n} - min(x_i)}{max(x_i) - min(x_i)} \tag{2}$$

4.3   Data Transformation

Data transformation unfolds features to unveil hidden data for training or prepare data for training and classification. Figure 3 shows the transformation of the *date* feature by extracting the *weekday, year, month,* and *year* features. These features are potentially good predictors since food intake is frequently associated with specific periods of the year (e.g., Christmas, summer, winter) or the week (e.g., weekdays or weekends).

Another data transformation is required to break down nonatomic features. *Food ids* are stored in the dataset, separated by commas in a single attribute. However, the breakdown of *food ids* results into a variable number of independent attributes. The one-hot encoding technique assigns the values in an attribute to multiple flag attributes and designates a binary value to them [13].

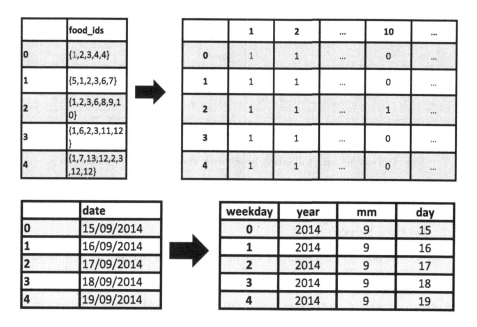

Fig. 3. Feature transformation.

4.4   Model Creation

The training process involves several stages:

– dataset breakdown into train, test, and validation data;
– feature selection using the Random Forest algorithm [3];
– analysis and selection of appropriate hyperparameters;
– model training using a multilayer perceptron (MLP) network [9].

We randomly select 70% of the dataset for training, 10% for testing, and 20% for validation.

5   Results

This section presents the experimental results obtained by applying the methodology described in Sect. 4.

5.1   Data Normalization

Figure 4 shows the training and validation losses with and without normalization. We kept the normalized data for the following learning stages due to the visible classification performance improvement.

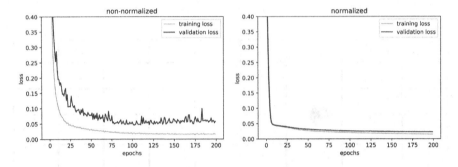

Fig. 4. Training and validation losses with and without normalization.

5.2   Feature Selection

Figure 5 presents the importance score of each feature selected by the Random Forest algorithm. The score provided by *user_id* shows that individual preferences greatly impact the selection of recommended food. As expected, the sequence – representing the day meal's number – is another important predictor since food intake patterns are associated with each meal during the day. A more surprising constatation is the score attributed to target goals, which unveils their higher discriminative power relative to meal nutrients. This result leads to the conclusion that the target nutrition goals of each person are fundamental food recommendation predictors.

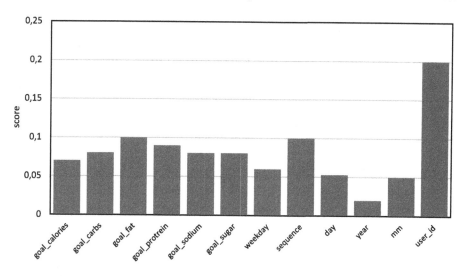

Fig. 5. Importance score of selected features obtained using Random Forest.

5.3   Hyperparameters Setting

Table 1 lists hyperparameters evaluated through different settings.

Table 1. List of hyperparameters evaluated.

hyperparameter	tests
epochs	1–1000
batch	1–128
hidden layers	1–30
units	1–3000
activation function	*ReLU*, *Sigmoid*, *Tanh*, and *Softmax*
loss function	*Binary Cross-entropy*, *MSE*, and *Cross Entropy*
optimizers	*SGD*, *AdaGrad*, *RMSprop*, and *Adam*

As observable in Fig. 6a, the *Sigmoid* and *Softmax* activation functions have the best performance. The mean square error exhibits the best performance of all loss functions (Fig. 6b). In contrast, the optimizers RMSprop and Adam (Fig. 7) outperformed the other evaluated optimizers. From the analysis of Fig. 8a, it is noticeable that the optimal setting is achieved using one hidden layer.

According to the previous results, the experimental setting for the remaining tests involved the *Sigmoid* activation function, the *MSE* loss function, and the *RMSprop* optimizer. According to Fig. 8c, the batch size is 32 provides the best results.

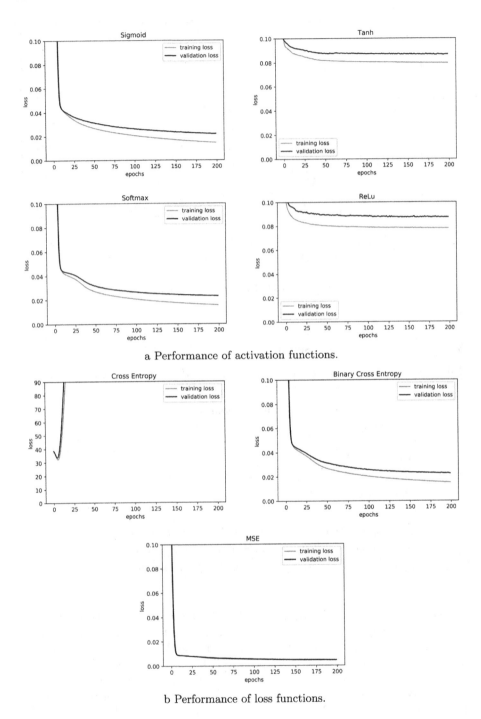

a Performance of activation functions.

b Performance of loss functions.

Fig. 6. Performance of activation and loss functions.

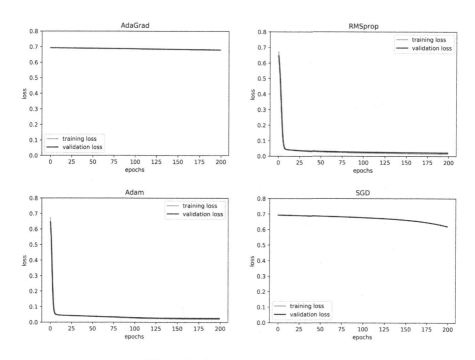

Fig. 7. Performance of optimizers.

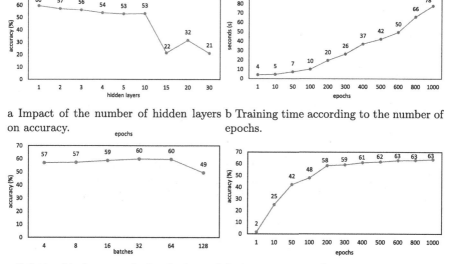

a Impact of the number of hidden layers on accuracy.

b Training time according to the number of epochs.

c Relationship between the batch size and accuracy.

d Accuracy according to the number of epochs.

Fig. 8. Experimental results.

5.4   Accuracy

The results shown that the maximum accuracy of 63% is obtained after 600 epochs (Fig. 8d) – i.e., the equivalent of 50 s in our machine (Fig. 8b).

6   Conclusion

Food recommendations can provide a significant contribution to the nutrition area. Food plans fail most of the time because people fail to accomplish the recommendations. It requires discipline to keep eating according to a plan. Plus, without proper education in the nutrition area, it is impracticable for regular people to change food when only equivalents are available or to evaluate the impact of extras on the target goals determined by the nutritionist.

This article contributes to state of the art on food recommendations by presenting an approach to help people choosing meals appropriate to their nutritional goals. Results have shown that energy and nutrient goals are essential predictors of meals. The user id's high discriminative power indicates that the accuracy levels of 63% can be improved by combining food recommendation models trained with historical data of a group of people with individual data. Thus, our future research will be aligned with the combination of models trained from people-group and individual datasets.

References

1. Alian, S., Li, J., Pandey, V.: A personalized recommendation system to support diabetes self-management for American Indians. IEEE Access **6**, 73041–73051 (2018). https://doi.org/10.1109/access.2018.2882138
2. Banerjee, A., Noor, A., Siddiqua, N., Uddin, M.N.: Food recommendation using machine learning for chronic kidney disease patients. In: 2019 International Conference on Computer Communication and Informatics (ICCCI), pp. 1–5 (2019). https://doi.org/10.1109/iccci.2019.8821871
3. Biau, G.: Analysis of a random forests model. J. Mach. Learn. Res. **13**(1), 1063–1095 (2012)
4. Chen, H.C., Chen, A.L.: A music recommendation system based on music data grouping and user interests. In: Proceedings of the Tenth International Conference on Information and Knowledge Management, pp. 231–238 (2001)
5. Gao, X., Feng, F., Huang, H., Mao, X.L., Lan, T., Chi, Z.: Food recommendation with graph convolutional network. Inf. Sci. **584**, 170–183 (2022). https://doi.org/10.1016/j.ins.2021.10.040
6. Ghongane, H.: MyfitnessPal Dataset. https://www.kaggle.com/datasets/zvikinozadze/myfitnesspal-dataset/discussion/194277
7. Herforth, A., Arimond, M., Álvarez-Sánchez, C., Coates, J., Christianson, K., Muehlhoff, E.: A global review of food-based dietary guidelines. Adv. Nutr. **10**(4), 590–605 (2019)
8. Mansoori, S., Liberatore, C., Ramirez, A., Chai, S.: Increased sodium consumption is associated with abdominal obesity in older adults. Curr. Dev. Nutr. **5**(Suppl._2), 1230 (2021). https://doi.org/10.1093/cdn/nzab055_040

9. Noriega, L.: Multilayer perceptron tutorial. School of Computing. Staffordshire University, vol. 4, p. 5 (2005)

10. Oh, S.W., Koo, H.S., Han, K.H., Han, S.Y., Chin, H.J.: Associations of sodium intake with obesity, metabolic disorder, and albuminuria according to age. PLoS ONE **12**(12), e0188770 (2017)

11. Oh, Y., Choi, A., Woo, W.: u-BabSang: a context-aware food recommendation system. J. Supercomput. **54**(1), 61–81 (2010). https://doi.org/10.1007/s11227-009-0314-5

12. Phanich, M., Pholkul, P., Phimoltares, S.: Food recommendation system using clustering analysis for diabetic patients. In: 2010 International Conference on Information Science and Applications, pp. 1–8 (2010). https://doi.org/10.1109/icisa.2010.5480416

13. Potdar, K., Pardawala, T.S., Pai, C.D.: A comparative study of categorical variable encoding techniques for neural network classifiers. Int. J. Comput. Appl. **175**(4), 7–9 (2017)

14. Rostami, M., Oussalah, M., Farrahi, V.: A novel time-aware food recommender-system based on deep learning and graph clustering. IEEE Access **10**, 52508–52524 (2022). https://doi.org/10.1109/access.2022.3175317

15. Schedl, M.: Deep learning in music recommendation systems. Front. Appl. Math. Stat. 44 (2019)

16. Song, Y., Dixon, S., Pearce, M.: A survey of music recommendation systems and future perspectives. In: 9th International Symposium on Computer Music Modeling and Retrieval, vol. 4, pp. 395–410. Citeseer (2012)

17. Zhang, J., Li, M., Liu, W., Lauria, S., Liu, X.: Many-objective optimization meets recommendation systems: A food recommendation scenario. Neurocomputing **503**, 109–117 (2022). https://doi.org/10.1016/j.neucom.2022.06.081

Author Index

Printed in the United States
by Baker & Taylor Publisher Services